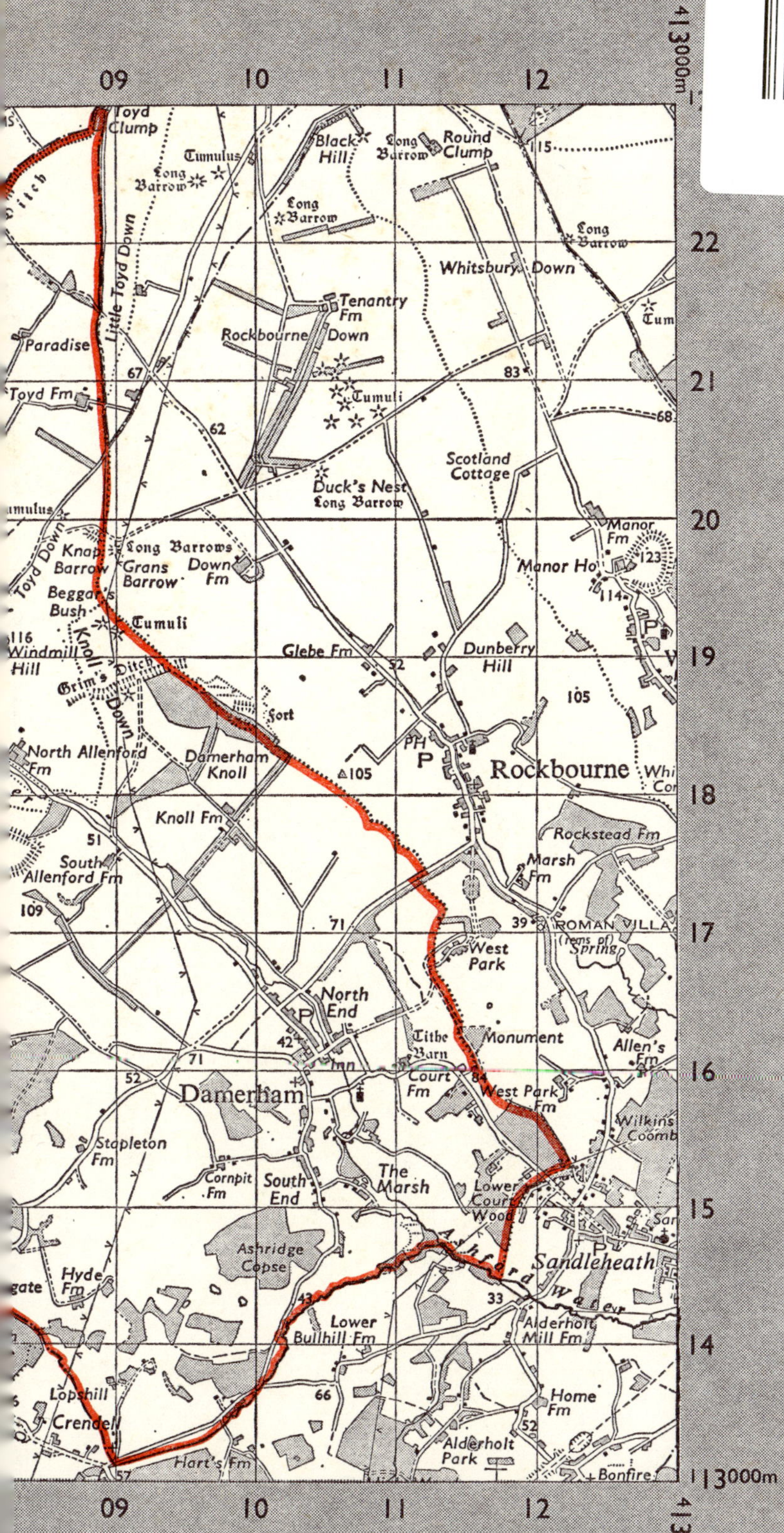
09
10
11
12
413000m
Toyd Clump
Tumulus
Long Barrow
Black Hill
Long Barrow
Round Clump
Long Barrow
Long Barrow
Little Toyd Down
Whitsbury Down
22
Tenantry Fm
Rockbourne Down
Paradise
Toyd Fm
Tumuli
67
62
83
21
68
Scotland Cottage
Duck's Nest Long Barrow
Manor Fm
20
Knap Barrow
Long Barrows
Grans Barrow
Down Fm
Manor Ho
123
114
Toyd Down
Beggar's Bush
Tumuli
116
Windmill Hill
Knoll Down
Grim's Ditch
Glebe Fm
52
Dunberry Hill
19
105
Fort
North Allenford Fm
Damerham Knoll
PH
P
105
Rockbourne
18
Knoll Fm
Rockstead Fm
51
South Allenford Fm
Marsh Fm
109
71
39
ROMAN VILLA
(rems of)
Spring
17
West Park
North End
P
Tithe Barn
Monument
Allen's Fm
42
Inn
71
16
52
Damerham
Court Fm
West Park Fm
Wilkins Coomb
Stapleton Fm
Cornpit Fm
South End
The Marsh
Lower Court Wood
15
Ashridge Copse
Sandleheath
Hyde Fm
43
33
Ashford Water
Lower Bullhill Fm
Alderholt Mill Fm
14
Lopshill
66
Home Fm
Crendell
52
Alderholt Park
57
Hart's Fm
Bonfire
113000m

…oximately.

DAMERHAM AND MARTIN

A Study in Local History

E. H. LANE POOLE

DAMERHAM AND MARTIN

A Study in Local History

CHAPTER HEADING DECORATIONS BY
PHILIP FREEMAN SAYER

COMPTON RUSSELL

First published in Great Britain 1976 by
Compton Russell Ltd
The Old Brewery, Tisbury, Wiltshire
and designed and printed by
The Compton Press Ltd

Set in Linotype Granjon

ISBN 0 85955 023 0

CONTENTS

LIST OF CHAPTER HEADING DECORATIONS

ACKNOWLEDGEMENTS

My first and greatest debt is to my brother, Dr. Austin Lane Poole, President of St. John's College, Oxford, for his help, advice and the use of his extensive medieval library. Next, I would wish to express my gratitude to the late Rev. H. W. Moule, Vicar of Damerham, for his kindly encouragement. Lastly, I gratefully record my indebtedness to Mr. Philip Jackson for having given me free access to the valuable collection of Court Rolls in his possession. Acknowledgements to others who have imparted information are gratefully made in the footnotes to the text.

E. H. LANE POOLE

Message from Mrs. E. H. Lane Poole

My daughter and I, now living in Australia, would like to record our thanks to Monty Trethowan for his work in making the publication of my husband's history possible. He was assisted by his friend Irvine Gray, F.S.A., who revised the footnotes, and his secretary Eileen Macey who dealt with the considerable amount of typing and correspondence involved. I hope that the book will give as much enjoyment to those who read it as my husband had in writing it.

ALISON LANE POOLE

FOREWORD

This book, which was the outcome of a long period of research after his retirement from the Colonial Service in Rhodesia, is sadly published many years after my uncle's death in 1961.

E. H. Lane Poole's life fell into two distinct parts, totally different in their setting and quality, but both perhaps dictated by the same underlying feeling: an intense love of his country, which he tried to serve first in active administrative work overseas, and then, on retirement, in scholarship – a kind of scholarship already of an established tradition in a family of historians, and although in his case dedicated to a detailed history of only two parishes, carried out with just such a meticulous imagination and control as was the work of his brother Austin Lane Poole, his father and uncle, Reginald and Stanley.

He loved the rural England which still survived, deeply rooted in the past, until the Second World War. This book, written when the downland sheep-walks were being broken up for arable, is a fitting memorial to a man who so enjoyed the rich legacy of rural continuity. His own words written to an archaeologist friend in 1944 show the awareness and pleasure re derived from scholarship applied to the two parishes he has so successfully portrayed in this history. 'Returning from a visit to Rockbourne,' he wrote, 'as I rode home over the knoll the sheep were folded on the turnips and three horse-drawn ploughs were working across a single large field and I could not help thinking how it exemplified what you and your work and your library stood for. "How jocund did they drive their teams afield".'

A number of friends have contributed to the improvement of this typescript, and I would like to express the gratitude of the family for their generous help. Mr. Collin Bowen, Dr. Isobel Smith and Mrs. Margaret Guido have read those parts concerned with the prehistoric period and have made some necessary revisions. The reader will appreciate that on the whole the book is being published more or less exactly as it was completed by the author in 1953. Some of the archaeological propositions would now be restated but revision of archaeological opinions is constantly taking place and to have attempted to revise the History taking into account all the new findings and opinions of the last twenty years would have been an impossible task. Mrs. Eames is to be thanked for her note on the medieval tiles, Mr. Philip Freeman Sayer for the decorations he has made for the chapter headings, and Vaughan Abigail and Clive Simmonds, from Bishop Wordsworth's School, Salisbury, for completing the unfinished index. Mr. Richard Sandell, Honorary Librarian of the Devizes Museum Library, has done much to promote interest in this book. Above all, Mr. H. M. Trethowan deserves our grateful recognition for all his enthusiasm and hard work in bringing the book finally to publication in spite of many difficulties.

CATHERINE DUPRE

I

INTRODUCTORY

THE parish of Martin up to the year 1895 was situated in the county of Wiltshire. The people of the village were, anciently, Wilsaetan, a branch of the men of the Wylie valley, whose capital was Wilton. By a Local Government Act of 1895, when adjustments were made to the county boundaries for convenience of administration, effect was given to the wishes of the parishioners, expressed eight years previously,[1] to be transferred to the county of Southampton, already the authority for the operation of the Poor Law and the Highway Acts. But although local government was henceforth administered from Fordingbridge and parliamentary representation included in the constituency of the New Forest, Martin retained many of its old associations with Wiltshire. Salisbury remained the diocesan see, and Chalke the rural deanery; Salisbury is still the market town, the shopping centre and the focus for rail and road communication. Wiltshire has imparted its influence upon agriculture, and the Wiltshire dialect is the common speech. Martin has never altogether adapted itself to 'The Forest'.

[1] Report on Areas and Boundaries, 1887. A report presented to Wilts Hilary Sessions 1888 pursuant to the Local Government Boundaries Act 1887. A copy is indexed as Wilts Tracts 95 in the library of the Wiltshire Archaeological Society at Devizes. It is interesting to note that in the same year the Dorset Committee urged that Damerham and Martin be transferred to that county.

From the earliest time of which there is record Martin was included in the Hundred of South Damerham. This hundred was composed of all the estates of Glastonbury Abbey in South Wiltshire and, besides Damerham and Martin, embraced the detached parishes of Deverill, Monkton and Compton Chamberlayne.[2] It was denoted South Damerham to distinguish it from the artificially created Hundred of North Damerham, which comprised the estates of the Abbey in North Wiltshire, Kington St. Michael, Grittleton, Nettleton and Christian Malford, excised in 1321 from the old Hundreds of Sterkely and Chippenham.[3] But there never existed a place called North Damerham; it was merely found convenient to denote the two groups of Glastonbury manors in this way.

The Hundred of South Damerham was at that time of considerable importance; in 1280, for instance, it was appointed the place for the return of writs from all the Glastonbury manors in Wiltshire, with one exception, from the north as well as the south hundreds.[4] The single exception was Idmiston which owed suit to Alderbury and was not brought into line with the other manors until the following century.[5] A consequence of the transference of Damerham and Martin to Hampshire was their incorporation in the Hundred of Fordingbridge, with the neighbouring parishes of Rockbourne, Whitsbury, Breamore and others.

Damerham, derived from the two old English words, 'domera' and 'hamm' is taken to mean, not too confidently,' an enclosure of the judges'.[6] It was divided into the tithings of Stapleham (now Stapleton), Damerham Parva or Coffyn, Northington (now North End) and Munstrestret[7] – the street, that is, leading to the minster or monastery. Martin comprised the

[2] *Nomina Villarum*, 9 Edw. II (1316), Record Commission, *Parliamentary Writs, etc.*, Vol. II.

[3] *Wiltshire Topographical Collections of John Aubrey, F.R.S.* collected and enlarged by J. E. Jackson, M.A., F.S.A., p. 124. Hereafter referred to as Aubrey, *Top.Coll.*

[4] *Calendar of Charter Rolls,* (1280) II, p. 226; See also *The Great Chartulary of Glastonbury*, ed. Dom Aelred Watkin (Som. Rec. Soc. LIX), Vol. I, p. 222; hereafter abbreviated to *G.C.*

[5] *G.C.* (1332), IV, p. 260; and *v. infra.* Ch. V.

[6] *Place Names of Wiltshire* (English Place Name Society) p. 400. Hereafter abbreviated to *P.N.W.*

[7] *Nomina Villarum* quoted by Sir Richard Colt Hoare in his Modern History of South Wiltshire, *Hundred of South Damerham* (hereafter referred to as Hoare, *H.S.D.*), but Hoare is in error in identifying Northington with a place near Alvediston in the Chalke Valley which was never part of the Glastonbury estates. He is wrong again in locating Munstrestret in the north-west corner of the Parish of Martin.

three tithings of West Martin, East Martin and Tidpit. Toyd and Allenford remained extra-parochial until the middle of the nineteenth century when they, too, were incorporated in the parish. In the medieval period Martin was seldom distinguished from Damerham: thus, in Domesday Book there is no mention of Martin, which is comprehended in Damerham, and in the earliest survey no attempt is made to separate the populations or tenements of the two villages.[8] Fifty years later a partial differentiation is made between the tenants of the two places[9] but the separation was not complete until the early Tudors. Ecclesiastically Martin was a chapelry under the perpetual vicariate of Damerham until 1847, when it was formed into a separate ecclesiastical district, and made a vicarage in the gift of the Vicar of Damerham in 1866. The manorial court was held at The Compasses, Damerham and occasionally at the White Hart Inn at Martin until 1920.

The parish boundaries are appended to a charter ascribed to about 945 by which Damerham and Martin were granted by King Edmund to the Abbot and Convent of Glastonbury.[10] They are demarcated by prehistoric earthworks and ancient roads; the south-western boundary follows the stupendous earthwork of Bokerley Dyke; the north-western coincides with the Roman road from Old Sarum to Dorchester; the northern boundary is a segment of Grims Ditch; the old English Wilton Way, passing between two neolithic long barrows, demarcates the eastern boundary. The south-eastern boundary between Martin and Damerham is not specifically described, but, for the assignment of grazing and apportionment of the water meadows, must have been made at the same time. It should be added that the schedule describing the boundaries is thought not to be coeval with the charter granting the land.[11]

Since 1895 Kitt's Grave has marked the convergence of the three counties of Dorset, Hampshire and Wiltshire. Before then the Ash at Padnore or Penegeford[12] at the confluence of the river Allen or Ashford Water, as it is here called, with the Salisbury Avon below Fordingbridge

[8] *Liber Henrici de Soliaco*, 1189 (Roxburgh Club, 1882), p. 127.

[9] *Rentalia et Customaria Michaelis de Ambresbury, c.* 1235, (Som. Rec. Soc., 1891), p. 108. Hereafter referred to as *Rentalia.*

[10] Birch, *Cartularium Saxonicum* (London 1885-1893), II, p. 579; hereafter referred to as Birch, *C.S.*

[11] *v. infra*, Ch. IV. for the boundaries in detail.

[12] Cf. in 945 (Birch, *C.S., loc cit.*), 'then to the ash at Penegeforde, that stands in Wiltshire, Dorsetshire and Hampshire'; and in 1227, perambulation 'to the Hasche at the waters of Padnore', *infra.* Ch. IV.

was the point of intersection of the boundaries of the three counties. Contiguous with the parish of Martin are the parishes of Cranborne and Pentridge (Dorset), Bowerchalke, Broad Chalke, Bishopstone, Stratford Tony and Coombe Bissett (Wiltshire) and Rockbourne and Damerham (Hampshire), all of which will recur frequently in subsequent pages.

In the centre of the parish, surrounded by the Downs, lies the village of Martin. Apart from the uncertain identification of the battle of Meretune in 871 with Martin,[13] the first authentic record of the name occurs in the charter of 945 already mentioned. Until the sixteenth century it was invariably spelt Mertone, Merton, or Meretune. The substitution of an 'a' for an 'e' in the first syllable begins in the second half of the sixteenth century,[14] coinciding with the expansion of the knowledge of writing and the spelling of the word as it was pronounced. The modern spelling with an 'i' in the place of an 'o' or an 'e' in the final syllable is first noted about 1670.[15] The meaning of the name is a farm or settlement on the boundary from the old English elements 'maere' and 'tun',[16] an apt name for a parish contiguous with three counties.

The Tithing of West Martin did not extend beyond Townsend Lane until about 1775, when houses began to be built on waste by labourers working in their own time after the day's work. Its southern limit was College, and the houses flanked the village street on either side. To visualise East Martin as it was a hundred years ago, the council houses and the vicarage must be expunged from the scene. Until the Reformation it was dominated by the large demesne farm of the Abbey of Glastonbury at what is now Bustard Farm. The third of the tithings is the hamlet of Tidpit, pleasantly set in its verdure of water meadows, once possessing a church and some half dozen farm houses, and lying astride the road which for five centuries was one of the principal approaches to the west of England.

Aubrey was the first to speculate upon the derivation of its quaint name.[17] Arguing from a phrase used in the vernacular of the north of

[13] *infra,* Ch. IV.

[14] Martyn, *Statutes*, 7. Ed. VI. Marten, *Visitation of Wilts* (1565), and *Survey of the Lands of the First Earl of Pembroke* (Roxburgh Club, 1909), hereafter referred to as *Pemb. S.*

[15] *Col. S. P. Dom.*, 1672, p. 679. Aubrey, Mon. Brit., *c.* 1670. Locally, however, the modern spelling was in use half a century earlier, as, for instance, in the Court Rolls.

[16] *P.N.W.*, p. 402. Merton is the form almost invariably used in Charters and in the Rolls. Mertone is the spelling of the local historians, Adam of Damerham and John of Glastonbury, as well as of the medieval surveys.

England that 'sheep tod the ground', he supposed the first syllable to mean manure and Tidpit to be none else but a dung pit. The late Dr. Grundy traced the first syllable to an Anglo-Saxon word 'dod', the name given to a plant known as catstail, said to be locally abundant.[18] But its derivation from a proper name, Tuda, with the meaning Tuda's Hollow now has general acceptance.[19] Tudeputte,[20] Toudeputte,[21] and Todeputte[22] were the commonest medieval forms, but the post-Reformation variants are surprising in their incongruity.[23]

Rising near the Coote Arms on the Salisbury-Blandford main road, the river Allen flows through the centre of West Martin. There are several rivers of this name in the south and west of England, but its meaning is still obscure. It is thought to be a back-formation from Allenford[24] which occurs in 1333 as Elingforde, in 1518 as Allingforde, and in 1569 as Alleniford. This place name suggests that the stream was not bridged on the Damerham-Martin road in the Middle Ages, but that a bridge spanned the stream at the boundary of the parish (where the present bridge is) in 1612 is proved by the obligation to repair it being imposed on the inhabitants of Damerham.[25] And the field name Bridgelonde (1518),[26] now Bridgeacre, shows that a bridge existed at Tidpit pond where the Holloway led to Martin Woods and Cranborne. Despite the field names Millhedge, Millbourne, Millfurlong (1518) and Millclose (1569) there is no evidence that there were any water mills either at Martin or Tidpit. Four mills in Damerham are mentioned in Doomsday and three in the Glastonbury Chartularies. Of these Little Mill and Corn Mill remain on the Ordnance maps today. The interruption of the stream by the ponds at Bustard and Tidpit suggest that another may well have been at one of those places. From the precautions taken in the past to preserve

---

17 *Aubrey,* Mon. Brit. pt. V.

18 *Arch. Journ.* LXXV, p. 112.

19 *P.N.W.*, p. 403.

20 *Book of Fees,* 1242.

21 *Register of Simon of Ghent* (Bishop of Salisbury), 1307.

22 *Foedary of Abbot Monyton,* 1335, hereafter abbreviated to *Foedary.*

23 The following versions of the spelling include Tutpyt, 1467; Tupputte, 1518; Tyttpitt, 1569; Typpett and Tittpitt, 1611; Sudpett, 1539; Badpytt, c. 1740; Dodsput and Dydpytt, 1661.

24 Ekwall, *English River Names,* p. 4; *P.N.W.*, p. 400.

25 Court Rolls *sub anno* formerly in the custody of Mr. Philip Jackson, Solicitor, Fordingbridge. (These are now in the custody of a member of the Coote family.)

26 *Terrarium Abbatis Ricardi Beere,* printed in Hoare, *H.S.D.*, p. 53; hereafter referred to as *Beere.*

the purity of the water in these ponds it may be assumed that they supplied a source of drinking water to many of the inhabitants: no sheep might be washed in them, no ducks or geese kept on them and no straw or dung pitched into them.[27]

The stream is what in Wiltshire is known as Winterbourne – flowing in winter, but desiccated in summer. Peter of Blois' description of Old Sarum, when, as a canon, he objected to compulsory residence on that arid hill top, might with aptitude be applied to Martin in the summer and autumn months: 'short of water, but full of chalke'.[28] Until a few years ago the water poured in a flood down the village street in winter and spring; the postman on foot, or later on cycle, was unable to deliver letters and children are said to have gone to school on stilts.[29]

Just before the beginning of the Second World War, the water was conducted underground by a culvert, which, while it drained Bustard Pond, afforded a dry passage to pedestrian traffic.

Archaeological sites on the Downs, however, show that there has been since the Romano-British epoch a subsidence of perhaps some fifty feet or more in the level of the water table.[30] Only on this assumption could the early inhabitants have obtained a drinking supply within reasonable proximity to their settlements. We must imagine that in their time the 'coombs', the 'slades' and the 'denes', the depressions, now dry, which furrow the slope of the Downs, were, like the Allen stream, flowing in winter with water sufficiently close to the surface to be easily drawn from shallow holes in summer.

The old White Hart Inn and the remnant of the village cross in the centre of West Martin stand at an altitude of 200 feet exactly above sea level. The highest elevation of over 500 feet is attained on the western boundary where Blagdon Hill projects from the range of Pentridge hills; the lowest at Allenford Farm which lies at 180 feet only above sea level.

Martin, without its girdle of downs, would lose much of its charm and fascination. The Downs exercised an influence both upon the type of agriculture and upon the life of the people. Their presence ensured that

[27] Court Rolls, 1754 *et passim.*

[28] Peter of Blois (c. 1135-1205): 'Est inibi defectus aquae, sed copia cretae'. These dexterous rhyming hexameters are quoted in the *Register of St. Osmund*, II.20.h. Peter was made Canon of Old Sarum in 1194.

[29] W. H. Hudson, *A Shepherd's Life*, chap. III, for an account of the village street about the year 1900. In *Beere*, 1518, Waterlane may refer to this street.

[30] Heywood Sumner, *Ancient Earthworks of Cranborne Chase*, p. 6: Pitt-Rivers in his excavation of Woodcutts estimated a water table a thousand years ago fifty feet higher than now.

Martin should be preeminently a sheep and arable village; they determined the avocation as shepherds of a large proportion of cottagers; this environment left an impress of reserve and taciturnity on those who spent much of their lives in close contact with it.

In its general features the village has, in all probability, altered little in the past five hundred years. Since houses are usually built of the materials nearest to hand, thatch, flint and timber predominate largely in their construction. Flints were collected by women and children from the arable fields, recently reclaimed from the Downs, as they became enclosed. Much of the timber, which in shape is often curvilinear, is said to have originated from broken-up ships. Waggons, which drove to Poole Harbour, laden with corn for shipment to Bristol, used to return with a load of ship's timber. Where stone was employed, it came from the Chilmark quarries.

Always excepting the church, the old White Hart Inn represents the oldest building in the village. No other building adapts itself so readily to the medieval *hospitium* as the White Hart. Built about the second half of the fifteenth century, it was held for a rent of 30/- a year, of which ten shillings was earmarked for the maintenance of poor females below the Abbot's gate at Glastonbury.[31] Opposite the inn there stood until recently an archway, possibly giving access to stabling in what is now King's Farm, which was thought to have been a survival from monastic times. The plinth (and at one time part of the shaft) of the village cross is extant,[32] and the stocks disappeared in the last generation.[33]

Domestic architecture provides an indication of the development of the village. About 1550 we have the Tudor manor house, shorn of one or perhaps two wings and grievously mutilated; about 1650 three half-timbered cottages,[34] once farms, with the centre one bearing the date 1653 and having hogging brickwork, distinctive of the period, set in its walls; about 1750 three mellowed red brick farm houses[35] of a more substantial style (on the chimney of the middle house is the date 1739), built at a period when the copyhold farmer had raised himself in the social scale

[31] *Beere*, 64: 'ad usum mulierum paupercularum infra portam Abbatis'.

[32] A water-colour sketch of the White Hart Inn with the decapitated cross in the foreground, dated 1805, is in the Buckler Collection in the library of the Wilts. Archaeological Society at Devizes. The White Hart is mentioned in the Court Rolls of 1609.

[33] The stocks were *in situ* on the village green in 1886, *v. Salisbury and Winchester Journal* of 21st Aug. 1886.

[34] Harris's, Simy's and another.

[35] Garrett's, Reade's and Williams's.

and was able to afford himself a relatively comfortable dwelling. The following hundred years saw the demolition of many old buildings and the erection of many new, a chapel (1829), a school (1857), and many private houses. But for all that the village remained a happy blend of old and new, a village which so endeared itself to W. H. Hudson that he returned to it again and again, and whose charm impelled him to describe it as he did in *A Shepherd's Life*. An elm tree on the green and a rookery at the end of the lawn of the manor house must have added to the picturesqueness of the village.

Many of the present farms derive their names from the customary tenants of Glastonbury Abbey, who occupied them upwards of five hundred years ago; John Swetapulle (Sweetapple), William Harries (Harris's), John Garrett (Garrett's) or Thomas Prynce (Prince's). Reade's, Thaine's and Hancock's date from the seventeenth century. Williams's and Talk's to the eighteenth. It was the same in the Middle Ages when farms were known by their former occupants; Mayshouse,[36] Godwyne's,[37] Drages', Aunger's[38] and others which cannot now be identified.

Martin was neither the birthplace nor the residence of any person of distinction. The Earls of Pembroke and Shaftesbury, the Dukes of Newcastle and Sir Eyre Coote at different times held extensive property in Martin, but none of them lived there. In the 250 years that succeeded the accession of Queen Elizabeth scarce half a dozen names were conceded the prefix 'Mr.' or the suffix 'Gent.' in the parish registers or Subsidy Rolls. And they were gentlemen farmers, each holding a number of copyholds in the seventeenth and eighteenth centuries: the families of Horsey, knights under the Tudors, of Garrett of Alderholt Park, of Reade[39] of Fryern Court, of Grove,[40] a branch of that family at Fern, near Shaftesbury, which played a distinguished part in the life of the county, and of Hancock, his neighbour at Tidpit. But most of the farmers at Martin were copyhold tenants of small holdings, one- or two-horse livings, as

[36] 1189.

[37] *Rentalia*, 1235.

[38] *Feet of Fines, Wilts.*, 1325.

[39] The Reade family at Martin were resident under Queen Elizabeth. The marriage of Joseph Reade with Jane Garrett, heiress, of Alderholt Park, brought him all the Garrett copyholds in Martin. George, the son of Joseph, married Barbara, daughter of Peter Rooke of Fryern Court, and so acquired that property also. Martin, however, was their first choice, and they are all buried in the churchyard.

[40] Thomas Grove 1664-1738 lived at Martin and was elected M.P. for Shaftesbury in 1713. He married Elizabeth Hooke of Tangier Park, Hants. *v.* Hutchins, *Hist. of Dorset,* III, p. 568 (hereafter referred to as Hutchins).

they came to be called. Only half a century ago, before the era of mechanical transport, at the end of the day's work some fifty or more wagons might have been seen trundling in slow procession homewards along the drove, and ten or more flocks of sheep grazing the herbage of the down. Martin was preeminently a village of farmers and workers on the farm.

> Along the cool sequestered vale of life
> They kept the noiseless tenor of their way.

John Aubrey, the antiquary of Wiltshire, writing in the last quarter of the seventeenth century declared: 'I take Merten [Martin] to be the best seated for healthy airs etc. and sports of any place in the county. The soile is gravelly and pebbly.'[41] Having lived many years at Broad Chalke he was well acquaintetd with Martin, and often rode there and over the Downs, hawking or in pursuit of his antiquarian proclivities. Aubrey may have been at fault in his geology: the longevity of the inhabitants, incised upon the tombstones in the churchyard, testify to the salubrity of the situation. For sporting amenities in that age the reputation of the locality was unsurpassed in the county.

Aubrey was not alone in extolling the amenities of South Wiltshire. Indeed the unanimity of writers at this period is truly remarkable. Here, for instance, is the panegyric of an anonymous author in the late seventeenth century whose purpose was to laud the beauties of Longford Castle and its neighbourhood:

'So that as to her sports either in point of exercise or curiosity . . . this country may boast with any other; whence eate we better rabetts than those which are taken in Auburne Chase and on Rockbourne Warren[42] . . . Where was there (before King James' days) any Hare Warrens in England, but the two in Wilts? Where was there so famous a Horse-Course in the South as those on Salisbury Plain? (one whereof is about 12 miles endways). Where can any pleasure in walking, fishing, bowling, playing of cricket or stop-ball, or in the field sports as coursing, setting, shooting, running or such as are beforenamed be taken with that ease, cheapness and satisfaction as in Wiltshire?'[43]

[41] Aubrey, *Nat. Hist. of Wilts*, p. 123. (Hereafter abbreviated to *N.H. Wilts.*)

[42] This is the Black Warren, marked on the Ogilby maps of the late seventeenth and early eighteenth centuries. Within living memory a black rabbit has been seen from this warren.

[43] *Wiltshire Archaeological Magazine* (hereafter abbreviated as *W.A.M.*), 187 (Dec. 1947): H. C. Brentnall, Longford MS. p. 20.

Celia Fiennes, herself a Wiltshire woman, a native of Newton Tony, strikes the same note: 'A fine champion country,' she writes in 1697, 'pleasant for all sports – Riding, Hunting, Coursing, Setting, and Shooting.'[44]

Clarendon Park and Cranborne Chase attracted to their forests nearly every King of England until the Hanoverian sovereigns gave drawing rooms a preference over the hunting field. Although the tradition that King John hunted regularly from Tollard Royal appears to be entirely without foundation, he hunted from Cranborne at least eighteen times in a reign of eighteen years, and from Clarendon, when he often stayed at Downton.[45] Blagdon was emparked as a royal park in 1321 by Edward II, and enlarged to include part of Martin Wood and what is now Kites Nest Farm in 1483 by Edward IV.[46] August was the month which gave the best prospects for hunting deer. Thus we find Edward VI prolonging his western progress to spend a week from August 21st between Woodlands and Wilton,[47] hunting among other places over Faulston Down, when 'he lost his courtiers, or his courtiers him, a hunting, and found him again in Falston Lane[48]. On August 24th, 1607, James I killed a buck in Vernditch and another in Howles' Walk, Cobley, dined at Woodyates Manor and took coach to Tarrant for the night. In August 1609, hunting from Cranborne, he killed twelve bucks in two days.[49] He was there again in 1621 and in 1623. Ten years later, Charles I was hunting in Blagdon, and when staying at Wilton would often fish for trout in the Ebble at Broad Chalke. Charles II hunted both from Wilton and Wimborne St. Giles. Royal patronage declined under the Hanoverian kings and the last of royal blood to shed the lustre of his name was Frederick, Prince of Wales (1707–51), who was Ranger of Cobley Walk.

Lord Arundel of Wardour kept a kennel of foxhounds at Breamore as early as 1705, and hunted the country of which Martin was near the centre, as far as Cranborne. His huntsman used to receive from the churchwardens of that place one shilling for every mask, presumably as destruction of vermin.[50] The Arundel family maintained a pack until

[44] *The Journeys of Celia Fiennes* (c. 1695), ed. Morris, p. 5. Also Defoe, *Tour through Great Britain*, I, p. 196, who takes exception to the Wilton Hare Warren.

[45] Sir T. Duffus Hardy, *A Description of the Patent Rolls*.

[46] *Col. Pat. R.*, 1476-1485, p. 336, *infra* Ch. II.

[47] King Edward's Journal, printed in Burnet, *History of the Reformation*, II, pt. II, p. 88.

[48] Aubrey, *N. H. Wilts.*, p. 69.

[49] Hutchins, III, p. 380.

[50] Extract from the Register of Cranborne Church.

1782 when it was taken over by Hugo Meynell to form the famous Quorn pack.[51] But Thomas Fownes is usually credited with being the first to have hunted this part of the country in the modern fashion. His kennels were at Stapleton near Shaftesbury, and about 1739 were known as the Cranborne Chase foxhounds.

A further attraction to the county gentlemen was the opportunity for racing. 'The Race' as the Salisbury course was at this time called, is said to have originated with the gift by the second Earl of Pembroke to the city of Salisbury of a silver bell, which in 1630 was converted into a gold cup to be competed for on the Thursday after mid-Lent Sunday.[52] Two races were run, one from Whitesheet Hill, near Alvediston, to Harnham Hill, a distance of some fourteen miles along the Harepath. It is not surprising to learn that this race, which must have been a kind of steeplechase, was seldom contested. The starting point of the other was a point known as Start on the boundary of North Down Farm, Broad Chalke to Hare Warren, a distance of about four miles. The finish of the shorter course, therefore, was about where the grandstand is today. Continuing in his familiar anecdotal strain, Aubrey adds that this course was covered in five minutes or a little more by a horse named Peacock, a bastard barb, and 'the most beautiful horse even seen in the last age'.

Charles II's patronage of racing is well-known. His racing mares were stabled at Rockbourne under the supervision of Sir George Marshall, who received £200 for his services.[53] Sir George had much to do with promoting racing at Malmesbury, and, dying there, gave directions for his body to be interred underneath the tomb of King Athelston, before the altar in Malmesbury Abbey,[54] much to Aubrey's indignation.

Nor has Martin and its neighbourhood been neglected in literature. Contrary to the author's express wish, it eventually transpired that under the pseudonym of Winterbourne Bishop W. H. Hudson had, in his best-known book, *A Shepherd's Life*, depicted the village of Martin; and the original of Hudson's shepherd, Caleb Bawcomb, is now known to have been one of Martin's own sons, James Lawes.[55] Hudson's visits to Martin extended over the decade 1895–1905, when he lodged in a half-timbered cottage, formerly belonging to an eccentric village character

[51] *Country Life*, Feb. 1951.
[52] Aubrey, *N.H. Wilts.*, p. 117.
[53] *Cal. S.P. Dom.* 1628-29, p. 389.
[54] Aubrey, *Top. Coll.*, pp. 258, 266.
[55] Poole in *Times L. Sup.* 23, June 1945. For further details *v.* Miss Lawes in the *Hants and Dorset Magazine*, June 1952.

named Malachi Martin, of whom (under the disguised name of Elijah Raven) some description is given.[56]

It is probable that in Thomas Hardy's *Tess of the D'Urbervilles* Trantridge may be identified with Pentridge,[57] which agrees better with the topography than does Boveridge.[58] Pentridge, as described in the book, is connected by a bridle path with Cranborne or Chaseborough, where the Fleur de Luce Inn still stands. Tess may have lost her virginity in Vernditch, abutting upon our parish, that wood of primevial yews and oaks, 'the oldest wood in England'. It would be about an hour's ride from the starting point and near enough to the highway for Alec D'Urberville to discern its contours by the light of a waning moon.

We have it on the dubious authority of Aubrey that Vernditch was the scene of the courtship of Roger Mortimer, first Earl of March, to Isabella, the Queen of Edward II, but he cites no evidence beyond his vivid imagination. 'If these oaks', he writes, 'were as vocal as Dodonas, some of the old dotards could give an account of the amours and whispers between the great Earl and the fair Queen Isabell.'[59] With greater probability Aubrey supposes Vernditch to have been the original of Philip Sydney's Arcadia. 'Those romancy plains and boscages did no doubt conduce to the heightening of his fancy. He lived mostly in these parts, and his most masterly touches of his pastorals he wrote here upon the spot where they were conceived. T'was about these purlieus that the muses were wont to appear to him and where he wrote down their dictates in his table-book, though on horseback. I remember some old relations of mine and other old men hereabout to have seen Sir Philip do this.'[60] The old relation was his great-uncle, Thomas Browne.[61]

Adjoining the northern boundary of the parish is Bishopstone, said to be Plumpstead Episcopi of Anthony Trollope's Barchester novels, from the spacious rectory of which the future Archdeacon Grantley drove in his gig to the Close of Salisbury. Silverbridge in the same novels is thought to be Fordingbridge, the capital town of the modern hundred.

Aubrey's opinion that Martin was 'the best seated for healthy airs' in the county no doubt influenced him in selecting this village as the site of one of his seven English public schools. Here 'under the eye of

[56] Hudson, *A Shepherd's Life*, Ch. XXIII.
[57] Lea, *Highways and Byways of Hardy's Wessex*, p. 145.
[58] Windle, *The Wessex of Thomas Hardy*, p. 312, prefers Boveridge.
[59] Aubrey, *N.H. Wilts*, p. 108.
[60] *Ibid.*
[61] Aubrey, *Brief Lives*, II, p. 248.

Lord Shaftesbury' and 'at Cranborne in Dorset by Lord Salisbury's, the finest place in England',[62] were to be established schools for the education of some fifty sons of gentlemen, destined to fill the high offices of state, conducted on principles far in advance of his time, which included good meals, ample sleep and the abolition of corporal punishment 'on the bare buttocks'. Aubrey's ambitious project came to nothing, and we who live here now have perhaps no cause to regret that our tranquillity remains undisturbed. In the eighteenth century spasmodic tuition in Grammar (the tedious insistence on grammar had evoked Aubrey's vehemence) and English and Latin exercises was given by altruistic persons in the churchyard,[63] and at the end of the century there had been some sort of a dame's school. The erection of the present school buildings in 1858 was described in an official report to be on the most approved plans, and it has done duty until the present day.

[62] Aubrey, *An Idea of the Education of a Young Gentleman.*
[63] Memorandum in the Parish Registers, 1719.

II

ROADS, DOWNS AND FORESTS

THE road system connecting Martin with the outer world has a local interest, not only on account of the antiquity of many of the highways, but also because it reflects the change of route and direction that has taken place in the past seventeen hundred years.

First, both in antiquity and importance, is the Roman road which runs from Old Sarum to Dorchester by way of Woodyates and Badbury Rings. It is believed to correspond with Iter XV of the Antonine Itineraries, the Ackling Dyke and, if this be so, Woodyates is identifiable with the Roman town of Vindocladia, as was suggested by General Pitt-Rivers.[1] It is not always appreciated that a large part – probably the greater part – of the vestiges of this Roman settlement lies within the boundaries of this parish. The two termini of the Via Iceniana were Silchester and Exeter and the intermediate posts are listed opposite.

From Old Sarum the road passed by Stratford-sub-Castle, and, crossing the race course, forded the Ebble at Stratford Tony, which places preserve the fact in their names Street Ford. That sector which bounds the

[1] Pitt-Rivers, *Excavations in Cranborne Chase* (hereafter referred to as Pitt-Rivers), III, *passim*. Woodyates is now generally accepted as the site in preference to Gussage, proposed by Hoare.

A Calleva		(Silchester)
Isca Dumnoniorum	m.p. 136	
Vindoni	m.p. 15	
Venta Belgarum	m.p. 21	(Winchester)
Brige	m.p. 11	
Sorbiodunum	m.p. 8	(Old Sarum)
Vindocladia	m.p. 12	(Woodyates)
Durnonovaria	m.p. 9	(Dorchester)
Moriduno	m.p. 36	
Isca	m.p. 15	(Exeter)

parish on the north-west was called Seven Street in the charter of 945 by which the land was granted by King Edmund to Glastonbury Abbey. Various conjectures have been made as to the meaning of Seven Street, of which the latest, advanced by O. G. S. Crawford, is its derivation from a proper name, Seofa.[2] But the possibility of its being connected with Seven Ditches a few miles further west along this road should not be altogether ignored. Along part of this section it is superimposed upon Grimsditch and where Grimsditch diverges to the south of the road, it is named in the boundaries annexed to the 945 charter, Street Ditch, the Ditch, that is, the adjoining section of which had been converted into a road. After leaving Woodyates the road is known as Ackling Dyke, and is raised above the level of the surrounding country so as to form a low causeway. Aubrey commented upon the pebbles employed in the metalling of the road, and supposed they had been transported thither from the sea, ignoring a more probable source on Pentridge Hill.[3] The intersections of General Pitt-Rivers give some idea of the magnitude of the construction: there were six strata of metalling, first a surface mould, second pebbles, third rammed rubble, fourth a tertiary gravel, fifth rammed chalk and finally nodular flints. It measured three feet from the surface line to the top of the road.[4]

It was along this road that the Saxons advanced against Romano-British peoples who constructed the earthwork of Bokerley Dyke; later again, the Danish incursion used this route before being repulsed by Aethelwolf in 851 on Oakley Down;[5] and, if we are right in our con-

[2] Crawford and Keiller, *Wessex from the Air*, p. 183.

[3] *Ibid.* 174.

[4] Pitt-Rivers, III, p. 74.

[5] Crawford and Keiller, *Wessex from the Air*, p. 173 for a discussion on the site of this battle.

clusion that the battle of Meretune in 871 was fought on Martin Down, it was along this road that the Danes advanced for their invasion of Wessex before meeting Aethelred and his brother Alfred in that engagement.[6]

The Roman road ceased to be used for regular traffic when, between 1229 and 1232, Robert Bingham, Bishop of Salisbury, in order to divert commerce from Wilton, to which it had up to this time gone, and to attract it to the new cathedral city, caused the bridge at Harnham to be built.[7] The translation of the cathedral church from Old Sarum is usually ascribed to the year 1217 and the new Salisbury received its charter from Henry III in 1227. It cannot be said that the Bishop lost much time in depriving Wilton of its supremacy.

The Wilton Way dates from the Saxon period. It is mentioned in the charter of 945 as well as in the charters of several neighbouring parishes. Its course has been traced in detail by the late Dr. Grundy.[8] It enters the extra-parochial district of Toyd, north of the farm, and passing between the two tumuli of Knap and Grans barrows, after crossing Grimsditch below Damerham Knoll, descends to the ford over the Allen river at Allenford pond. Thence it continued to Damerham along what is now the Martin-Damerham road. When Wilton ceased to be the capital of Wiltshire, this road still remained the main route from Damerham to Salisbury and was in constant use until well on in the nineteenth century.[9] It gave its name to Wilton Field, and what is now Paradise Farm was only a hundred years ago called Wilton Field Barn.[10]

As the main arterial road to the West of England the Roman road was superseded by what later became the coaching road from London to Poole Harbour. Indeed, within a few years of the building of the bridge at Harnham this road was styled 'a great royal road'.[11] Leland, writing about 1540, gives the following description of the country as he travelled on horseback from Cranborne to Salisbury: 'I passed about 2 mile or more all by playne champain ground, leving Blackdon (Blagdon) the King's park hard on the left hand. Thus a 6 miles by like ground to

[6] *v. infra.* Ch. IV.

[7] S. H. Cassan, *Lives of the Bishops of Salisbury*, (1824), p. 177. Camden, however, attributes it to Bishop Giles of Bridport (1256-62).

[8] G. B. Grundy, in *Arch. Journ.* LXXV, p. 112.

[9] Cf. Inclosure Award, 1831, where it is shown as the Damerham-Salisbury main road, and was by statute forty feet in breadth.

[10] Martin tithe map, 1846.

[11] Dugdale, *Monasticon Anglicanum*, I, p. 57: 'magna via regalis.'

Homington, and so to Saresbyri, al champain ground a 2 miles.'[12]

The itinerary is to be found in Ogilby's *Britannia Depicta*, in his maps drawn at the end of the seventeenth century, and later in the tabulated routes of Patterson's *Roads*. Connecting London with Weymouth and Poole, this road passed in succession through Basingstoke, Stockbridge, West Tytherley, East Dean and Dunkton (Downton). The next stage was by Tipput (Tidpit) to Cranborne. Thence it went via Wimborne Allhallows, Lower and Mid Gusset (Gussage), Tarrant Monkton, Blandford, Dorchester, to Weymouth and via Horton Inn and Wimborne Minster to Poole. By the eighteenth century a quicker and more direct route was opened to Weymouth and Exeter, but the road over Toyd Downs to Tidpit and on through Martin Wood to Cranborne was still used for the mails and coaches to Poole, as it had been frequently used for the passage of troops by both sides in the Civil War. So important a place at this time was Poole that coaches were advertised to make the journey from London in a single day. Several milestones, in remarkably good condition, survive along this road, in particular one on Blackheath bearing the legend 'From Poole Gate XIX miles. From Cranborne III miles'.

In 1818 a Turnpike Trust was formed styled the Poole Trust with the object of converting it into a turnpike road. From Poole as far as Tidpit the road was much improved, but the section from that point to Coombe Bissett, where it united with the new Salisbury-Blandford road, was never completed. It was not until 1835, however, that the scheme was finally abandoned.[13] Coaches at this date travelled at between seven and eight miles an hour, and on this route the coach was advertised to leave Salisbury at 6.0 a.m. and might be expected at Tidpit about 7.30 in the morning. On the return journey the coach left Poole at 4.30 in the afternoon and, arriving at Tidpit about 7.30 p.m., reached Salisbury in time for supper at half past eight. It was, for those days, an expensive mode of travelling, costing about 1s. 6d. a mile. But as early as 1658 the stage coach travelled from the George Inn at Aldersgate to Salisbury in two days at a cost of no more than twenty shillings.[14] Inhabitants of Tidpit may be surprised to learn that this road, passing as it now does through a narrow hollow-way, was by regulation defined to be forty feet in

[12] Leland, *Itinerary*, III, p. 87; *v.* also 'Lelands Notes in Wiltshire' by Canon Jackson in *W.A.M.* XXIX, p. 100; and Strype's *Cranmer*, III, pp. 325-28.

[13] Hutchins, III, p. 399.

[14] Trevelyan, *English Social History*, p. 250.

breadth, and its maintenance raised from a rate levied upon the fields on either side.

In its turn this road was superseded by what is still commonly called the Turnpike. It is popularly supposed to have been built for the convenience of George III and his queen for their visits to Weymouth, but, whereas the road was constructed in 1757, George III did not make his first expedition to Weymouth until 1789, when he stayed at Gloucester Lodge, now the Gloucester Hotel, on the esplanade. The first stage out of Salisbury was at Woodyates, where horses were changed at the inn of which the grandfather of Robert Browning was at one time the landlord.[15] Famous coaches to use this road were the *Regulator*, the *Eclipse* and the *Royal Mail*. The trust was, however, badly administered, and by 1867 became involved in a debt of £8,570 and was soon afterwards wound up.[16] There were six toll gates on the forty-seven miles between Salisbury and Dorchester.

Most characteristic of the village, however, were the droves, those green ways along which sheep were driven to the downland pastures or the neighbouring markets. At Martin they also served as accommodation lanes from which a plough team or a waggon could deviate into the open fields on either side; they afforded grazing to horses, cattle and pigs, except for the summer months from May Day to Lammas, when the corn crops were growing to maturity. Like the highways, the droves were under the protection of the manorial court: It was an offence to remove soil from a drove,[17] and the tenants were under an obligation to contribute towards the cost of a man to catch moles in the droves.[18] The chief of them was The Drove (la Drove of the survey of 1518), flanked by the drove closes and terminating at Drove End. Many ways, which we now call roads, were formerly sheep droves.

The catastrophic condition of English roads until the invention of metalling the surface, is the subject of comment in numerous diaries and biographies. Yet for equestrian traffic they adequately met the needs of the time in the summer months, and some quite remarkable feats of travel were accomplished. For instance, in 1205 King John rode from the Tower of London to Cranborne Manor in one day,[19] an achievement

[15] A tablet to his memory may be seen in Pentridge Church.

[16] *Report on Turnpike Trusts*, 1867.

[17] Court Rolls, 1759. This seems to have been of common occurrence. The parson of Bishopstone in 1275 'affossavit de via regalia (The Roman Road) et inclausit in curia sua et mutavit viam regalia ad alium locum'. Rot. Hund. II, p. 257.

[18] *Ibid.* 1613.

which was probably unsurpassed until the era of railways. The first Earl of Shaftesbury was a frequent traveller on horseback to London. The route which he most recommended was that via Winchester and Guildford. A century later the stage from Salisbury to Winchester received approbation even from Arthur Young, who usually found little to admire in the road system. But whether Shaftesbury travelled by Winchester, Basingstoke or Andover, he never spent more than two nights on the road.

The upkeep of the main roads until the nineteenth century was a duty imposed upon the parish under the supervision of waywardens, and enforced by the court leet. Those villagers who did not possess carts were required to collect stones in heaps by the roadside, while others, who had vehicles, conveyed them to the site needing repair.[20] The Manorial court also had jurisdiction over encroachments upon the highway such as digging a hole or erecting a fence within the stipulated width.[21]

The most conspicuous feature of the environment are, however, the Downs. In successive pages, and more especially when treating of sheep-farming, we shall have occasion to refer to them with greater particularity, and here we shall do no more than name them and give some conception of their area and position, as they were in the Middle Ages.

Martin Down, which lies like a kind of no-man's land between the verge of cultivation in the Open Fields and the Wiltshire-Dorsetshire boundary, has for thousands of years seen the browsing of multitudes of sheep. But its seemingly eternal repose was abruptly disturbed by the advent in 1943 of tractors and bulldozers, whose devastating action, irreverent of historic prescription, reduced its virgin expanse by half, and left to the commoners of West Martin the least usable moiety. If evidence, besides the supple texture of the turf, were required to show that the Down had never been encroached upon, it may be found in the fact that it was surveyed in the Middle Ages at approximately the same area as it was five years ago; then 787 acres, now 798, a remarkable example of the accuracy of medieval admensuration. At the earlier date what we now know as Hanham's Hill was called Blackheath Common, and the remainder Sheepdown.

---

19 Sir T. Duffus Hardy, *A Description of the Patent Rolls*, Introduction.

20 Court Rolls, 1609.

21 *Ibid.* 1611.

Martin Down was reserved exclusively for sheep, but many years previously West Martin had lost its Cow Down. What singularity of soil or conformation determined our ancestors to assign the watershed which separates the Ebble from the Allen to cattle is now a mystery to us. But from Bowerchalke to Coombe Bissett the Ordnance map reveals a succession of cow downs, with an ox-drove traversing the ridge. In the Middle Ages it was called Rotherdown,[22] and many of the field names, such as Great Cow Down or Knat's Cow Down, perpetuate its original purpose. Later, the western part became known as Lodge Down, so-called after Verndítch Lodge, situated on the slope above, of which the field name Lodge Down Ground and Long Lodge Ground are a reminder. At the end of the Middle Ages the Rotherdown was surveyed to contain an area of 500 acres.

Bustard Down at one time supplied 420 acres of pasture to East Martin. A part was converted to arable in the seventeenth century by the process of 'burnbaking',[23] and the remainder is traditionally said to have been ploughed during the Franco-Prussian War of the 1870s. It is now contained in Paradise Farm.

Sometime before 1755 *Tidpit Common* surrendered forty acres to the plough, but has remained unchanged in other respects since the Middle Ages when it was surveyed as 165 acres. It had this difference from other village downs, that it was at once both a sheep down and a cow down. In many ways it is, perhaps, the most attractive of all downs. Irregular in size and shape, it contains the remains of the only prehistoric village in the parish, and a remarkably well preserved section of Grimsditch. It is the habitat of curlew, wheatear and stonechat, of buzzard, or even an occasional peregrine. It commands a panorama of country, comparable with any scenery in the neighbourhood. May the Common long be spared!

The undulating expanse of the sheepsleight of Toyd gave way to corn crops in the Second World War.

This picture of downland in the Middle Ages enables us to visualise the more easily how it was possible, as will be seen in a later chapter, to sustain four or five thousand sheep on the down pastures. Since we shall return to them again, they may be tabulated as follows:

[22] *Beere*, p. 56. From the Old Eng. hryder, meaning cattle. *v.* also Pemb. S. II, p. 313.

[23] *v. infra.* Ch. VIII. In the Tithe Map of 1846 an area is marked 'Burnbaked part of Bustard Down'.

DOWNLAND IN THE MIDDLE AGES:	ACRES
Martin Down (Sheepdown & Blackheath Common)	767
Bustard Down (Estmerton Down)	420
Tidpit Common	165
Whitcombe (Wydecombe)	72
Allenford (extra-parochial)	318
Toyd[24] (extra-parochial)	147
Total Sheepdown	1889
Cow Down (Rotherdown)	500

If any dependence could be placed upon the mensuration of pasture in Domesday Book and through the Middle Ages, it might be possible to appraise the progress of reclamation of the Downs and their conversion to arable. At the time of Domesday pasture was estimated at 4,320 acres, at the end of the Middle Ages at 3,300, and at the beginning of the twentieth century at 3,066 acres. Unfortunately these figures disclose the reverse of the truth; for while in the earlier period enclosure was small and gradual, in the four centuries following the end of the Middle Ages it was extensive and rapid.

No description of Martin would be complete without some account of Cranborne Chase. The controversy concerning the claims to the Outer Bounds as against the Inner Bounds for some six hundred years evoked incessant complaint, constant litigation and a spate of polemical literature. At the same time the issue was worth arguing about. For, whereas the Inner Bounds, situated wholly in Dorset, were computed to comprise 40,000 acres only, the Outer Bounds, delimited by the rivers Stour, Nadder, the Salisbury Avon and the Dorsetshire Allen, were estimated to contain some 800,000 acres, of which a large part lay in Wiltshire and Hampshire.

Cranborne Chase is thought to have originated in the possessions inherited before the Conquest by Brictric.[25] Having passed to Matilda, the wife of William I, they came in the middle of the twelfth century to William, Earl of Gloucester. On his death in 1183, after remaining in the

[24] Toyd is a corruption of Two Hide. In *Rentalia* 1235, p. 114, 'Apud duas hydas' is used. For variants *v. P.N.W.*, p. 403.

[25] Dugdale, *Monasticon Anglican* (hereafter cited as Dugdale); *v.* also Freeman, *Norman Conquest* IV, p. 709, and *Som. Rec. Soc.* XLVII, p. 169.

hands of the King for six years, the honour was granted to William's third daughter, Isabella, the wife of John Plantagenet, who afterwards succeeded to the throne as King John, and passed with her, after her divorce and on her remarriage to Geoffrey of Mandeville. When in 1215 King John granted the Chase to Geoffrey de Mandeville, he granted precisely what had been held by William,[26] and directed a perambulation to be made to ascertain exactly what this was. Had this perambulation survived, there could have been little argument about the true bounds. The appropriation of the Outer Bounds is believed to have been an act of King John,[27] and the claim to them was stoutly maintained throughout the ascendancy of the Earls of Gloucester in the thirteenth and early fourteenth centuries. They were held to have been established by a perambulation made by John, when he held the title of Earl of Gloucester, before he became king, and to have been confirmed by another in 1245.[28] A recognition of the Outer Bounds seems to be implicit in the question put to John Bisset when in 1236 he applied to enclose Rockbourne Park, as to how far Cranborne Chase would be curtailed by such action.[29] The proceedings of Quo Warranto in 1280 when perambulations were cited to support both contentions, were inconclusive, and after the extinction of the Honour of Gloucester and when the Chase passed to the Crown, the opposing arguments were allowed to subside. But they were challenged again in 1612 when 'the whole chase, free chase and free warren in the Chase of Cranborne, and all privileges and jurisdiction and liberties in the counties of Dorset, Wilts and Southampton'[30] were granted to Robert, Earl of Salisbury.

Nevertheless, the owners of monastic and ecclesiastical estates within the Outer Bounds remained under a sense of grievance, and in the course of the second half of the thirteenth century a number of incidents caused them to give utterance to it. The Abbess of Wilton complained of trespass in Vernditch in 1250,[31] the Bishop of Winchester objected to a toll being exacted from his men of Downton when they took their produce to Salisbury market,[32] the Rector of Bishopstone (another manor of the

[26] *Rot. Litt. Claus.* (Record Commission), p. 216.

[27] Hoare, *H.S.D.*, quoting Adam of Damerham, p. 26: 'quaedam loca confinia tanquam extra chaceam appropriavit de quobus fuit manerium de Domerhame'.

[28] *Placita de Quo Warranto*, 3 Ed. I. (1276), p. 184(b).

[29] *Close Rolls*, 1236, p. 280.

[30] *Cal.S.P.Dom.* 1611-18, pp. 412 and 452.

[31] *Rot. Hund.* (Record Commission) II, p. 295 (1275).

[32] *Ibid.* p. 257.

Bishop of Winchester) remonstrated when deprived by the foresters of a cartload of thorns,[33] and finally the Abbot of Glastonbury was roused to action when one of his men at Martin was summarily hanged in the streets of Cranborne.[34]

Towards the end of the thirteenth century doubts of the validity of the Outer Bounds were cast by the perambulation of Walter Scammell, Dean of Salisbury in 1279. This perambulation held that the Chalke valley had belonged to the Abbess of Wilton 'from a time of which no memory remains' and that Vernditch and the downlands of Wiltshire,[35] since they had been afforested during the reign of Henry II, should be disforested as contravening the provisions of the Carta Foresta of 1217. Moreover, concessions were made within the Chase incompatible with the terms by which the Chase was granted. Thus, in 1232 the Abbot of Glastonbury was permitted to ditch and fence against deer his estates at Damerham and Martin, and in 1331 was granted free warren on his demesne lands.[36] As time went on, moreover, the enclosure of parks within the Chase still further complicated the issue. Blagdon was emparked as a royal park in the reign of Richard II, and private parks were enclosed at Wilton, Rockbourne and Breamore. Adam of Damerham recounts the grievances of the parishes at length: 'The manor of Damerham was greviously oppressed by the powers of the Count [sc. Earl] of Gloucester by reason of the Chase at Cranborne, because no villein of the manor, even when so permitted by the Abbot, could enter the woods of the said Abbot, or take anything away from thence or even from their own plantations [*ortulis*] without first showing it to the Count's foresters; nor to drive off the Count's beasts from their own crops and orchards, without being arrested by the foresters and compelled to answer in the Count's court as much for verdure as for venison, and as well for persons as for beasts. The foresters entered even into the houses of the villeins and into their gardens.'[37]

An instance of the grievances complained of by Adam of Damerham is given in the Hundred Rolls of the year 1275:[38] 'The said foresters, that

[33] *Ibid.*

[34] *Ibid.* p. 253. Adam of Damerham, II, p. 572 (Printed by Hearne, 2 vols., Oxford 1727; hereafter cited as Adam).

[35] West, *A History of Cranborne Chase* (1818), p. 75. Legal memory dated from the accession of Richard I (1189).

[36] *Close Rolls*, 1330, p. 169.

[37] Adam, II, p. 572.

[38] *Rot. Hund.* (3 Ed. I) 253.b.

is to say, a certain Savicus and Walter Brice, on the authority of Geoffrey of Leuknore, came to Martin, and in the county of Wiltshire, to the house of John the Bor and there by force took a certain man of Forton[39] and, accusing him of a felony, led him to Cranborne in the county of Dorset, and there, at their own will and without reason, hanged him. And having hanged him they came to Bredeme[40] in the county of Wiltshire and there took two cows from the cows of Peter of Skidemore, saying that they belonged to the felon that was hanged, and by force took those cattle to Cranborne and detained them there. And they went to the house of Richard of Martin and took a horse belonging to the man who was hanged, valued at 10/-. And they found in the home of the hanged man a silver mark and a silver buckle, valued at 8d.'

Similar episodes were reported in 1281: 'William of Cunishasele and some foresters of the county came to the house of John of Martin and there took a certain man and led him as far as Cranborne and there hanged him the same day. And William with his associates so oppressed the men of Martin that they could not pasture their draught horses in La Heze without suffering damage and loss. And the said foresters did attack John de Calve[41] in his house at Martin and took him to Cranborne, and refused to allow him to return until he had paid a fine through John of Martin. And the said foresters did arrest Geoffrey Godwine at Martin, a villein of the Abbot, to answer in the court at Cranborne, because he had captured a wild beast, and he was fined half a mark.'[42]

There has probably never been an epoch when Martin was without its poachers. Vernditch, in particular, was a favourite resort of poachers. In 1738, for example, after a keeper had been killed in a struggle, the poacher, condemned at Salisbury Assizes, was hanged in chains at the scene of the crime. But his body was cut down a few days later by his confederates and concealed at the bottom of a deep well.[43] Such incidents were of constant occurrence. W. H. Hudson[44] recalls other incidents in later centuries. But these men and their predecessors, whether poachers

[39] Ibid., p. 249; the same grievance emanates from the Hundred of Chalke. In this Horton is read for Forton and is probably correct. Horton is a village in Dorset, not far from Cranborne.

[40] Probably Bridemore in the parish of Berwick St. John in the Chalke Hundred. Hutchins III, p. 408 adopts this translation for the textual Brideme. For variants *v.* *P.N.W.*, p. 201.

[41] John Calvus appears as the holder of a virgate in the *Rentalia*, p. 109.

[42] Hoare, *H.S.D.*, p. 25.

[43] Chafin, *Anecdotes and History of Cranborne Chase* (1818), p. 34.

[44] Hudson, chapters III and VII.

or innocent parties, made parish history. They championed a cause against the formidable Earl of Gloucester, the lord of the Chase, and secured valuable concessions both for themselves and the Abbot.

In consequence of vigorous protests by the Abbot of Glastonbury, John of Taunton, a meeting was arranged with the Earl of Gloucester at Sherborne, 1281. The result must have been gratifying to the abbot who obtained all he could have hoped for: all offences in future were to be tried in the abbot's court; no attachments were to be made except for persons taking venison captured in the act; permission was granted to the abbot to take six beasts a year with his own hounds and in view of the Earl's foresters; the earl's claim upon Boulsbury Hayewode was abandoned; finally the abbot was permitted to ditch and fence against deer. In return for these concessions the Earl of Gloucester was allowed to post a forester at Blagdon, who, however, was denied his customary perquisite of exacting food and drink from the villagers, nor were foresters permitted to levy cheminage against the Abbot during the fence month.[45] 'Thereafter', writes Adam of Damerham, 'no forester dared enter upon the crops of the villeins.' The terms of the settlement are a negation of the claim to the Outer Bounds of the Chase.

It remains only to add that Edward III in 1330 at his court at Woodstock granted the Abbot and Convent of Glastonbury free warren in all their demesne lands at Damerham[46] which included Martin wood.

To complete the story of the Chase, actions for trespass though they never came into court impelled the Earl of Salisbury to dispose of Vernditch, the largest deer walk in Wiltshire[47] to the Earl of Pembroke in 1621, and the remainder of the Chase to the Earl of Shaftesbury in 1671 for the sum of £5,300. In 1692 it was sold to Thomas Freke of Shroton for £3,500, and by the will of Elizabeth Freke passed by reversion to George Pitt of Strathfieldsaye. It descended in 1776 to George Pitt, first Baron Rivers and remained in this family until its disfranchisement in 1829.

In the eighteenth century the legal and historical arguments were abandoned and the case against the Chase founded on the grounds of immorality and its being prejudicial to society as conducive to poaching,

[45] Adam, II, p. 572; Hoare, *H.S.D.*, p. 26. Cheminage was the toll exacted from all carts and waggons using a road through the forest during the fence-month, that is, for a fortnight before and a fortnight after midsummer, when the does might be expected to drop their fawns. Strictly, it was an incident of forest law and was not applicable to a chase.

[46] *Close Rolls*, 1330, p. 169.

[47] Alderholt in Dorset was the largest deer walk in the Chase.

stealing and smuggling with their consequences, the idleness and profligacy of the rural population. It is, however, significant that the advocacy for disfranchisement coincided with the phase of enclosures all over England. In the latter part of the century a committee of landowners was formed which, meeting at Woodyates in 1787, offered Baron Rivers a house and £200 a year which was reckoned to be a good deal more than the deer were worth, if sold.[48] A second meeting in 1790 led to a subscription list being opened, but it was not until 1829 that the Chase was disfranchised, after the annual hunt at Tollard which for generations had succeeded the session of the Chase Court, and the hunt at Handley which traditionally terminated the sitting of the Manorial Court had, to the indignation of the public, been prohibited.

The most extensive woodlands in the hundred are those at Damerham. According to a recent survey they enclose 904¾ acres. These must be the woods referred to in Domesday as measuring, with a high degree of inaccuracy, five quarentines (furlongs) in length and four in breadth, or about 200 acres only. The only comment necessary is to refer to Maitland's conclusion that Domesday measurements conveyed the idea of shape rather than size.[49] They were conterminous with Rockbourne Park and the boundary between them through the dense undergrowth was not clearly defined, since the necessity for delimiting it a second time arose in the thirteenth century. The woods on the Rockbourne side of the boundary contained deer in 1226.[50] At Damerham in 1307 there were said to have been 100 acres of large oaks and undergrowth worth 13s. 4d. a year.[51] There were poachers at Damerham, too, as well as at Martin, for in 1313 during the minority of John Bisset, who held the manor of Rockbourne, his guardian, John Drokenford, Bishop of Bath and Wells, complained that 'persons took deer, and with ferrets, nets and other engines, took rabbits in their burrows.'[52] At the suppression of Glastonbury Abbey in 1536 the woods were described as 'very well fett with oaks, ashes and maples, now ready to be sold, and valued at £514.13.5.' In addition, the growing timber was assessed at £555.16.7 and the yearly revenue accruing from the sale of wood and timber was reckoned at £26.0.10. There were also 'two eyes of fesauntes which always

48 Baron Rivers, *An authentic account of a late negotiation for the disfranchisement of Cranborne Chase* (1791), p. 10.

49 Maitland, *Domesday Book and Beyond*, p. 371.

50 Maddox, *Anglicana Baronia*, p. 53. I.P.M. 35 Ed. I, p. 53.

51 *I.P.M.*, 35 Ed. I.

52 *Cal. Pat. R.* 1315, p. 133; *ibid.* 1307-1313, p. 603.

have bred here.'[53] When the first Earl of Pembroke acquired this property in the reign of Queen Elizabeth, the four coppices known as Court Copse, Edmondshill, Middle Coppice and Drakenorth comprised 120 acres of 'hazels, willows, thorn trees and ashes of various ages and different species of oaks for timber.'[54]

These famous woods were sedulously preserved and judiciously replanted by successive members of the Coote family, so that at the sale of the property in 1941 the timber in the immediate vicinity was valued at £23,018. The woods were advertised to contain 6,024 oaks, 350 ash, 127 elm, 429 beech, 228 sycamore, 265 chestnut, 613 scots fir, 18 larch and 128 Wellingtonia, exclusive of hardwood poles.[55]

Mention must be made of Blagdon Park, which, though it was situated solely in Dorset, when first emparked by Roger Damory in 1321, expanded into the parish of Martin in the fifteenth century. Blakedown, as it was originally spelt, the cold, bleak upland, was bounded on the east by Bokerley Dyke, then known as Blakedounsditch,[56] and contained some 500 acres. It was a royal park, and in order to improve its hunting amenities, Edward IV had it enlarged in 1483 by an additional 240 acres. This enlargement coincided with the property of Kite's Nest farm, together with the down and heath land lying to the north of the Cranborne road. The text of the grant is as follows: 'Grant in frankalmoin to John,[57] the Abbot and the Convent of St. Mary, Glastonbury, of the manor of Sevenhampton Denys with Knights' fees and appurtenances, county Somerset, in recompense for 240 acres of pasture adjoining the King's Park of Blakedon, county Dorset, and pertaining to their manor of Estmerton, county Wilts, which they have granted to the King for the enlargement of his park.'[58]

Kite's Nest is probably not so recent as the present buildings suggest. It may well have been the forester's post in the thirteenth century to which allusion has already been made. Until about sixty years ago it was called North Blagdon farm[59] as distinguished from West Blagdon farm on the Dorset side of the boundary and at the same time retained in the

[53] Valor Eccles., and Dugdale, I, p. 18.

[54] *Pemb.* 1569, II, p. 312.

[55] Sale Catalogue, 1941.

[56] 'ad magnum fossatum de Blakedounsditch' in a document dated 1257 quoted by Dugdale, I, p. 57.

[57] John Selwode, Abbot of Glastonbury, 1457-93.

[58] *Cal. Pat. R.* 1476-85, p. 336.

[59] It was so named in the Tithe Awards, 1846, and locally until the end of the last century.

name its connection with Blagdon Park. Somewhere about 1890 the name was changed to Kite's Nest farm, named after Kite's Nest wood, which lies at the angle formed by the Tidpit-Cranborne road with Bokerley Ditch. Presumably the wood was at one time the haunt of a pair of kites.[60]

Since the grant above cited, Kite's Nest has always run with Cranborne rather than Martin. 'A warren of conies' in the Blagdon park was held to belong to the Prior of Cranborne in 1552.[61] Blagdon was disparked in 1570, and granted to John Scuddamore in 1577. John Hanham, who may have given his name to Hanham's Hill, acquired the property in 1582. The next owners were the Hoopers of Boveridge, who in 1788 sold it to Henry Brounker of the same place.

Vernditch (Fern Ditch) was at one time more extensive than it is today. The Roman road in Aubrey's day passed through it instead of along its southern boundary[62] and that part which lay to the south of the road belonged to this parish. Something has already been said about its connection with hunting and literature. John Aubrey, who lived at Broad Chalke was well acquainted with this part of the Chase and he learnt more from his relation who lived at Woodminton. The deer, Aubrey tells us, were already decreasing in his day (c. 1675). According to his estimate, whereas about 1650 there had been between one thousand and twelve hundred deer in Vernditch alone, some twenty years later there survived not more than five hundred.[63] Even so, it was more heavily stocked than any deer walk in the Chase proper. Though they weighed less than the Grovely deer, buckskins from Vernditch and Cranborne fetched sixpence a hide more. The native fallow deer were supplemented

[60] Smith, *Birds of Wiltshire*, p. 83, gives 1867 as the most recent record of a kite in Wiltshire. In his list of place-names referring to breeding places (e.g. Kite's Tree, Kite's Wood), he has omitted Kite's Nest, which deserves to be placed on record.

[61] *I.P.M.*, 2 & 3 Phil. & Mary.

[62] Aubrey, Mon. Brit.

[63] *A Chronicle of Cranborne* (1841), p. 315, gives the following view of deer, extracted from the Court Rolls:

	1645	1657
West Walk	170	105
Bursey Stool	80	20
Rushmore	185	160
Cobley	317	350
Staplefoot	80	55
	832	690

in the eighteenth century by an importantion of red deer from Horton Park, but they did not survive long. Wild boars were introduced from the New Forest in the time of Charles I, but, as they mated with domestic pigs, they were easily destroyed in the Civil War.[64] Vernditch was also renowned for its Martens, now almost extinct in England, whose skins in the seventeenth century fetched as much as 4s. 6d. apiece.

In the eastern part of the walk, north of the parish boundary, stood Vernditch Lodge, now demolished, though its foundations, still clearly visible, reveal the magnificent views in two directions which it commanded. So ideally sited was this house that a sportsman writing in the early years of last century declared of it, 'A trout stream running down Chickengrove bottom, and Vernditch Lodge would beat Paradise out and out.'[65]

The parish of Martin contains only 132 acres of woodland, of which 84 acres lie in Martin Woods. In the Middle Ages they were not separable from Boulsbury Hayewode, the chief cause of friction between the abbot and the Earls of Gloucester. Its name indicates that it was fenced for deer, and further suggests 'leaps and creeps', with enclosures for their capture. The forester of Hayewode was an important person on the Glastonbury staff and cannot have had an easy time. He had his farm at Boulsbury in the thirteenth century, and was allowed special privileges by the Convent of Glastonbury, among which was free pasture for his pigs and the top and lop of all trees felled.[66]

[64] Aubrey, *N.H. Wilts.*, pp. 58ff. A Parliamentary garrison was stationed at Falstone, only a few miles distant.

[65] Chafin, *Anecdotes and History of Cranborne Chase*, p. 86.

[66] *Rentalia*, p. 114.

III
THE PREHISTORIC PERIOD

WHEN such authorities as General Pitt-Rivers, Heywood Sumner, Professor and Mrs. Stuart Piggott[1] and others have done so much original work, it may seem both impudent and supererogatory in a layman to intrude in the realms of archaeology. Yet the omission of a brief account of prehistoric earthworks and their sites would leave a lacuna in what purports to be a parochial history. The following summary is offered with less diffidence because so much of it has been collated from the works of those authors.

The Neolithic period is represented by long barrows, of which there are at least four within the parish. Features, common to them all, are that in elevation they are sited above the 300 foot contour (the fourth to be hereafter mentioned is a few feet below it), and in direction they are orientated between the north and west points of the compass. Most conspicuous, both on account of their length and position, are Knapp and Grans Barrows,[2] which project prominently from the slope of Toyd Down. Their length entitles them to be ranked among the longer of

[1] To Professor and Mrs. Stuart Piggott, besides their generous help, I am deeply indebted for the privilege of examining their photostat copy of Aubrey's *Monuments*, from which I have freely quoted.

[2] Although only the former is within the parish (the boundary with Rockbourne passing between them) the two cannot well be dissociated.

long barrows, but their local reputation of being the longest in England is not substantiated by fact. Under the name Langeberge they formed a point on the boundary of the parish, as it is defined in and annexed to the Charter of 945. The Anglo-Saxon Wilton Way, also part of that boundary, so far from avoiding the barrows (though avoidance presented no difficulty) passes between them, using the barrows, it would almost seem, as a guide post. Their situation, as viewed from the village, on the slope rather than the summit of the Down, would appear to be a fine illustration of the theory of 'false crests' evolved by Stukely and explained by his biographer.[3] It indicates that the settlement, in which those who constructed the barrows dwelt, lay in the direction of the present village, and at that elevation at which they were most conspicuous. Until recently Grans Barrow was embellished by a cincture of conifers; now only a single specimen survives to denote what was once named Martin Clump.

A third barrow is situated in Burnbake field, a reclaimed part of Tidpit Common Down. Now ploughed almost flat, it never aspired to the length and prominence of the two just mentioned, and is, in fact, classified as a 'short' long barrow. At an elevation of over 400 feet, it lies south of and adjacent to Grimsditch and Hoare commented upon the fact that the ditch was deviated to avoid the barrow.[4] Examination of the site, as of the Ordnance map, leaves the opposite impression; that Grimsditch was diverted to come in contact with the barrow. Hoare would seem to have drawn the inference that the barrow was avoided out of reverence for a monument of the dead; in fact it would appear that the excavators were so far indifferent as to make use of the barrow as one side of their ditch. A quarter of a mile eastward of the barrow is the only ancient village site within the parish.

The fourth barrow is at the end of Long Barrow Lane, which deviates to the right from the road leading from Martin to the Turnpike. It was a familiar object to open field farmers in the Middle Ages, who described the furlongs in its vicinity by their position in relation to it, e.g. above, below, beyond or at Long Barrow.[5] Four trackways or paths converge upon it, and it was a point on the boundary demarcating the tithings of West and East Martin.

The former existence of a long barrow at Kitt's Grave, the point where

[3] Stuart Piggott, *William Stukely*, p. 71.

[4] Hoare, *H.S.D.*, p. 223.

[5] *Beere*. In, apud, super, desuper, stubtus, ultra Langberge.

the counties of Wiltshire, Dorset and Hampshire now meet, rests mainly on documentatry evidence. In local legend it is the place where a girl, in some versions a gypsy, having committed suicide, and no parish claiming her corpse, lies buried at the point where the parishes of Bowerchalke, Pentridge and Martin converge.[6] It is situated about 100 yards north of Grimsditch and close to the western end of Verndicth. A mound is said to have been visible there within living memory, and the traces that remain indicate a 'short' long barrow.

Cotelesburgh mentioned in the boundary appended to the charter of 945 is identifiable with Chetoles Beorh of an earlier Bowerchalke Charter of 917, and their indentification with Kitt's Grave has been put beyond controversy by Dr. Grundy.[7] In 1100 the Abbot of Cranborne, by virtue of holding Pentridge, collected the tithes of Coetel;[8] at the end of the Middle Ages the Abbess of Wilton, who held the Hundred of Chalke, built a gallows at Chutelborghe, and the Abbott of Glastonbury, holding the parish of Martin, protested.[9] The demands of three conventual heads of great monastic foundations upon the tithing of Cotelsburgh tend further to confirm its position at the convergence of three parishes and its identification with Kitt's Grave.

In the *Pembroke Survey* of 1569 a description of the Rotherdown in the parish of Bowerchalke is given, 'which begins at the western end of Verndicth at a certain barrow called Gallowes Barowe and extends by the ditch which divides Chalke and Martin and ascends to the plain by well-known bounds to the highway leading eastward'.[10] The ditch dividing Chalke from Martin can only be Grimsditch, and the barrow at the western end of Verndicth would seem to be none other than Kitt's Grave. Here, then, is a sinister ascription to Kitt's Grave as far back as the beginning of the sixteenth century to relate with the local legend of today.

Martin Down and Tidpit Common, both virgin turf, undisturbed by the plough from time immemorial, together extend over 910 acres,[11] on which are concentrated in three groups thirteen round tumuli. How many in cultivated areas have been levelled by the plough must be a matter of

[6] Edith Olivier and Margaret Edwards, *Moonrakings*, pp. 72, 74.
[7] *Arch. Journ.* LXXXI, p. 68.
[8] Hutchins, III, p. 382.
[9] Beere, p. 64.
[10] *Pemb. S.* I, p. 90.
[11] A large part of the down was ploughed up during the war but is not now under cultivation.

speculation, but the density on the Down suggests that not so many have vanished as is sometimes supposed. In the old days of the horse plough it was not so easy to erase all traces of a barrow; on the other hand, when three years ago the Ministry of Agriculture introduced the bulldozer to Martin Down, two round barrows were completely obliterated. Barrows are conspicuous features and furlongs in the open fields were often denoted by their situation with regard to them, as in the case of the long barrow mentioned above. It is a fact, not without significance, that wherever in the medieval terrier of Martin a field is named after a barrow, that barrow survives today; examples are Whitebarrow fields at the top of Smallend Lane, Stopland Barrow field, where Grimsditch camp now stands, and the Long Barrow fields already mentioned.

But nowhere within the parish is there evidence of such an ubiquity of tumuli as were at one time visible in the contiguous parish of Pentridge, west of Bokerley Dyke. Aubrey writes of them: 'There are a little within the line [i.e. Bokerley] nineteen barrows and some of them very great. Here are also two or three circular trenches with a little tump or two which were possibly the places *combustione cadaverum*. Mem. The many barrows between this and Pentridge, and in the Chase is a coppice called Barrow Coppice, where are many barrows.'[12]

At Thornhill, where Martin Down is narrowest and cultivation approaches nearest to Bokerley Dyke, there was a group of five, a trio and a pair.[13] They lie close to that ditch which diverges in a northerly direction from Bockerley and passing south of Martin Down enclosure, proceeds to Vernditch, and is ascribed by General Pitt-Rivers to the Bronze Age.[14] A second group is contained in the obtuse angle formed by the intersection of Grimsditch with Bokerley. Between the latter and Whitebarrow field along a distance of about a thousand yards are eight round barrows. To the west again lies the third concentration near the ancient village on Tidpit Common ascribed to the Romano-British period. One of these was the subject of an anecdote by Aubrey. 'In a barrow', he writes, 'above Todpitt, vulgo Tippit, in the parish of Merton, by digging for a windmill post A.D. 1650 an urne was found with small pieces of buried bones in it and a spear's head and the tusk of a boar with a hole in it as if to put a string in it. I had it but gave it to the Repository of the

[12] Aubrey, Mon. Brit. pt. IV; cf. also Heywood Sumner, *Ancient Earthworks*, p. 48, quoting Stukely.

[13] This pair has been erased by the Ministry of Agriculture, as mentioned in a previous paragraph.

[14] Pitt-Rivers, IV.

Royal Society. About this Todpitt and other parts hereabout are pitts of great antiquity. I could never learn why they were made.'[15]

Since that date there has been extensive despoliation of barrows, and in the past fifty years important scientific excavation and systematic preservation of their contents. But this round barrow above Tidpit can claim the distinction of having been among the first to have been examined by an antiquary with a conception of the value of his discovery, and the exhibits must have been among the earliest to have been presented to the Royal Society, which, though it had been founded some years before, was not incorporated by charter until 1662. Unfortunately there survives no record of Aubrey's donation in the archives of the Society.[16]

The most recent addition to the literature of Grimsditch[17] most importantly establishes that it is not a homogeneous whole, but a complex system of earthworks of which a part, probably the greater part, dates from the Bronze Age and part from the Iron Age. Two intersections of the ditch, where it is crossed by the Wilton Way on the southern and northern perimeter, determined this new fact: the sector on the south near Damerham Knoll was found to be of Iron Age construction,[18] that on the north near Toyd Clump to date from the middle or late Bronze Age.[19]

Any theory as to the purpose of Grimsditch must, therefore, take this new discovery as its starting point. It follows from it that the excavators of the northern sector did not contemplate *ab initio* an enclosure, or, if they did, never completed it. The final link which created the enclosure – if indeed that was the purpose and not two independent boundary lines – was not made until several centuries later.

The superficial area of this irregular 'enclosure' is estimated to be some fourteen square miles, and its circumference about sixteen or seventeen miles, with continuations of the ditch at the north-east and north-west corners. The average depth is given as five to six feet.

The purpose for which Grimsditch was excavated still remains an enigma. Archaeologists have, however, cleared the field of conjecture by the negative process of eliminating what it can *not* have been. Thus,

[15] Aubrey, Mon. Brit., pt. V; *v.* also Hoare, *H.S.D.*, p. 223.

[16] So I was informed by the Secretary.

[17] C. M. Piggott, in *Antiquity*, XVIII, p. 65; *v.* also H. C. Bowen in *Recent Work in Rural Archaeology*, ed. P. J. Fowler.

[18] Sumner, *Ancient Earthworks*, p. 28.

[19] C. M. Piggott, *loc. cit.* p. 67.

it can never have been a defensive ditch, because, apart from its being too shallow, the spoil has been cast up on either side at the whim of the diggers or as the terrain offered greater facility. It is improbable again that it was ever intended for the confinement of cattle; our early ancestors were capable of numerous devices more economical of human effort than the excavation of a ditch of such length, and one, moreover, which allowed cattle easy egress.

The view, first propounded by Aubrey,[20] that the ditch might be a trackway, providing intercommunication between the settlements situated near it, some of which are coeval with the ditch, is an attractive one. Against it two objections have been opposed: first, that at both intersections the ditch was found to be V-shaped with steep sides and a base of not more than two feet. But this is not in itself decisive; native paths in central Africa seldom exceed two feet in width and are often as narrow as nine inches. A two-foot path is sufficient for pedestrian traffic and for the transit of livestock. The second point is mentioned only in connection with the southern (or Iron Age) cutting, that the base reveals no evidence of having been trodden.[21] We should perhaps be cautious of accepting this single observation as conclusive, or of making it applicable to the whole circuit of the ditch.

The preponderance of archaeological opinion, however, from Warne and Hoare to Sumner and Mrs. Piggott, favours a tribal boundary of some sort, whether of people or fields. Within the 'enclosure' there are no settlements coeval with the ditch (we exclude the cattle post on Martin Down and the later farm on Rockbourne Down) unless their vestiges have been destroyed by cultivation. This suggests that the ditches were constructed by people living outside them, probably either to the north or to the south.

Grimsditch is mentioned twice in the boundaries appended to the 945 charter: in the northern sector it is called Strete Ditch, after the metalled Roman Road, at one point aligned on the top of it. In the southern sector it is named Wide Ditch, its overall measurement averaging 50 or 60 feet.

Among post-Conquest documents Grimsditch is mentioned under that name in a perambulation of Cranborne Chase dated 1275.[22] The *Pembroke*

[20] Aubrey, Mon. Brit.

[21] Sumner, *Ancient Earthworks*, p. 61.

[22] *Placita de Quo Warranto*, 184(b). The earliest reference given in *P.N.W.*, 16, is in an I.P.M. of 1380, Grymsditch.

Survey of 1569, as has already been said, referred to the northern sector as 'le trench which divides Chalke and Martin'.

Aubrey, at the end of the seventeenth century, was the first by personal investigation and diligent inquiry to attempt to discover the direction, extent and purpose of this and other ditches. It has been imputed to him that he confused Grimsditch with Bokerley.[23] But the error he really made was to align the Dorset-Wiltshire (new Hampshire) boundary with Grimsditch instead of with Bokerley. A source of confusion is indeed presented to the readers of his *Monumenta* by his having illustrated the ditches by a map, accompanied by various symbols in Part II, the key to which is to be found in Part III. The most easterly ditch is described as: 'At Chalke Southdown runs a rampart having its graff westward: it is upon the division of Wiltshire and Dorsetshire and runs into Cranborne Chase.'[24] This is Grimsditch along which he has erroneously demarcated the county boundary. It is the same earthwork of which in an earlier passage he wrote: 'Over Blackdon Hill (west of Merton) there runs a great crooker ditch which comes from Cranborne Chase. T. Golden told me it is called Grimsditch. Quaere, how far it runs? It parts Dorsetshire and Wiltshire.'

The middle ditch is: 'ββ a great work (perhaps in the nature of the Picts' wall) with the graff eastwards.'[25] This is an unmistakable description of Bokerley dyke. Then: '. . . a work of the like nature with the last but not so great, having the graff also eastward.'[26] This way may be identified with the first or easternmost of the Seven Ditches. Aubrey's diagram is reproduced opposite.

The overall horizontal measurement of the massive earthwork of Bokerley averages 82 and the vertical 20 feet, exceeding in altitude both Wansdyke and Offa's Dyke. To the men of Martin, Bokerley is always that immense ditch and rampart which frowns upon the western flank of their Down; but to the archaeologist the less spectacular sector, next Woodyates, named by General Pitt-Rivers (with more regard to aptness than euphony) Bokerley Junction, has a greater interest. It has been minutely and methodically excavated:[27] the ditch here bifurcates into the Rear and the Fore Dykes; it is intersected by the Roman road from

[23] O. G. S. Crawford, in *Antiquity*, XVIII, p. 71.
[24] Aubrey, Mon. Brit., pt. III.
[25] *Ibid.*
[26] *Ibid.*
[27] Pitt-Rivers, III.

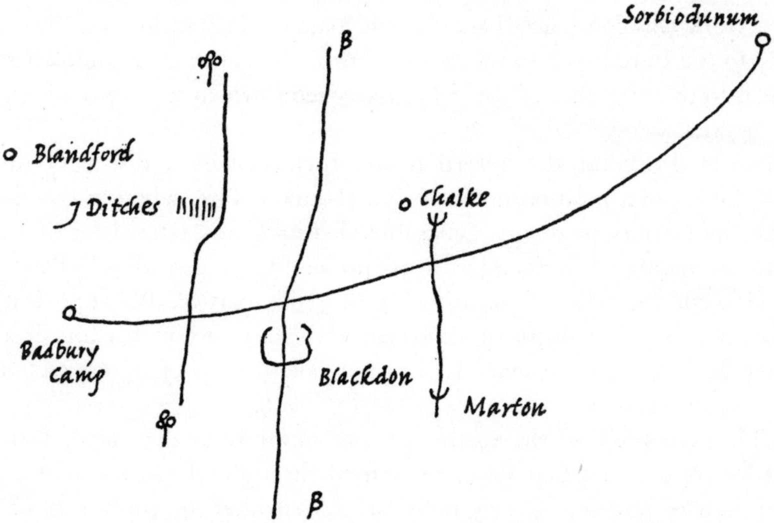

Old Sarum to Dorchester and lastly it is claimed to be the site of the Roman Town of Vindocladia.[28]

Writers since General Pitt-Rivers have been unanimous in ascribing a post-Roman date (or at any rate one contemporary with the last of the Emperors to rule over Britain) to the earthwork and have assumed it to have been constructed as a defensive fortification, to oppose an incursion advancing along the Roman road from Old Sarum.[29] This view has remained unchallenged for fifty years until Professor Hawkes recently expressed a doubt whether it was substantiated by the General's discoveries.[30] On General Pitt-Rivers himself must rest a large share of the responsibility for any misconception, since his statements are not free from ambiguity. 'The dyke', he writes, 'is now proved to have been thrown up no earlier than the reign of Honorius (395–423) and possibly by the Romanised Britons as a defence against the Saxons,'[31] And again:

[28] The site of Vindocladia is still open to discussion.
[29] Sumner, *Ancient Earthworks*, p. 55.
[30] *Arch. Journ.* CIV, pp. 62 *et seq.*
[31] Pitt-Rivers, III, p. 20.

'Bokerley Dyke was not thrown up until at or after the time of the evacuation of Britain by the Roman legions in A.D. 407.'[32] It is hardly surprising that it should be inferred from such passages that the whole earthwork was constructed subsequent to 407, whereas, in fact, they refer only to the Fore Dyke to the north-west of the Salisbury-Blandford road, that is to that member of the defensive scheme which was chronologically the latest.

The evidence for this assertion was furnished by a discovery in the Fore Dyke, in a position on the original surface line, where it could not, either by fortuity or design, have intruded itself at a later date, of a coin of the Emperor Honorius (395–423) and another of Arcadius.[33] The coins provide conclusively a *terminus a quo* for this part of the work, but for this section only. Failure to appreciate the exact site of this find has led to the application of its evidence to the whole instead of to one section of the earthwork.

The main body of the earthwork has never been excavated. General Pitt-Rivers believed that what he termed the right flank, the centre and right centre terminated originally at the epaulement south-east of the Salisbury-Blandford road.[34] The epaulement itself was, on the evidence of a coin of Magnentius, not earlier than 350–53,[35] and it has been assumed that the centre and right flank are contemporary with it.

Such being the position left by the excavations of General Pitt-Rivers, the archaeologists are under a debt of gratitude to Professor Hawkes for putting Bokerley Dyke in its proper perspective in a critical examination of the evidence in the *Archaeological Journal*.[36] He has propounded for the separate parts a chronology, which, unless future excavations disclose unexpected material, is not likely to be disturbed. For the right flank and central portion (Hawkes's 'A') he ascribes the date 325–30,[37] mainly on the evidence of fragments of pottery found at the epaulement, the extreme northerly limit of this sector of the dyke. The Rear Dyke, a purely military earthwork, is precisely dated to the year 367, when the south of England was invaded by a force of Saxons.[38] The discovery of a

[32] *Ibid*, p. 152.

[33] *Ibid*, pp. 14, 64. The rear dyke is ascribed to the years 308-313 on the evidence of a coin of Maximinus.

[34] *Ibid*, p. 292.

[35] *Ibid*, p. 90.

[36] *Arch. Journ.* CIV (1947), p. 62.

[37] *Ibid*, p. 70.

[38] *Ibid*, p. 76.

coin of Valens (364–68) in the re-filling of the ditch where it cut across the Roman road from Old Sarum to Dorchester was an important factor in determining the date with such exactness.[39] The Fore Dyke (Hawkes's 'C') is shown to be an improved version of the Rear Dyke, and on the strength of the Honorius coin was thrown up about the year A.D. 405.[40]

It must be acknowledged that Professor Hawkes's analysis of the voluminous material has produced a complete and satisfactory explanation of all the known data; but in his development of a conjecture of the late Professor Collingwood that Cranborne Chase may have been an imperial estate for the exploitation of sheep farming,[41] and in his supposition that the right flank and centre of Bokerley Dyke may have formed one of its boundaries comparable with the Bitberg Walls in Germany, he does not, perhaps, carry complete conviction.

This theory of the primary purpose for which this section of Bokerley Dyke was constructed raises a number of difficulties, for it assumes that defence against barbarian incursions was only a subsidiary reason.[42] It may be asked why this colossal earthwork should have been constructed, when the older Grimsditch, sited on an almost parallel alignment, was already there and ready to be utilised. Again, if this be one boundary, where are the others? If a deterrent to stock-theft was the object,[43] why was it considered necessary to build a fortification so massive and in character so obviously defensive? The precipitousness of the rampart and the profundity of the ditch were, surely, designed not against sheep-stealers, but to oppose an army.

To those who attached a significance to the comment of General Pitt-Rivers that not a single fragment of evidence of Saxon occupation had been observed,[44] the conclusions of Professor Hawkes may not come as a surprise. But the Roman origin of all sectors of the dyke has effectually demolished the hitherto accepted notion that it was constructed in the turbulent years that followed the Roman evacuation as a defence against the invaders of Wessex.

The dyke is referred to in the Charter of 945 in the passage 'along the ditch to Widegate' (Woodyates),[45] where the boundaries of the grant

[39] *Ibid*, p. 73.
[40] *Ibid*, p. 78.
[41] Collingwood & Myres, *Roman Britain and the English Settlements*, p. 224.
[42] *Arch. Journ.* CIV, p. 71.
[43] *Ibid.*
[44] Pitt-Rivers, III, p. 153.
[45] Birch, *C.S.*, II, p. 579.

to the convent of Glastonbury are defined. In a perambulation of 1237 it is called Blakedounsditch,[46] i.e. Blagdon ditch, after Blagdon Hill, which it traverses. The word Bokerley has not been found earlier than the end of the seventeenth century, when Aubrey spells it Bocally.[47]

In the next chapter a claim has been advanced that the site of the battle of Meretune in 871 was Martin Down, but there is no historical evidence that any battle was fought on the Bokerley Dyke position. Nevertheless, so formidable a bastion may well have served its purpose by deflecting an invading army, such, for instance, as that which captured Old Sarum in 552, from further penetration into Wessex. It is tempting to conjecture that the isolated find of a Saxon sword at Toyd[48] might be connected with some such campaign. An invading army, having landed at Southtampton Water, defeated the Britons at Cerdicsford (identified with Charford, between Downton and Breamore) in 519, and again at Old Sarum. If, as Sir Oscar Crawford suggests, their route took them beyond Downton to Odstock,[49] it brought them within three miles of the Saxon sword and eight of Bokerley Dyke.

Martin Down enclosure has achieved archaeological distinction, not so much because of its revelations, as on account of the systematic and exemplary method of its excavation by General Pitt-Rivers in 1895.[50] It is a small rectangular enclosure, containing only about two acres, with a low ditch and bank and two entrances. It is surmised to have been a cattle post or a small pastoral settlement, and though never densely populated, is thought to have been occupied over a considerable period of time. Pottery ascribes the site to the Bronze Age. Besides the domesticated animals, ox, sheep, horse and pig, large specimens of red and roe deer were found. Sir Oscar Crawford formed the opinion that invaders in the period 700–500 B.C. were responsible for rectangular encampments of this type.[51]

No more need be said after the General's meticulous account of his excavations, but an allusion may be made to modern fables. The legend that it was the original site of Martin village appears to have originated with the excavations of 1895. A decade later, when W. H. Hudson

[46] Dugdale, p. 57.

[47] Aubrey, Mon. Brit., *passim*.

[48] Now in the Salisbury Museum. Neither the donor, nor the exact locality of the find are known.

[49] *Antiquity* XX (1931), p. 441.

[50] Pitt-Rivers, IV, p. 185.

[51] *W.A.M.* 43, p. 129; also O. G. S. Crawford, *Professional Papers*, No. 7.

wrote *A Shepherd's Life* and Martin came to be identified with his Winterbourne Bishop, the Down Enclosure was invested with a church and a bishopric. The site is today known locally as Church Bottom.

The Roman Occupation of England is represented on the map by areas in which either the villa or the village predominated. Cranborne Chase, Salisbury Plain and, indeed, Wiltshire generally, are distinguished by the paucity of Roman villas and the frequency of Roman villages.[52] Close to the parish boundary, but outside it, there are many examples of the village: within the parish there is but one, situated on Tidpit Common Down. Formerly described on Ordnance Surveys as British, more recently and less committally as ancient, it is now believed, subject to the verdict of excavation, to be Romano-British. It lies on the exterior edge of Grimsditch and in the vicinity are visible square Celtic linchet fields. Only half a mile distant, slightly to the south-east, and separated by a reentrant, from which presumably water was drawn, is another Romano-British village, which indicates a fairly close settlement on the Downs here at this period.

Only a quarter of a mile away from the latter site, in the parish of Damerham, is the enclosure of Roman date called Soldier's Ring. It is a pentagonal enclosure, surrounded by a shallow bank and ditch, superimposed upon some older Celtic fields. It has several entrances (some of which are recent), its total area is between twenty-six and twenty-seven acres and its purpose is a mystery. Until more conclusive evidence is available, the view that it was an enclosure for cattle is open to revision.

The attractive suggestion has been made that Soldier's Ring was the original site of Boulsbury, which lies about three-quarters of a mile from the Ring.[53] An early form of Boulsbury is Ballesbergh,[54] which may be connected with La Balle,[55] a field name in 1518 and Ball Hill Copse of the present day, neither of which are far away. Soldier's Ring occupies the eastern part of Blackheath Down, which runs with the Boulsbury property. For the name Soldier's Ring we must probably look to recent times. It was known by that name to Sir Richard Colt Hoare writing about 1830, who, however, qualified it by the adverb 'vulgarly' Soldier's Ring. By 1870 it had become 'Soldier's Ring Camp'. It is the sort of name that may have originated no further back than the Napoleonic

[52] Collingwood and Myres, *Roman Britain*, pp. 210, 222.

[53] Grundy, in *Arch. Journ.* LXXXI, p. 71.

[54] *P.N.W.* p. 400. The earliest forms are Baltesberg and Baulesberg (Inq., 1189). Rudulfus de Baltesburgh also occurs in Inq., 1189.

[55] *Beere*, p. 42.

wars, when the militia were in that state of constant mobilisation in Wessex, described by Thomas Hardy in his novel *The Trumpet Major*. It may have been no more than the summer camping ground of the local militia. In 1779 George III, when staying at Wilton, rode out to review his troops on Tidpit Down.[56] And the last of the Hoopers, Captain Edward, locally known as the 'Father of the militia', trained at Boveridge a company so smart and disciplined as to earn the admiration of all who saw them reviewed in Hyde Park.[57] Captain Hooper trained his company in his own grounds at Boveridge, but may well have prescribed for them exercises on a ground so admirably adapted for parade and so conveniently near to his own residence.[58]

Few of those who live in Martin realise that a considerable part of the Roman settlement of Vindocladia lies beneath the soil of their parish. For, since General Pitt-Rivers identified Vindocladia of the Antonine Itineraries with Woodyates, it has been associated with that parish rather than with Martin. Yet the angle formed by the present Salisbury-Blandford road with the county boundary running northwards from 'Bokerley Junction' is covered with vestiges of this settlement. The magnitude of the discovery may be judged from the fact that over 1,200 Roman coins were found in addition to 800 in Bokerley ditch and rampart. Skeletons, pottery, bronze and iron artefacts, fragments of bones of animals, domestic and wild, hypocausts and drains were among the profusion of remains discovered. The General has devoted a large part of his third volume to this excavation.

But perhaps the most familiar of Roman survivals is the road which connects Old Sarum with Dorchester, which over much of its length through the parish is in excellent preservation. A description of it finds a place in an earlier chapter in which the road system at Martin is developed.

Occasionally field names may give an indication of the Old English heathen epoch. There are, perhaps, two such names in this parish. La Burelle or Les Burelles is given as a field name in the east field of East

[56] Lord Herbert, Henry, Elizabeth and George. Letters and Diaries of the 10th Earl, 140.

[57] Hutchins, III, p. 385. Boveridge is under two miles from the Ring.

[58] Adjacent to Soldier's Ring is Knight's Copse. It is possible that Knight's Copse may recall a knight's fee, on the analogy of Erlesford as has been suggested, deriving from the Lopshill knight's fee. From the Knight to the Soldier is no great step. And perhaps for the origin of both the copse and the ring we should look to the knight's fee of the Wife of Hugo, *v. infra* Ch. IV.

Martin in Beere's survey of 1518. Like the Burrells at Rowde, near Devizes, it may have its origin from Byrgels, meaning, in old English, a burial place.[59] The site of the field cannot now be identified. The other is Wedone, which occurs in the same survey, a furlong in the east field of Tidpit, also unidentified. It is derived from the old English 'weoh', meaning a shrine or sacred precinct.[60]

[59] *P.N.W.*, p. 425.
[60] Stenton, *Anglo-Saxon England*, p. 101.

IV

KING ALFRED TO DOMESDAY

HISTORIANS are not yet in agreement as to the site of the battle of Meretune, contested in 871 by King Aethelred and his brother Alfred against the Danish forces invading Wessex. Various localities have been proposed; Merton in Surrey,[1] Morton in Berkshire,[2] Merton-on-Otmoor in Oxfordshire,[3] Marden in Wiltshire,[4] Marten near Great Bedwyn in the same county,[5] and Martin in Hampshire.[6]

From this selection preference has until quite recently been given to Marden, situated in the Pewsey Vale. The identification of the site of the battle with Marden seems to have originated with Camden, who in 1586 suggested that 'Marden might probably enough be the Meretune or Meredune of the Saxon Annals, famous for the battle between King Ethelred and the Danes in 871'.[7] Besides local tradition and vestiges of

[1] Freeman, *English Towns & Districts*, p. 183. Oman, *Hist. of England*, p. 37.
[2] Lingard, *History of England*, I, p. 188.
[3] Kennett, *Parochial Antiquities*, I, p. 48.
[4] Britton, *Beauties of Wiltshire*, p. 17; Hodgkin, *Pol. Hist.*, I, p. 280.
[5] Grundy, in *Arch. Journ.* LXXV, p. 191.
[6] Warne, *Ancient Dorset*, p. 267; Major, *Early Wars of Wessex*, p. 124.
[7] Camden, *Britannia*, (Gough, 2nd Edition, 1806), I, p. 159.

entrenchments, his grounds for this supposition were that near Marden he found a barrow in altitude second only to Silbury Hill. The myth of the Hatfield Barrow, as it is usually known, was only exploded when the excavations of William Cunnington and Sir Richard Colt Hoare in 1809 disclosed, besides charred wood, only 'a few small fragments of human bones'.[8]

Such evidence, in the light of modern archaeology, is not likely to gain wide acceptance. While it is acknowledged that barrow burial persisted into late Saxon times, it is not argued that the common soldiery, defeated in battle, were so interred – unless, indeed, as secondary interments, which pre-supposes an earlier date for the barrow. Barrow burial is believed to have been reserved for persons of distinction, but the only person of high rank known to have been killed in this battle was Heahmund, Bishop of Sherborne, who was buried at Keynsham near Bath.[9] Indeed, if an ubiquity of barrows were an indication of a battle site, the claim of Martin would take precedence. Aubrey, who shared Camden's opinion that the prevalence of barrows was evidence of slaughter on the battlefield, wrote of the barrows west of Martin Down: 'West of the work [Bokerley Dyke] there has been a terrible fight . . . So great a sign of slaughter I never found not heard of in England. One may plainly see that the chace of victory runs westwards. I have observed, when I have been hawking, at least one hundred barrows, sparsim, in the Downs and elsewhere.'[10]

The relevant extract from the *Anglo-Saxon Chronicle* furnishes the following account of the battle: 'Two months later the Kings Alfred and Aethelred fought against the army at Merton; and there were two divisions and they put them to flight and far into the day were victorious. And there was great slaughter on both sides, but the Danes held possession of the battle place. And there were slain Bishop Heahmund and a great many good men. And after this fight there came a summer force to Reading. And the Easter after Aethelred died, and his body lies at Wimborne Minster. A month later Alfred beat the Danes at Wilton. . . .'[11] The only contemporary authority who might have been able to amplify this account was Asser, Bishop of Sherborne and the biographer of King

[8] Hoare & Cunnington, *Ancient Wiltshire*, p. 6; also Meyrick in *W.A.M.*, pp. 52, 217.

[9] Aethelweardus, IV, p. 2: 'in loco Caeginshamme;' *v.* also *Six English Chronicles* (Bohn), p. 67.

[10] Aubrey, Mon. Brit., pt. III.

[11] *Anglo-Saxon Chron.*, *sub anno* 871.

Alfred, who, for reasons which his editor explains, omits any mention of the battle.[12]

The best manuscript of the *Anglo-Saxon Chronicle* gives the spelling Meretune. It was written at Winchester about thirty years after the battle was fought,[13] and should, therefore, be a good authority on the spelling of local topographical names. The great majority of post-Conquest chronicles follow the same spelling.

Now, the names Marten (Wilts) and Martin (Hants) are alike derived from the old English words 'maere', meaning a boundary, and 'tun', meaning a farm or settlement.[14] Marden, on the other hand, is thought to be a combination of the elements 'merh', meaning fertile and 'dene', meaning a valley.[15] The identification of Meretune with Marden involves the assumption that the chronicler wrote '-tun' when he meant '-dene'.

The first syllable of Meretune has not the same relevance to the argument. But the late Dr. Grundy, deriving it from 'mere', meaning a pool, found the settlement by the pond adapted itself fittingly to a description of Marten, just as Warne a century earlier had translated the elements in Martin as *oppidum paludosum*,[16] an apt description of the village when the stream flowed down the main street.

Nevertheless, the topographical argument which appealed to earlier Anglo-Saxon scholars gave way to the cogency of the etymological evidence among modern historians.[17] Marden, then, rejected for these reasons, was superseded by Marten, near Great Bedwyn. Grundy, who favoured this site, emphasised that close to Marten passed the Roman road from Mildenhall (Cunetio) to Winchester, along which the English forces might retire in the event of defeat. It is, however, not without significance that they retreated not upon Winchester, but to Wimborne, a journey of almost twice the distance.

The Danish army was based on Reading, where they had fortified the angle at the confluence of the Kennet with the Thames.[18] The event pre-

[12] *Asser's Life of King Alfred*, ed. Stevenson, p. 239.

[13] Stenton, *Anglo-Saxon England*, p. 680.

[14] *P.N.W.*, pp. 307, 402. But Ekwall (*Oxf. Dict. of English Place-Names*, gives as the most likely meaning 'Settlement (*tun*) by a lake', adding that the lake has in many cases disappeared.

[15] *P.N.W.*, p. 321.

[16] Warne, *Ancient Dorset*, p. 267. 'The swampy village'.

[17] Earl and Plummer, *Two Saxon Chronicles*, p. 88; Plummer, *Life and Times of King Alfred*, p. 95. T. Hodgkin, *Pol. Hist.*, I. p. 280; R. H. Hodgkin, *History of the Anglo-Saxons*, p. 548.

[18] *Asser* (Stevenson), p. 87.

ceding the battle of Meretune had been the encounter at Basing towards the end of January, in which the English army was defeated; the event following it was the engagement at Wilton about the twentieth of May. Both these battles suggest that the Danes were exploiting a southerly rather than a northerly route, possibly even an advance upon Winchester itself. After the defeat at Basing the English line of retreat would naturally be such as would cover Winchester and protect the approaches to the west, rather than a deviation to the north with the risk of communications with the capital being intercepted.

Close to Basing is Silchester, the Roman Calleva, and the eastern terminus of the Via Iceniana of the Antonine Itineraries, which, passing through Winchester and Old Sarum, proceeded to Dorchester and Exeter. Astride this road lies Martin Down defended by the massive earthwork of Bokerley Dyke. The road was the historic gateway into Wessex. The dyke had been thrown up to protect the approaches against just such another invasion.[19]

The battle was fought on the twenty-second of March, the date being determined by that day having been appointed in the calendar for the commemoration of the martyrdom of Bishop Heahmund.[20] The date coincides with the vernal equinox, not usually a propitious season for campaigning. This fact alone may have predisposed the armies in favour of the Roman road founded upon six strata of metalling.

Although the Danes remained in possession of the field of battle, they were not in a position to give pursuit, and Aethelred was able to withdraw to Wimborne Minster, only fourteen miles from Martin. It is pertinent here to revert to Marten and to enquire why, if it were the scene of the battle, the king did not retreat upon Winchester, to which the road was open. If, as the inscription on his tomb at Wimborne suggests, he was severely, perhaps mortally, wounded in the battle, it might be expected that he would retire to his capital to be interred with the bones of his father Aethelwolf and his grandfather Egbert. Instead, he makes a much longer journey to a nunnery at Wimborne with which his family had had hitherto very little connection. On the other hand, from Martin retreat to Winchester would have been impossible, because the Danish army was interposed between the king and his capital. So Aethelred, in his wounded state, was compelled to make his way along a road that was not under threat from the enemy, to the nearest sanctuary at Wimborne.

[19] Hawkes, in *Arch. Journ.* CIV, p. 76.
[20] Plummer, *King Alfred*, p. 92.

The itinerary of Aethelred after the battle seems a fatal objection to the identification of the site with Marten.

The original brass on Aethelred's tomb in the Minster was seen by Leland, who copied it, apparently incorrectly, for he gave the date of the King's death as April 13th. But the *Chronicle* is conclusive that he died after Easter, which in that year fell on April 15th. The inscription runs: 'In hoc loco quiescit corpus Sancti Ethelredi regis West Saxonum, Martyris, qui Anno Dom. DCCCLXXII; XXIII die Aprilis per manus Dacorum paganorum occubuit.'

The proposition advanced, then, is that Meretune of the *Chronicle* is to be identified with Martin.[21]

The earliest documentary reference to Damerham is contained in the Will of King Alfred,[22] ascribed to a date between 880 and 885,[23] and is accepted as genuine by Anglo-Saxon scholars. The final paragraph reads: 'And I will that there be given to the convent of Damerham their charters and their liberty to choose such land (lord) as may be most desirable for them for me and for Aelflaed and for the friends for whom she has interceded and I intercede.'[24]

The text has been taken to mean the Alfred wished the people of Damerham to be free,[25] which, without laying too much emphasis on the implications of freedom at this date, is a justifiable paraphrase. They are enjoined to transfer their land and their liberty to the house at Damerham that they may have a lord of their own choice.

Damerham was at this time royal demesne in the possession of the king and was not alienated until some sixty years later, when King Edmund bequeathed it to his wife with reversion to the Abbey of Glastonbury. The evidence for the existence of a convent there rests upon Thorpe's translation of this passage, and upon this passage alone. Although the word used in the Latin version is 'domus' and in the early English text 'hows',[26] there is no evidence whatsoever that there ever was

[21] *v. W.A.M.* CXCIV, p. 36, where the writer has discussed the site of this battle in greater detail, and *W.A.M.* CXLVI, p. 362, where Lt. Col. Burne furnishes strategical and tactical reasons in favour of a site on Martin Down, north-east of Bokerley Ditch.

[22] Birch, *C.S.* II, p. 176.

[23] Stevenson (*Asser*) LXVII, regards it as probably earlier than 884. Kemble and Birch place it between 880 and 883.

[24] Thorpe, *Dipl. Aev. Sax.*, p. 492.

[25] *V.C.H., Hants*, IV, p. 586.

[26] The translation given in *English Historical Documents* (1955), I, 495, is as follows: 'And I desire that the community of Damerham be given their title-deeds

a convent at Damerham. Had one, in fact, existed, it is inconceivable that it could have escaped the notice of Glastonbury historians from William of Malmesbury and Adam of Damerham to the late Jason Armitage Robinson and Professor Knowles.

There is no notice of a convent in Asser's biography of King Alfred; nor is it mentioned in the grant of Damerham by King Edmund,[27] though the land is described in considerable detail, and the presence of a convent on the estate might be supposed to interest Glastonbury; it is not mentioned in the Will of Aethelflaeda, Edmund's widow; it was not known to Adam of Damerham, who might be expected to claim antiquity for a convent in his native village. Moreover, the mass of material relating to Glastonbury manors, which has in the past sixty years been published under the auspices of the Somerset Record Society, is entirely silent about a convent at Damerham.

On other grounds its existence is wholely improbable. The degeneration of monastic life in England in this reign is notorious and will be referred to later. Since it can not have been a survival of the early missionary venture, it follows that it must have been a foundation of King Alfred himself. He founded a monastery at Athelney and a nunnery at Shaftesbury, and contemplated the New Minster at Winchester. Had he founded also a convent at Damerham, it could hardly have been omitted from his biography.

It remains to find an adequate translation of the 'hows' or 'domus' of Alfred's Will. The name Damerham, derived from Domrahame, is said to mean an enclosure of the judges,[28] and throughout the Middle Ages as well as in modern times there has always been a building called the Court House – an appropriate depository of charters. It has been pointed out that the places mentioned in the Will are the private property of the king and his family.[29] Thus later his grandson, Edmund, as the owner, was in a position to leave it in his will to his wife, with a reversion to Glastonbury. Confirmation of this is furnished by his widow, Aethelflaeda, signing herself 'Queen aet Domrahame'[30] in 946, that is to say at the royal residence at Damerham. This, then, seems to be the meaning of the word, a royal residence, situated on a private estate of the

and freedom to choose whatever lord they prefer, both for my sake and for Aelfflaed and for the friends for whom she used to intercede and I intercede.'

[27] *infra* p. 50.

[28] *P.N.W.* p. 400.

[29] Plummer, *King Alfred*, p. 90.

[30] *Anglo-Saxon Chronicle* (Rolls Series), II, p. 90.

king.[31] His interest in the villagers thus becomes explicable and intelligible.

The Charter,[32] on which Glastonbury Abbey relied for its title, consists of a grant by King Edmund of land to his wife, Aethelflaeda, conditional on her demising it to the 'ancient church of Our Blessed Mary in the monastery of Glastonbury', of which Dunstan was at that time the abbot. The estate consisted of 100 *mansae* 'at Domerhame cum Mertone et Pentrintone', and included also arable, downland, pasture, meadows and woods.[33] The charter is undated, but must be assigned to between the year 944, when Edmund's firs wife died, and the year 946, when he died himself. Athelflaeda,[34] the daughter of Ealdorman Aelfgar and second wife of Edmund, the 'Queen aet Domrahame' of the *Anglo-Saxon Chronicle*, discharged her trust in a will dated not earlier than 975.[35] In it neither Martin nor Pentridge are mentioned, although, according to William of Malmesbury, quoted by Adam of Damerham, they were expressly included in the original grant.[36]

The date of Edmund's grant is significant. As has been seen above, during the preceding century monasticism had declined almost to the point of evanescence. Before the time of Dunstan, Glastonbury was said to be the only place where a few monks kept to the Rule,[37] and they have been described as a *familia* of clerks,[38] possibly supervised by thanes instead of an abbot.[39] Its revival was due to the appointment of Dunstan as abbot by King Edmund in 943. With Dunstan was associated a lady, Aethelflaeda, who built herself a house to the west of the abbey,[40] accepted the ministrations of the abbot and devoted herself to his service.

The identity of this Aethelflaeda has not been solved, though some details about her are known. It might be supposed that she was the widow

[31] If this surmise is correct the site was probably that occupied later by Glastonbury, now Court, Farm.

[32] Birch, *C.S.* II, p. 580. Kemble, *Codex Dipl.*, III, p. 271; Adam of Damerham, II, p. 72; John of Glastonbury, I, p. 121. In Birch the grant runs '. . . delecte conjugi vocitimane Aethelflaeda . . . ut derelinquat ad ecclesiam vetustam Beatae Virginis Marie Glastoniense'.

[33] 'campis, pascuis, pratis, silvis, donans donabo libertatem'.

[34] Napier and Stevenson, *Crawford Collection of Charters*, pp. 86-87, unravels the perplexing relationship of Aethelflaeda.

[35] Birch, *C.S.* III, p. 600; Whitelock, Anglo-Saxon Wills, p. 34.

[36] Adam, II, p. 72: 'Ejus uxor Aethelflaeda ejus jussu dedit Domerhame cum Mertone et Pentingtone C. hidas.'

[37] Cockayne's *Leechdoms*, III, p. 435.

[38] Knowles, *Monastic Order*, p. 34.

[39] Armitage Robinson, *Times of St. Dunstan*, p. 21.

[40] *Memorials of St. Dunstan* (ed. Stubbs), p. 17.

of King Edmund, the beneficiary of the estate at Damerham and the testatrix of that estate, in accordance with the will of her husband, to Glastonbury. But the editor of the *Memorials of St. Dunstan* expressly affirms that she was not Aethelflaeda of Damerham[41] and inclines to the identification of her with Aethelflaeda of Ramsey, daughter of Ealdorman Ethelwold.

The coincidence of date of the grant of King Edmund with the revival of the monastery at Glastonbury cogently suggests that the grant, with the expectation of the considerable revenue accruing from so large an estate, may have been the principal endowment of the re-founded convent. The liberality of Edmund towards Glastonbury is mentioned both by William of Malmesbury and by the author of the memorials.[42] The hundred hides of this charter was by far the largest area conveyed by a single grant, exceeding by a large margin the seventy hides at Wedmore or the sixty hides at Shapwick. After Glastonbury itself, it was also the richest manor. Henry of Blois was justified two centuries later in describing it as the chief of the Abbey's manors.[43]

No special significance need be attached to the description of the area as 100 *mansae* or hides. The term implied no more than sufficient land for the sustenance of one hundred families. The figure was, no doubt, a round number, but as an estimate of the population at that date probably not far from accurate. It presupposed a population of some 500 souls,[44] apportioned among the three villages, a figure that is not an unreasonable inference in the light of Domesday statistics. According to the Glastonbury Use, which reckoned 160 acres to the hide, the area contained 16,000 acres.[45]

Although not contemporary with the charter of 945, the boundaries afford much interesting material to the student of topography and place-names, upon which Dr. Grundy has helped to throw much illumination.[46] They are considered to have been an addition of the Middle Ages. They circumscribe the parishes of Damerham and Martin only, and therefore must have been defined after the alienation of Pentridge and

[41] *Ibid*, p. 18. She was a niece of Athelstan.

[42] William of Malmesbury, *Gesta Pontificum*, p. 196; *Memorials of St. Dunstan*, p. 92.

[43] Adam, II, p. 313: 'sic quoqu mannerium quod ante praecipuum dicebatur . . . re vera praecipuum feci'.

[44] Adopting Maitland's formula of multiplication by five. (*Domesday Book and Beyond*, p. 408).

[45] *Infra*, Chap. XII. The equivalent of about 12,667 *statutory acres.*

[46] Grundy, in *Arch. Journ.* LXXXI, p. 65.

the detachment of Woodyates. Pentridge was held by the Abbey in the reign of Edward the Confessor, but at the time of Domesday was crown demesne[47] and thereafter followed the descent of the Earls of Gloucester together with Cranborne Chase. Woodyates, a hamlet of Pentridge, was still part of the Abbey's estates in Domesday Book, all its four hides being held by the wife of Hugo,[48] who also held three hides in Damerham Parva. But, although it was held together with Damerham Parva until the end of the fourteenth century, it is evident that after the Domesday compilation Woodyates came to be regarded as a separate Dorsetshire manor. Thus the medieval boundaries of Damerham and Martin exclude from their terms both Pentridge and Woodyates, but appear to be older than the two amendments which followed.[49]

Two perambulations were made over sectors of the boundary in the thirteenth century; one in 1227 defining the bounds between Rockbourne and Damerham,[50] the other in 1246 demarcating the boundary from Biddlesgate to Bokerley.[51] In the former the point at issue was the right of pasturage, and it was brought to a final concord; in the latter, encroachment by the Abbot of Tewkesbury was in dispute. Both affected the parish of Damerham only, and although in the latter the Abbot of Tewkesbury lost some ground to his brother of Glastonbury, no material change was made. On account of their topographical interest and the light they throw upon the evolution of place names, the texts of the three perambulations are given below.

(i) Perambulation appended to the Charter, Birch II.580:

'From the Ash at Penegeford,[52] along the brook to Erlisford, from thence to Brinesford and so along to Mereborne to Heghebrugge and so along to Brockleford and to Thulewe and along the White Lake up to King's Berwes[53] and then right up to Brokhurste and along the lake to the hide of Lopushale[54] and so by Talayate[55] and then to the ditch by West

[47] 'Ipse ecclesia *tenet* Pentryc, T.R.E. et geld pro VI hidis. Terra est VI carucatis. Rex tenet modo in dominio'.

[48] 'Ipsa ecclesia tenet Ódeyete et uxor Hugonis de Abbate. T.R.E. geldavit pro IV hidis'.

[49] *Beere*, p. 64, mentions a perambulation made by Abbot Adam of Sodbury (1330-1345) to which the boundaries which follow may have belonged.

[50] *Feet of Fines, Wilts*, 17. Folio 15, p. 54.

[51] Dugdale, I, 57, *Infra* Ch. V.

[52] Elsewhere Padnore Ash, gave its name to Ashford Water at the confluence of the Allen stream with the Avon below Fordingbridge. At this date it was the beacon where the counties of Dorset, Wiltshire and Hampshire converge to a point.

[53] King's Barrow, 6″ O.S.

Widemere[56] and so along the riggis to Upiate[57] and thence along the ditch[58] to Wideyate[59] and then to the Gore,[60] and so to Cotelesburgh[61] and thence to Seven Strete,[62] and to Cotelshed[63] and so along the Streteditch[64] to Wiltonweie[65] and so along that way to Langeberghe[66] and then to Wideditch[67] and thence over the Knoll[68] to Acclei[69] and so to Hedstokke, and thence to Drakenhorde[70] and so along the ditch to the Frimditch and so to the Mere and from the Mere to the Landsherestokke and thence to Coppenthorne[71] and then to the Ellenbaum,[72] and then to Presteyate up to Holebroke Hill and so to Sladishevede and then to the Ash at Penegeford that stands in Wilts, Dorset and Hants, whence it began.'

(ii) The perambulation of 1227 (Cal. F. of F. Wilts, 17, Folio 15,54):

'From the corner of Damerham Park to Leiborne, to Wilkestile, to Holbroke Estrode, to Holbroke as far as the Hasche to the Water at Padnore.'

(iii) The perambulation of 1246 (Dugdale, *Mon. Angl.*, I, 57):

'Starting from Biddlesgate the boundary shall go always in a straight line along the whole length alongside the old ditch, the ditch remaining with the Abbot of Tewkesbury; and from that ditch in a straight line as far as a certain tree called Le hijs; and from that tree through the middle of Kentelscombe and from Kenelscombe [*sic*] as far as the croft of

---

54 Hyde Farm, Lopshill.
55 ? Biddlesgate.
56 Meare's Pond in Boulsbury Wood.
57 Either the Peak or Bokerley gap.
58 Bokerley Dyke.
59 Woodyates.
60 Triangular ploughland: an angle.
61 Chetoles Beorh of the Bowerchalke Charter of 917, now Kitt's Grave.
62 Sarum-Dorchester Roman Road, *v.* Crawford & Keiller, *Wessex from the Air*, p. 183.
63 Chettlehead. This order of names must be due to transposition; the only intelligible sequence is Gore-Cotelshed-Cotelesburg-Seven Strete-Skete Ditch.
64 Grimsditch from the point where it diverged from the Roman Road.
65 The Wilton Way, the Anglo-Saxon road from Damerham to Wilton.
66 The two Longbarrows on Toyd Down, known as Knap and Grans Barrows.
67 Grimsditch, at the base of Damerham Knoll.
68 Damerham Knoll.
69 Oakley Field.
70 Drakenorth 6″ O.S. Drakenhorde, 'the dragon's hoard' or treasure, must refer to some local legend.
71 Pollarded Thorn Tree.
72 Elder Tree.

William Schortefriende of Overtone; and from the corner of that croft as far as the great royal way, and so by the length of that way as far as the great ditch of Blagdonditch.'[73]

A survey of the boundary of the hundred was made with meticulous precision from field to field in 1817.[74] Apart from its remarkable conformity with the boundary annexed to the Charter, it is noteworthy chiefly for the number of boundary posts mentioned in it which have since disappeared. One of these was a Hoare stone at the point where the boundary intersects the Cranborne-Tidpit road which, however, being on the local boundary between Martin and Damerham, is not mentioned in that perambulation. It is plotted on the map annexed to the Damerham Inclosure Awards, in which two adjoining fields are named Hoare Stone Grounds. The author of *A Chronicle of Cranborne* described it as 'a large block of conglomerate, called a "wurstone".'[75]

By the time of Domesday, the 100 *mansae*, equated by Glastonbury with 100 hides, had become reduced to fifty-two. The difference can only partially be accounted for by the alienation of Pentridge and the detachment of Woodyates, together containing ten hides. Another hide at Lopshill had been lost to the Abbot of Cranborne. But the social and economic hide of Edmund had been replaced by the fiscal hide of William I; the hide was now a unit for purpose of taxation.

The Domesday survey of Damerham, which includes Martin, is as follows:[76] 'The church of St. Mary at Glastonbury holds Dobreham and it was assessed T.R.E. at 52 hides. Here are 30 ploughlands. Sixteen of these hides are in demesne where are 4 ploughlands and six Servi and 38 Coliberti. 14 Villani and 17 Bordarii occupy 19 ploughlands. 4 mills pay 20 shillings and here are 26 acres of meadow. The pasture is in length 3 leucae and one leuca broad. The wood is in length 5 quarentinae and in breadth 4. Of this land Serlo holds 5 hides. The wife of Hugo 3 hides. Roger 8 hides and 8 acres. Those who held them T.R.E. could not

[73] Dugdale, I. 57. I am indebted to Miss E. Clarke of Cranborne for the suggestion that Kenelscombe may be identified with Kennel Pond, one-and-a-half miles west of Boveridge.

[74] Court Rolls 1817.

[75] *A Chronicle of Cranborne*, (1841), p. 312.

[76] *D.B.* 66(b). It may be conveniently studied in Penruddocke Wyndham's *Wiltshire extracted from Domesday Book*, published in 1788, p. 97, but since his day research has thrown a new light upon Domesday nomenclature. His most egregious mistranslation of *coliberti* as fishermen, is, it is only fair to say, corrected in a footnote to page x of his preface. In the twelfth line the words 'ibi sunt 3 carucatae et dimidium' are not translated.

be separated from the church. There are three ploughlands and a half.

'The whole manor T.R.E. was valued at £36. It now pays £61, but it is not appraised by the men at more than £45 on account of the confusion of the lands and because the demesne is rated too high. The land of the military tenant is worth £7.15.0.

'The same church [i.e. the Abbey of Cranborne] holds one hide at Dobreham. Here is one ploughland and a half. The Abbot holds one ploughland and 5 Bordarii half a carucate. The value is 20 shillings.'[77]

Domesday Book is fortunate in having been analysed with exceptional erudition. But it may not be irrelevant to emphasise some of the more salient features connected with this parish. There were six serfs at Damerham and Martin. While it would seem that in Wiltshire the abbesses, e.g. of Wilton or Shaftesbury in Dorset, had proceeded with the emancipation of slaves more rapidly than the abbots, the latter were a long way ahead of the royal manors, where a far larger proportion of the village population remained in a state of serfdom. The class of *coliberti* or freedmen were more common in Wessex than elsewhere in England, but at Damerham and Martin, not only were they the largest single class, but, numbering thirty-eight, they constitute more than half the persons engaged in agricultural operations. At none other of the fourteen Glastonbury manors in Wiltshire were there any coliberti at all. On the thirty-five Glastonbury manors in Somerset there were only nineteen, and on the six Dorset manors thirteen, all at Sturminster. They occur in Wiltshire more commonly on royal than on monastic manors.[78]

The *coliberti* have been equated with the Buri or Geburs, and were a class of emancipated slaves. The adjoining parish of Bowerchalke where (with Broad Chalke) there were ten *coliberti*, is derived from the word Buri.[79] In status they were inferior to the *villani*, and as a class disappear from later surveys. From the kind of work they had to do the *coliberti* seem to correspond with the holders of half virgates a hundred years later. It is attractive to suppose that the convent of Glastonbury through its manor at Damerham exercised its influence in securing the emancipation from servitude of this exceptionally large number of freedmen, in compliance with the wish of King Alfred expressed two centuries before.[80]

[77] *Ibid.* 144.

[78] e.g. Melksham, 31; Westbury, 16; Aldbourne, 15; Warminster and Bedwyn, 14 each, all royal manors. Bradford-on-Avon (Abbess of Shaftesbury) had 18, and Broad Chalk (Abbess of Wilton) 10.

[79] *P.N.W.*, p. 204. *v.* Stenton, *Anglo-Saxon England*, 467-70.

[80] *v. supra.*

The *bordarii* are classified as indistinguishable from cotsettlers[81] or cotagers. They are seldom found together on the same manor; thus where, as here, there are *bordarii*, there are no Cotsettlers. But the rule is not universal; on twelve of fifty-nine Glastonbury manors both *bordarii* and cotsettlers were found at the time of Domesday. A hundred years later, at Damerham the *bordarii* have disappeared and cotsettlers, who had no place in the Domesday Survey, have taken their place.[82] Fifty years later again, the cotsettlers are superseded by the tenants of a quarter virgate, the ferling or ferdel.[83]

Domesday Book introduces us to those who held land which later became knights' fees. In the Hundred of Damerham there were three. The *servitium debitum*, or the number of knights which Glastonbury Abbey was under an obligation to produce, when called upon by the king was about the year 1159 forty knights, and sometime earlier it had been sixty.[84] But the figure remained at forty for the next hundred years.[85] The Abbey, however, relieved itself of its responsibility by leasing or sub-infeudating its fees; one was so let to Serlo and his successors, the Martins at Tidpit, another to the wife of Hugo and his successor, Alfred de Nichole at Damerham, and the third to Roger and his successors, the de Gurnays at Lopshill. In turn they often sublet, as, for example, Nicholas Martin sublet part of his fee at Tidpit to Ralf de Baskerville. The revenue accruing from the rents, dues and services attached to the fee enabled the tenant to retain one knight, fully armed, equipped and trained. Thus in the rent-rolls and customaries of the twelfth and thirteenth centuries, the people living on the knights' fees are not included because their rents, dues and labour services were rendered not to the Abbey, but to the tenant responsible for providing the knight. There is, for instance, no mention of any villein tenants at Tidpit paying rents or owing labour service to the Abbey in the surveys of 1189 and 1245, because they discharged their rents and services to the holder of the knights' fee.

Service in the field at an early date was commuted for scutage, an arbitrarily fixed sum of money, usually one pound, or, as in the great scutage of Toulouse in 1159, two marks on the fee. The levy was not an

[81] Stenton, *Anglo-Saxon England*, p. 470. The only distinction seems to be that Borde is derived from French, and Cot from English.

[82] Inq. 1189, p. 129.

[83] *Rentalia*, 110; and *v. infra*, Ch. XII.

[84] Round, *Feudal England*, p. 251.

[85] *G.C.*, p. 234.

inconsiderable one, involving a total from the Abbey of Glastonbury of £53.4.0.[86] But by the time of the episcopate of Jocelyn, of Bath, it had been reduced to £30.[87] In 1242 Alfred de Nichole paid £10, i.e. £2 for each of his five hides; in 1267 his son paid the same amount for the expedition to Wales, and when the fee was divided, Robert Fitzpain paid £6 and William de Guise £4.[88]

Adam of Damerham transcribed in his *Historia* such excerpts from Domesday Book as concerned the Glastonbury estates, and a later scribe added interest to them by inserting an occasional note in the margin. Against the extract of Damerham there are two such notes: the hide held by Roger is annotated with the name Mallet, which does not occur elsewhere in the history of the village, and the five hides held by Serlo with the name Martin.[89] Martin has nothing to do with the village, which at this time was invariably spelt Meretune or Mertone. It records, as is corroborated from other sources, that the fee of Serlo descended to a family named Martin. It was situated at Tidpit and, according to the Glastonbury method of reckoning, comprised 640 acres. It, therefore, must have embraced beside the arable in the open fields, also the meadow and down pasture.[90] More probably, however, it represented an area of land estimated to be worth £20. The subsequent history of this fee is given in the *Foedary* of Abbot Walter Monyton[91] as follows:

'Serlo was the first predecessor of William the son of Martin. He held of the Abbey five fees and half a knight by military service that is to say a fee of five hides. They were made up:

	hides
at Netherhamme in the manor of Hamme, Somerset	5
at Pulle in the manor of Pulton	5
at Overton in the manor of Monkton	2
at Hornblowton in the manor of Dychesgate	5
at Todeputte in the manor of Damerham, Wilts.	5
	22

86 Round, *Feudal England*, p. 278.
87 John of Glastonbury, p. 404. (Hereafter abbreviated to John of G.)
88 *Foedary*, p. 31. 'sub nomine scutagii de scutagio currente'.
89 Adam, p. 651.
90 The medieval open fields contained about 350 acres of arable and the downs 237 acres of pasture.
91 *Foedary*, p. 25.

Afterwards the fees were held by William, son of Walter, i.e. in the time of King Henry. Then by Robert the son of Martin. Then by the son of Robert the son of Martin who acted as intermediary between the Abbot and Ralf de Baskerville, knight, the tenant in demesne of the said five hides at Tudeputte. Ralf de Baskerville ceded the five hides by charter to the Abbot and Convent of Glastonbury in free and perpetual alms together with the advowson of the free chapel and the services of freemen and villeins of the same manor of Tudeputte.'

This brief summary, however, exposes several omissions and needs to be supplemented from other sources. Martin of Tours, who accompanied the Conqueror to England, received for his services, in addition to a grant of land in Pembrokeshire, the barony of Martin in Somersetshire, by tenure.[92]

Serlo (c.1086) was succeeded by Robert Martin, who flourished in the reign of Henry I.[93] His name is omitted from the *Foedary* of Abbot Monyton, but manifestly a life must have intervened between that of Serlo and William, the son of Walter, the next, according to the *Foedary*, in succession. William, the son of Walter, held the fee in 1166,[94] paid homage to Henry de Sully, Abbot of Glastonbury, in 1189[95] and died in 1209.[96] Though in actual possession of the fee William does not appear to have been related to the Martin family, whose representative during his lifetime was Robert, to whom the fee was restored in 1255.[97]

All the lists of fees of the Martin barony tabulated in the *Foedary*[98] agree in placing Robert, son of Martin, in succession to William, son of Walter, but the *Historic Peerage* interposed a William, who died in 1215. Robert, the son of Martin, married in 1224 Juliana,[99] an alliance which formed a connection with Ralf de Baskerville, who later became closely connected with this fee. Robert was succeeded by William, the son of Robert, the son of Martin,[100] a tenant intermediate between the Abbey and Ralf de Baskerville.[101] He was succeeded by Nicholas, of whom Ralf de

[92] Nicolas (ed. Courthope), *Hist. Peerage*, p. 316.

[93] *Ibid.*

[94] The Red Book of the Exchequer (Rolls Series), p. 223.

[95] *Foedary*, p. 56.

[96] *Cal. Pat. R.* (1224) p. 463.

[97] *Som. Rec. Soc.*, XLVII, 'Wulfric of Haselbury' by John Abbot of Ford, edited by Dom Maurice Bell, where the descent from Serlo is given.

[98] *Foedary*, pp. 86, 87, 109, 113, at Ham, Monkton, Pylle and Horblotton.

[99] *Cal. Pat. R.* (1225), p. 586.

[100] *Foedary*, p. 25, in the descent of the Tidpit fee, gives only 'the son of Robert, the son of Martin', but all other lists supply the Christian name, William.

Baskerville in 1242 held half the fee of one knight.[102] Nicholas succeeded to the fees at Ham and elsewhere, but his name is omitted from the descent of Tidpit, and it would appear that he had surrendered it to Ralf de Baskerville. The latter in 1255 conveyed it, with the chapel and advowson, to the Abbey of Glastonbury.[103] It was held in demesne in 1260.[104] In 1264 Nicholas did homage to the abbot, Robert of Petherton, when he expressly excepted Tidpit from the number of his fees.[105] In 1275 the Abbey held it direct from Nicholas.[106] In 1282 Nicholas died.[107] By his marriage with Maud, the heiress to the barony of de Traci, that honour became merged in the barony of Martin.[108] His successor to the fee was his grandson, William,[109] who died in 1325, and from his son, another William, the barony passed through his sister, Joan, to the Audley family.[110] After the dissolution Tidpit was disposed of to John Barwick and Robert Freke.[111] The connection of the Audleys with Tidpit was revived in the sixteenth century when John Tuchet, heir to the united baronies, acquired the advowson of the chapel of Tidpit,[112] although it had long been disused. It was then sold to John Webb, of Salisbury, and soon afterwards acquired by the Earl of Pembroke.

Ralf de Baskerville belonged to a distinguished Herefordshire family. He married Petronilla,[113] sister of that Juliana who had married Robert the son of Martin. In return for his conveying the Tidpit fee to the Abbey, he received in exchange the manors of Idmiston and Grittleton for his life.[114] He also held a third part of a virgate in the village of Tidpit, which he had bought for fifteen marks from Walter Boteler, who had earlier purchased it from Robert de la Felde. Walter Boteler is described as of Compton (Chamberlayne) and his daughter Juliana subsequently

---

101 *Ibid.*
102 *Book of Fees*, p. 732.
103 *Foedary*, p. 25.
104 *Rentalia*, p. 230.
105 *Ibid*, p. 234.
106 *Rot. Hund.*, II, p. 253.
107 Cal. Gen. I, p. 321.
108 Nicolas, *Hist. Peerage*, p. 479.
109 Cal. Gen. I. Henry III – Ed. I. p. 11. *Foedary*, p. 25.
110 Nicolas, *Hist. Peerage*, p. 316.
111 *Cal. Pat. R.* 3 Ed. VI, pt. XI.
112 *Wilts I.P.M.* (series of) CLIX, 74; *v.* Ch. IX.
113 *Close Rolls* (1258), p. 90.
114 Hoare, *H.S.D.*, p. 14.

renounced her dowry in Tidpit. The deed, witnessed by William of Martin, must belong to the last half of the thirteenth century.

The three hides held by the wife of Hugo in Domesday Book[115] comprised the tithing of Damerham Parva, Little Damerham or Coffyn, in which were situated the manor and vicarage houses. These alternative names are given in the *Nomina Villarum* of 1316.[116] The manor house was known as Damerham Parva Farm[117] until the nineteenth century was well advanced. The name Coffyn first occurs in 1216 when Elias Coffyn was granted lands in Damerham belonging to his brother Ralph.[118] About 1235 Matilda Coffyn, having set up her own jurisdiction at Damerham in opposition to that of the Abbot Michael of Amesbury, was deposed to her proper status.[119]

The fee of the wife of Hugo descended to Alfred de Nichole who made homage to the Abbot Henry de Sully in 1189.[120] He held it upon a tenure of sergeantry, obliging him to set before the abbot on his birthday the first dish, and if he were not invited to take part in the abbot's hospitality he would go without dinner, and entering by the back door, proceed about the abbot's business to obtain his summons and so discharge his relief.[121]

When his son, Alfred, died without issue in 1264, his fees were divided among the heirs of his three sisters.[122] Robert Fitzpain, son of the eldest sister, inherited Damerham Parva, and did homage to Robert of Petherton, Abbot of Glastonbury in 1264 for a third part of five and a half fees.[123] He was succeeded by his son Robert, who died in 1315[124] and a grandson who died in 1335, also named Robert, and a great grandson, Robert, who held three hides in Damerham Parva and died in 1354.[125] On his death the capital lordship of the manor lapsed to the Abbey of Glastonbury,[126] but his son Thomas who held the manor of Rockbourne, and a

115 *Wiltshire Domesday*, p. 96.

116 Hoare, *H.S.D.*

117 Inclosure Awards, 1818.

118 *Rot. Lit. Claus.* (Hardy), 274b. (1216).

119 Adam, 507; *infra* Chap. V. An Ada Coffyn occupied the Abbey's Grange (Bustard Manor Farm) at the end of the fifteenth century, and Coffyn was still the name of the tithing in 1605 (Court Rolls).

120 Inq. 1189, p. 7.

121 *Ibid.* 'in die natalis si inter fuerit.'

122 *Som. Rec. Soc.* XLVII, p. 154 gives their descent.

123 *Rentalia*, p. 234.

124 Adam, I, CXVI.

125 *Foedary*, p. 24.

126 *V.C.H. Hants*, IV, p. 588.

descendant, another Thomas, who married Joan Romsey, held also certain hereditaments in Damerham (infra).

As mesne tenants under Alfred de Nichole in the thirteenth century were the family of St. Quintin, of whom John is mentioned c.1290, followed by the family of St. Martin, of whom the first was William,[127] succeeded in 1297 by Reginald, who died in 1314, and Lawrence de St. Martin, on whose death in 1385 the name disappears from Damerham, but through the marriage of his sister Joan into the family of Calstone, this mesne lordship descended to Thomas Calstone, under whom it was heir to Daniells and apparently lapsed about the middle of the fifteenth century.

As sub-tenants under them were the family of de da Mare, who held extensive estates in Wiltshire, upon a tenure of sergeantry which involved the duty of supervising the harlots entering the King's Court.[128] Peter de la Mare held in 1242 the knight's fee in Damerham Parva of John de St. Quintin, who held of Alfred de Nichole, who held of the Abbey.[129] His daughter Marjorie, married Hugh Peverel, who in 1265 held a tenement in Damerham Parva worth a hundred shillings.[130] At the time of his death about 1296 he held forty-eight acres of Reginald de St. Martin for the eighth part of a knights' fee.[131]

In 1258 when the church of Damerham was ordained a vicarage, the greater and lesser tithes of a tenement belonging to William Peverel in Damerham Parva was assigned to the vicar as part of his stipend by the Bishop of Salisbury.[132] No other notice can be found of William, but Thomas Peverel, when he died in 1300, held in Damerham one carucate of Reginald de St. Martin by the service of one quarter of a knights' fee, the capital messuage, and fifty-seven acres of arable worth 2d. an acre, the whole estate being valued at sixty shillings and sixpence.[133]

Joan Peverel, his sister and heir, married John de Wraxhale, who sold half the manor to John Bisset (ob.1306), already the lord of the manors of Coombe Bissett and of Rockbourne, inherited from his mother, Ela. His son, John, died without issue in 1334, and the property descended to his sister, Margaret, who married, as her first husband, Sir Walter Romsey.

127 *Rentalia*, p. 230.
128 A. L. Poole, *Obligations*, p. 74.
129 *Book of Fees*, Part II, p. 732.
130 *Cal. Inq. Misc.*, I, p. 281.
131 *Cal. I.P.M.*, I, p. 248.
132 *G.C.*, I, p. 58.
133 *Wilts. I.P.M. Ed. I. – Ed. II*, I, p. 248.

Their son Thomas married Joan,[134] whose first husband had been Thomas Northlode, the heir to the manor of West Martin and Stapleton, after the death of William of Martin about 1300. Their son Thomas and grandson John Northlode succeeded. In 1430 he held also a hide of land at Stapleton of the Abbot of Tewkesbury. John and his two aunts, Cecilia and Maud, died without issue, and in default of heirs the succession devolved upon Joan Romsey, the widow of Thomas Pain, and the great grand-daughter of Sir Walter Romsey, by his second wife Alice Fyllol.[135]

John de Wraxhale, the husband of Joan Peverel, alienated only half the manor of Damerham Parva. The other half descended to their daughter, Maud or Matilda, who married William de Baddeby.[136] On his death in 1374 the estate was escheated, but restored when their daughter Edith married Oliver Servington. In 1419 he is shown as holding in Little Damerham messuages and land,[137] but in the following year, 1420, when he died, also 'the manor of Damerham, near Martin'.[138] His grandson, David Servington, in 1456 held the same.[139] The manor remained in the Servington family until 1554, when it was sold by John Servington to Sir John Cooper.[140] It was about this time mortgaged to Anthony Ashley, who held the *capitale messuagium* in 1569.[141] In the early part of the seventeenth century Sir Anthony Ashley represented at the Damerham court leet the Servington freehold[142] and the property was so described until the end of the century. The manor house was sold by Lord Shaftesbury to the Egremont family in 1856.

Reverting now to Joan Romsey, the widow of Thomas Pain, as the heir to the family estate she held, in her own right, the manor of Rockbourne, and messuages and sixty acres of arable and 8/- in rents at Damerham, and a messuage and a virgate of arable at Martin.[143] By her marriage with Thomas Fitz Pain she became allied with the descendant of Alfred de Nichole; by the death of John Northlode without heirs she became next of kin, inheriting that part of the manor which had

[134] *Cal. I.P.M.*, IV, p. 520.
[135] *V.C.H. Hants*, IV, p. 586.
[136] *Cal. I.P.M.*, II, p. 332b.
[137] *Ibid.* IV, p. 41.b.
[138] *Ibid.* IV, p. 50.a.
[139] *Ibid.* IV, p. 272.b.
[140] See *V.C.H. Hants*, IV, p. 586, for the descent from Peter de la Mare.
[141] *Pemb. S.* p. 309.
[142] Court Rolls, 1607–1613.
[143] *Col. I.P.M.*, III, p. 272.b.

been sold by John de Wraxhale to the Bissets; and from the inheritance of Thomas Northlode at the beginning of the fourteenth century of land held by William of Martin, she acquired the manor of West Martin and Stapleton.[144]

In the person, therefore, of Joan sometime before 1447 there had become concentrated the immense properties of the Bissets, Romseys and Pains. About 1447 she died without issue, and the next in succession was her second cousin, William Horsey. William was the son of Eleanor, who had married into the Dorsetshire family of Horseys. Eleanor was the daughter of Mary, a sister of Sir Walter Romsey, who had married a Byngham. William Horsey was, therefore, a grand-nephew of Sir Walter Romsey. He did not survive long. At an Inquisition taken in 1447 after his death, it was proved that he held the manor of Rockbourne; half the manor of Coombe Bisset; 2 messuages and 6 shops in New Sarum; 5 messuages, 70 acres of arable, 60 acres of pasture, 10 acres of meadow, and 20/- in rents at Damerham and West Martin;[145] 15 messuages, 2 carucates of arable, 10 acres of meadow, 20 acres of woodland, and 20 acres of pasture, of which Stapleham (Stapleton) is a part.[146] The descent of the Horseys is traced in a later chapter,[147] up to the sale of the Damerham property in 1564 and the Martin Estate in 1621 to Sir John Cooper.

The third knight's fee which corresponds with the land held at the time of Domesday by Roger, was at Lopshill and is recalled today by Hyde Farm. In the following century it descended to William Fitzjohn, who did homage to Henry de Sully in 1189 for one quarter of a knights' fee.[148] It passed to his grandson, Robert de Gurnay, who paid homage to Robert of Petterton, Abbot in 1269.[149] The fee was afterwards held by Anselm de Gurnay[150] and a John de Gurnay, who left it to Elizabeth, the wife of John Apadam.[151] A John Apadam did homage to Geoffrey Fromond, Abbot, in 1359,[152] and soon afterwards, in default of heirs, it lapsed to Glastonbury Abbey.

144 *Foedary*, p. 27.
145 Est Merton in the text must be an error for West Merton.
146 *Cal. I.P.M.*, IV, p. 236.a.
147 *Infra*, Chapter VI.
148 *Foedary*, p. 24.
149 *Ibid.*
150 *Rentalia*, p. 230.
151 *V.C.H. Hants.*, IV, p. 589.
152 *Foedary, loc. cit.*

A tenant of Robert de Gurnay in 1242 was Elias de la Hyde, who held one sixth part of one knights' fee.[153]

Towards the end of the thirteenth century, it was annexed by the foresters of the Earl of Gloucester, operating in Cranborne Chase, one of whom, Nicholas Scorditch, sold it to the Prior of Cranborne. In 1428 the Prior held one quarter of the fee, and, jointly with Isobel Martin, Roger of Bradonston and William of Buttlesgate (Biddlesgate) the other quarter as tenants of the Abbey.[154]

153 *Book of Fees*, Pt. II, p. 732.
154 *V.C.H. Hants.*, IV, p. 589.

V

THE MIDDLE AGES

THE vicissitudes of Glastonbury Abbey during the twelfth century call for some comment. In 1082 in conformity with the Conqueror's policy of substituting Normans for Englishmen in ecclesiastical posts, Aethelnoth, the West Saxon Abbot, was deposed, and Thurstan appointed in his place. One of his innovations was to supersede the old Gregorian chants by new fashioned modulations devised by William of Fecamp.[1] When the monks resisted, he introduced archers into the Abbey Church, who from the triforium shot down upon the monks, terrified and cowering in the choir, killing three and wounding eighteen more. Although removed on account of this and suchlike behaviour by William I, his recall was among the first acts of William II. In this reign the manor of Damerham was alienated from the Abbey. Thurstan had dissipated the lands and the revenues of the Abbey on his own perverted lechery.[2]

The annexation of a hide of land at Lopshill in the southern part of the parish of Damerham by Robert Cotele, with the consent and on the suggestion of Herlwine,[3] who became abbot in 1102, is not inconsistent with

[1] John of G., p. 158.

[2] William of Malmesbury, *Gesta Pontificum*, p. 196.

[3] Adam, p. 312. The words are those of Henry himself, quoted from his *Scriptura Henrici Blessiensis*.

the alienation of the manor. Henry of Blois expressed himself indignantly about the irregularity of the procedure, and Henry de Sully at the end of the century candidly criticised the transaction as having been done over the head of the abbot.[4] On the death of Herlwine Richard Cotele claimed it to be his by the gift of the Abbot, and bequeathed it to his wife and children, as though it were an hereditary possession.[5] This hide is said to be distinct from that held at Lopshill by Roger at the time of Domesday,[6] but it is admittedly difficult to find territorial space for two hides of the area of a Glastonbury knights' fee (640 acres) in this part of the hundred.

This hide, together with parts of the manors of Camerton, Pucklechurch, Ure and Poulting descended with the Cotele family. A successor, Richard Cotele, made homage to Henry de Sully in 1189 for six hides of which one and a half were at Lopshill,[7] held for the service of one knight, and for the service of constable, at the option of the lord of the manor.[8] It was of him that the Glastonbury scribe complained that he did not know how much was in a hide.[9] In 1235 Richard Cotele, presumably his son, held twelve hides, inclusive of the Damerham fee, for the service of one knight only.[10] Later, he acquired '20 librates' which 'belonged to the monks' table and to the demesne, for which he renders no service at all'.[11] A marginal note, mutilated, explains that they were situated at 'Horbloton, Ham, Monkton and . . . deputte [Tidpit]'. Under Abbot Roger Forde, Elias Cotele makes homage again for eight hides and for the castle at Ure.[12] In 1275 the Bishop of Bath, Robert Burnell, held here three parts of a knights' fee direct from the king *in capite*, and Elias Cotele was his tenant.[13]

The election of Henry of Blois brought to the direction of affairs at the Abbey a man not only of exceptional administrative and financial abilities but also one with considerable influence owing to his close relationship with the reigning monarchs. He was brother to King Stephen and

[4] *Inq.* 1189, 5.
[5] Adam, *ibid.*
[6] *Supra,* Ch. IV.
[7] Adam, *loc. cit.*
[8] Inq. 1189, p. 127.
[9] *Ibid.* 5 'Nescit quantum amuntat in hida', *cf.* Vinogradoff, *Villeinage*, 245, who surely had missed the irony of the remark.
[10] *Rentalia*, 4.
[11] *Ibid.*, p. 176.
[12] *Ibid.*, 230. His heir was William (*G.C.*, I. 204)
[13] *Rot. Hund.*, 3. Ed. I, p. 253.

nephew of Henry II. Educated at Cluny, he was elected Abbot of Glastonbury in 1126 and preferred to the bishopric of Winchester, in 1129, holding both offices in plurality until his death in 1171. He found the monastery on the verge of ruin and the monks in want of all necessities of life.[14]

There is no explicit evidence from which the date of his visit to Damerham can be determined. It has, however, been pointed out that his administrative work on behalf of the Abbey was chiefly accomplished before 1154,[15] when he retired to the monastery at Cluny. Much of it was delegated by Henry to Robert, whom he had appointed Prior of St. Swithun's, Winchester,[16] until his promotion to the see of Bath in 1135. Henry himself was made Papal Legate in 1139, and his official duties were in consequence appreciably multiplied. The employment of the first personal pronoun makes it quite clear that Henry visited Damerham in person. The date of the visit may perhaps be still further narrowed by placing it between the elevation of Robert to the bishopric of Bath and the date of Henry's legatine appointment, viz, between 1135 and 1139.[17] At the same time, Henry himself regarded this manor as the most important of the Abbey's possessions, as, indeed, it was also the largest and richest, and he would not lose time in restoring to the Abbey a manor which had been lost through alienation and in reorganising its administration and finances.

The passage in the *Scriptura Henrici Blessiensis*, quoted by Adam of Damerham, in which he describes having found at Damerham six persons who were called canons,[18] has usually been taken to mean that the church had become collegiate.[19] But it is suggested, with diffidence, that the text does not necessarily sustain that interpretation. The paragraph is divided into two distinct parts, the first dealing with the demesne, the second with the church.

In the first part, Henry's concern is that the proceeds of the demesne were being applied to the improper purpose of providing prebends for the so-called canons. 'Neither by entreaties nor by bribes could I be

14 Adam, p. 305.

15 Knowles, *Monastic Order*, p. 288.

16 Armitage Robinson, *Somerset Historical Essays*, p. 56.

17 Knowles, p. 287, ascribes Henry's activities on behalf of Glastonbury to the years 1126–1129.

18 Adam, II, p. 313, 'in manerio de Domerhame inveni sex, qui dicebantur canonici, singulas prebendas possidentes.'

19 Hoare, *H.S.D*, p. 5, and those who have followed him.

deflected from my purpose of restoring to the demesne what was due to it.' But not to act precipitately, he allowed each canon in turn to die before depriving them of their prebend.[20] He says nothing about the canons serving in church; if they had done so, he, as Bishop of Winchester and abbot of the premier Benedictine monastery, could hardly have acquiesced in their continuance in the church till their death. Nor did he replace them by a chaplain; the appointment of a chaplain was a parochial matter referred to in the part concerning the church. The crucial word seems to be *dicebantur*: they were called canons, called themselves canons, or were so-called canons, because they subsisted upon the revenues of a lay estate, like prebendary canons of a secular cathedral.[21] This account, at all events, is striking evidence of the deplorable state into which the manor had relapsed.

The second part of this passage evokes the hope that it may throw some light upon the architectural history of this inscrutable church. Henry did three things; first, he restored it, secondly he repaired the ecclesiastical ornaments, and thirdly he appointed a chaplain to secure the rights of the church.[22]

This is not the place to digress into the architecture of this remarkable building, of which no satisfactory description has yet been given. When the account was written at the beginning of this century for the *Victoria County History*, sprawling ivy usurped the exterior walls and plaster covered the internal faces, together obscuring many informative dating features. Some twenty years ago Mr. A. R. Greene corrected some of the erroneous conclusions of the *County History*, but the church still awaits an authoritative biographer. It may, however, be permissible to suggest that too late a date has been propounded for the original fabric of the church.

In support of this opinion three observations may be made; first, that the church must have been standing some time to have been in need of restoration ('renovate' is the word employed); secondly, that the church at Martin is assigned to the early Norman period, between 1090 and 1130. It was only a chapelry, dependent upon the parent church at Damerham, and cannot in point of antiquity have taken precedence. Finally, the church at Damerham must have been of some size and importance to have merited exceptionally fine church furniture and ecclesiastical ornaments.

[20] Adam, *loc. cit.*

[21] *See* E.H.R. (XVII), 1952, p. 383 where the relatively late use of the word Canonicus is argued.

[22] Adam, *loc. cit.*

What Henry of Blois did can only be conjectured when a more precise chronology has been assigned to the different parts of the building.[23]

That Henry should have repaired the church ornaments so that they reached a higher quality than was usual in parish churches evinces his evident affection for Damerham. Church furniture in inventories of this period are classified commonly as of books, ornaments and vestments,[24] but in the smaller churches doubtless all three were embraced in the term ornaments, which would include cross, candlesticks, thurible, pyx, ambry and processional equipment.

The phraseology employed in the appointment of a chaplain (*convenienter locavi*) suggests that Henry found one without difficulty in the village. This is very possible. A William of Damerham was about this time rector of Winford,[25] and in the following century Walter Scrianti of Damerham and Symon of Damerham are found attesting documents. In 1386 Nicholas Damerham held the prebend of Charminster and Bere[26] and William of Bardenay, Archdeacon of Wells, when overcome by gout, retired to end his days at Damerham.[27] The village must have been a nursery from which many alumni passed on to Glastonbury, as did its most famous son, Adam of Damerham.[28]

The apparent paradox of the Bishop of Winchester intervening in a church in the diocese of Salisbury is explained by the fact that Henry was acting in the capacity of abbot, not of bishop. Since the grant by King Edmund in 945, the Convent of Glastonbury became the owner of the land, and of the church built upon the land. By virtue of this ownership the abbot was vested with the right of presentation, and was thus entitled to appoint a chaplain and restore the church.

His preoccupation with the church did not prevent Henry from giving as much attention to the manor. Damerham and certain other manors he found alienated (distracted) and in a state of dilapidation. He strove energetically to enlarge them, recovered them and restored them to the convent.[29]

[23] Since this was written Prof. Stuart Piggott has furnished a plan of the Church, with a chronology, which is Appendix III.

[24] *Register of St. Osmund*, II, p. cxli.

[25] Adam, p. 619. Probably before 1150.

[26] *G.C.* I, pp. 167, 206.

[27] Adam, 478. 'Gutto enim . . . in pede arripiens ad Domrahame vitam finire coegit.' *v.* Le Neve, *Ecclesiastical Dignitaries* (1716) p. 43. He was made Archdeacon in 1210 and retired in 1243.

[28] *G.C.*, II, p. 46.

[29] John of Glastonbury, p. 166. *v.* also *Monasticon*, I, p. 4.

Henry ends his account of Damerham with one of those sentences in which his fondness for the epigrammatic tends to obscure his real meaning. 'Thus', he writes, 'the manor, which before was said to be the chief, consisting of harmonious buildings raised upon not unharmonious foundations, I indeed made the chief.'[30] The buildings may be assumed to be the various units composing the Court House and farm, but there is no description of them until towards the end of the next century.

Henry of Blois, despite a moral character which impelled St. Bernard in a moment of anger to call him the Whore of Winchester and to apply to him a scurrilous quotation from Ovid,[31] ranks with Michael of Amesbury in the following century as one of the greatest benefactors, and one of the most sagacious administrators, among the Abbots of Glastonbury.

Henry of Blois made two grants of land in the parish of Martin. To William the son of Helya he granted one hide (perhaps 160 acres) for the rent of one mark. In addition, William held half a virgate (perhaps twenty acres) free of rent. That this grant represented the manor house at West Martin and its appendant land is put beyond doubt by two marginal annotations, added by later scribes, in the *Foedary* of Abbot Monyton. The first of these is the name Northlode, the second, in a yet later hand, that of John Horsey,[32] both of whom we know from other sources to have held the manor of West Martin.

From William it descended to Peter Helya de Merton, about 1235, and from him to William of Martin, who was alive in 1300.[33] Through his wife Isobel it passed to the Northlodes and thence, as has been seen in the previous chapter, to the Horseys, from whom it came into the hands of Lord Shaftesbury. The recent discovery of an encaustic tile, ascribed to the fourteenth century in the manor house of West Martin indicates a substantial and imposing building in the time of the Northlodes.

About the same time a grant of two hides was made to Robert Peytevyn, who paid a rent of one mark and a sextarius of honey to the medarius (an obedientiary official) of Glastonbury.[34] In 1518 it was a freehold held by

[30] Adam, 313.
[31] Knowles, *Episcopal Colleagues of Thomas Becket*, p. 35.
[32] *Foedary*, 27.
[33] *F. of F., Wilts.*, 1300.
[34] *Foedary*, 27. Peytevin also appears as Pictavensis, of Poitou. The contributions of

the medarius, and may perhaps be identified with the property known today as Bustard Manor Farm. Both William the son of Helya and Robert Peytevyn made homage in 1189 to the Abbot, Henry de Sully.[35] Robert Peytevyn was followed by Roger, whose successor, Robert, alive under Abbot Adam of Sodbury, is shown as holding one hide only, and to have commuted his rent in honey to money.[36]

After Robert, the Prior of Winchester who succeeded Henry as abbot, Glastonbury Abbey lapsed to the crown until the election of Henry de Sully in 1189. Under his instructions was compiled the *Liber Henrici de Soliaco*, better known as the *Inquisition* of 1189, of which the surviving portions contain the first and only twelfth century survey of Damerham and Martin.[37] He was translated to the bishopric of Worcester in 1193.

In 1192 Richard I on his return from the Crusades, having been shipwrecked and cast ashore on the coast of Istria, came into the power of the Emperor Henry VI, and spent the year in captivity. The contribution towards his grievously heavy ransom exacted from Damerham and Martin amounted to £31.4.10,[38] composed of two aids, and a hidage, levied at 20/- on the knights' fee.

1st Aid	£21.13. 6
2nd Aid	3. 5. 4
Hidage	6. 6. 0
	£31.4.10

In the same year Savaric was appointed to the see of Bath, his predecessor, Reginald Fitzjocelin, having been translated to Canterbury, though he never lived to be consecrated archbishop.

The elevation of Savaric to the bishopric of Bath had, however, serious consequences for the Abbey. A member of the large and influential family of Bohun, Savaric was a cousin of Jocelyn, Bishop of Salisbury and of

the county manors to the Obedientiaries at Glastonbury were substantial. Towards the salaries of the Cook and another servant Damerham paid sums totalling annually nearly £18. *G.C.*, III, pp. 717-18.

35 Inq. 1189, p. 127. *Foedary*, p. 27.

36 *Foedary*, p. 28.

37 *v. infra*, Ch. XII. The *Inquisitio Hilberti Cantoris* made after the death of Henry of Blois has recently been discovered from MSS in Trinity College, Cambridge.

38 *Abbreviatio Placitorum*, 15a. Rich. I – Ed. II; *v.* also Maitland, in *Pipe Roll Soc.*, Vol. XIV.

Reginald, his predecessor at Bath, and in some obscure way was related, through his mother, with the Emperor, Henry VI.[39] Through his connection with Jocelyn he was appointed Treasurer of Salisbury Cathedral in 1176, made a canon of Heytesbury[40] and a prebendary of Beaminster.[41] Owing to his relationship with the Emperor, Savaric was the principal mediator in the negotiations for the king's release, and, as a condition of his services, exacted the promise of the Abbey of Glastonbury in exchange for the cession of the city of Bath to the crown. He united the abbacy with the bishopric, an arrangement confirmed by the Pope, Celestus III, and held both offices until his death in 1205. As a result Glastonbury became a Cathedral monastery and Savaric styled himself Bishop of Glastonbury,[42] a title assumed by his successor Jocelin until 1219. Against the resistance of the monks he forced open the door, garrisoned the convent with troops, and converted the abbot's lodging into a bishop's palace. The Abbey lost its tithes and by a decree of Innocent III yielded to the bishopric a quarter of its estates.[43]

Throughout the prosecution of its cause against the bishop the Abbey received loyal and indefatigable support from Master Martin de Summa. Martin de Summa was the Pope's subdeacon, and held under the Abbey the perpetual vicariate of Budleigh (Butleigh) on payment of a pension of one mark to Henry of Aliburne.[44] Also he hypothecated a payment of one mark to the Abbey for the reversion of the church at East Brent.[45] He was strongly opposed to the policy and behaviour of Savaric, and acted as the intermediary between the Abbey and the Pope. When the pecuniary resources of the Abbey were seriously deflated by the exactions of the bishop, Martin supplemented them from his own means. He had powerful friends at the Papal Court,[46] and his efforts and influence alike greatly interfered with the projects of Savaric. On his journey to Rome he was robbed of his money, his possessions and his riding equipment by the bishop's agents outside Winchester.[47] At London he was detained as a prisoner. He reached his destination only by adopting various dis-

[39] Adam, p. 425.
[40] *Reg. St. Osmund*, I, p. 312.
[41] *Fasti Eccles. Salusb.*, p. 257.
[42] Cassan, *Lives of the Bishops of Bath and Wells*, p. 113.
[43] Adam, p. 410.
[44] *G.C.*, I, p. 65.
[45] *Ibid.*, p. 66: John of G., p. 388.
[46] Adam, p. 371.
[47] *Ibid.*, p. 388.

guises and by following unfrequented routes.[48] As a last resort, to deflect him from his course, Savaric offered him the manor of Damerham if he would withdraw from the petition and the defence of the monks.[49] Nonetheless, the petition was duly presented, and in 1202 Innocent III responded to it. His injunction issued to the bishop required him, *inter alia*, to restore to Martin everything that had been taken from him and to make satisfaction to him within two months for loss and injury incurred by him.[50]

The Abbey at this time was gravely impoverished; indeed, another fifty years were to elapse before its chronicler could pronounce it free of debt.[51] It was unlikely to be in a position to pay Martin's expenses within several years, and although there is no direct evidence to connect the award of Bishop Jocelyn in 1233 with the order of Innocent III in 1202, equally there is nothing else in the account of these years by the two Glastonbury historians to explain it. Curiously, neither Adam of Damerham nor John of Glastonbury mention the award, thereby suggesting that the Abbey had been at fault or, at any rate, remiss in not having defrayed Martin's expenses before. Damerham was the richest of the Abbey's manors; it had not been appropriated to the bishopric; its revenues, tithes and advowson had remained intact; it had before been offered to and rejected by Martin; he was entitled to the tithes of Budleigh, of which he was the vicar. Damerham for these reasons was an obvious manor to pay Martin's costs, and perhaps, the only manor capable of discharging the debt. The terms of the award are as follows:

'Award of Joscelin bishop of Bath in a dispute between Robert abbot of Glastonbury and the convent on the one part and Master Martin de Summa the Pope's subdeacon on the other that the abbey shall pay the tithes due and accustomed of the church of Bodeclya to wit of hay, mills, vaccaries, fisheries etc., and the usual log against Christmas, also the tithe of Domerham park according to the custom of parks in the archbishopric of Canterbury, and shall pay £100 at Domerham in ten half-yearly instalments for rents, arrears, costs, the maintenance of four horses and as many servants, and all other disputed claims, under pain of five marks at each term to the fabrics of Wells and Salisbury; Master Martin shall withdraw all plaint and action, shall before Midsummer give up all

48 *Ibid.*, p. 371.
49 *Ibid.*
50 *Ibid.*, p. 419.
51 John of G., p. 223.

instruments concerning the same, and if any be hereafter produced to the prejudice of the abbey they shall be of no effect; the said Martin shall leave the abbey immune, and in such case the payments aforesaid shall cease; if he die during the next five years, he may dispose of the unpaid instalments by will; payment shall if necessary be made of the rents of Domerham, Marton and Ydomeston, and the steward of the abbey, the servants and reeves of those manors shall be sworn to keep back enough of such rents to content the same, and the pain incurred; any error or obscurity herein to be corrected by the bishop and his successors. Accepted by the parties, submitting them to the bishop to enforce his award, the said Martin being sworn that he has not parted with any instruments, and Albert his nephew abjuring all claim. Done in the chapter of Glastonbury, the morrow of St. Benedict 27 bishop Joscelin' (1233).[52]

For the action of Savaric in uniting the Abbey with the bishopric precedents had been created in recent years by Henry of Blois and in the eleventh century by Sigar. But under both the Abbey had flourished; under Savaric it deteriorated. Nor did the Abbey's anxieties cease with the Bishop's death, but it may well have agreed with the last line of his epitaph: 'Sic suprema dies fit sibi prima quies.'

It was not until 1218, after a prolonged struggle that Glastonbury obtained its divorce from the bishopric, nor until 1275 that the negotiations were brought to a final concord at the cost to the Abbey of four manors and five advowsons.[53] Although the Abbey succeeded in retaining Damerham, its largest and most valuable manor, for the next fifty years it was preoccupied in revoking the alienations of land that occurred in this period and in reasserting the authority it had lost since the days of Henry of Blois. The monetary costs in lawsuits and appeals to Rome were enormous, and large contributions were exacted from the Damerham manor, which, while the dispute lasted, had been almost neglected.

William Pica, a 'master', was excommunicated immediately after his election by the convent and died, it was rumoured by poison, soon after preferring his appeal to Rome. William Vigor, the cellarer, led the opposition to the bishop until his death in 1223, but was not recognised as abbot outside the convent. The monks, however, retained grateful memories of him on account of his order to strengthen the gravity of beer. His successor was Robert, the Prior of Bath, appointed against the will of the convent.

[52] Hist. MSS. Comm., *MSS of Dean and Chapter of Wells*, i, 473–4.
[53] Adam, p. 551.

A case between the abbot and John Bisset in 1227 was settled before the itinerant justices at Wilton.[54] It concerned the eastern boundary of Damerham, where John Bisset, lord of the manor of Rockbourne, was alleged to have created an enclosure. The proceedings have, indeed, been cited as an early instance of enclosure,[55] but the real object seems to have been the demarcation of the boundary. The abbot acknowledged the right of John Bisset to enclose this portion of the park, and, in consideration of the acknowledgement, the latter conceded the right of free commonage for twelve beasts to two of the Abbot's tenants. The record established the eastern boundary of the manor from the corner of Damerham Park as far as 'Hasche at the water of Padnore'.[56] Rockbourne Park, it may here be mentioned, was claimed at this time by the Earl of Gloucester to be part of Cranborne Chase, for in 1236 an Inquisition was held to find out to what extent the Chase would be curtailed, if John Bisset enclosed the park.[57]

By the succession of Michael of Amesbury in 1235, Glastonbury had for the first time since the beginning of the century an abbot, elected unanimously by the convent. Among his first acts was a visit to Damerham, where his chronicler relates 'among other good things he did there, he convicted Nicholas of Haversham,[58] Godfrey the chamberlain and Matilda Coffyn,[59] of with-holding suit to the Hundred Court at Damerham and degraded them to their proper station. The cucking-stool of Matilda, according to law, he overturned.'[60] At the same time he took the opportunity to recover from Richard de Limesi forty acres, alienated by Savaric, and restored them to the church. The farm house and an enclosure, however, was returned to Richard for his life, in 1235.[61]

The grant of two virgates to Henry Hammond at Martin for an annual rent of one mark is dated to Michael of Amesbury. The tenement passed to Robert Hammond and from him to another Robert, who was a customary tenant under the abbot (Adam of Sodbury), was a witness to a deed of 1329, and did homage to John de Breynton in 1336. His

[54] *F. of F., Wilts.* (1227), p. 17.

[55] Gray, *Field Systems*, p. 34; *W.A.M.* LI, p. 141; Tate, *Wilts Inclosure Acts.*

[56] *Supra,* Ch. IV.

[57] *Close Rolls* (1236), p. 280.

[58] Sheriff of Wiltshire.

[59] Coffyn was an alternative name for the tithing of Little Damerham or Damerham Parva. *v. supra*, Ch. IV.

[60] Adam, p. 507: 'et tuberellum dictae Matildia per judicium prostravit.' *v.* also John of G., p. 217.

[61] *F. of F. Wilts.* (1235), p. 26.

land passed to William Sturton.[62] The Hammonds may have lived in East Martin, and their name may survive in the field called Hamonstyle.

In 1246 the Abbots of Glastonbury and Tewkesbury combined in a perambulation of their common boundary near Boveridge, and a considerable acquisition of territory at the expense of the latter was the consequence. The initiative came from the crown the previous year when the Sheriff of Wiltshire was ordered to Summon twelve 'discrete' knights of the shire for the purpose.[63] The land in dispute was a certain pasture, worth an annual rent of twenty shillings, which was recovered from the Abbot of Tewkesbury.[64] At the same time Thomas of Pentridge (Pentone) who had been granted by Robert, the Prior of Bath, half a hide of arable and four farms at Kentelfuorth was evicted and the land restored to the Abbey.[65] Reginald of Stapleham was ejected from one and a half virgates and from the post of custodian of Boulsbury Highwood, which he claimed to be vested in his family by hereditary right.[66]

These substantial enlargements rendered necessary a redemarcation of the boundary at Boveridge (Boworth), which has been described in detail in the previous chapter.[67]

More closely connected with the parish is the grant in frankalmoin by Roger Peytevyn to the Abbey of four acres 'which lie in the field called Tohyde [Toyd]'.[68] His ancestor Robert Peytevyn has already been noticed earlier in this chapter, but after a Robert, who flourished about 1300, and a successor, William, about 1350,[69] the family disappears from Martin. But the field survived longer. In 1518 the Medarius of Glastonbury paid twelve pennies to the sheriff every Hocktide for a free tenement called Peytwynsfelde, which John Sellwood, the abbot in the latter half of the fifteenth century, retained in freehold.[70] In 1569 there is a reference in the *Pembroke Survey* to 'four acres at Twoyde, where the lord's wethers are folded in tempestuous seasons',[71] which is certainly the same field.[72]

[62] *Foedary*, p. 28.
[63] *Close Rolls* (1245), p. 35.
[64] Adam, p. 507.
[65] John of G., p. 217.
[66] *Ibid.* and Adam, p. 507. In 1518 this forester is called the *Custos nemorum* (of the groves) of Boulsbury.
[67] *Supra*, Ch. IV.
[68] John of G., p. 391. Hoare, *S. Wilts.*, p. 27.
[69] *Foedary*, p. 26.
[70] *Beere*, p. 54.
[71] *Pemb. S.*, I, p. 312.

Michael of Amesbury's title to permanent distinction rests upon his *Customaria et Rentalia*, which will always constitute a principal authority on thirteenth-century rents and labour services. This survey demands a chapter to itself. He left the Abbey free of debt, its herds and flocks greatly multiplied and its lands cultivated to the best advantage.[73] Abbot Michael's heart and soul were in the country with his agricultural estates, and he endears himself to us for his fondness for sheep. A line from his epitaph runs 'Ovibus debita rura suis.'

Michael of Amesbury retired before old age incapacitated him, and was granted a pension of £160 a year, the manor of Mere and valuable perquisites from the Abbey's kitchen.[74] He was followed by the cellarer, Roger Forde (1252–61). He supplemented the *Rentalia* of Michael with his *Extente*.[75] Whereas Michael of Amesbury's *Rentalia* had concerned itself with persons, rents and services, Roger Forde's *Rentalia* dealt with land. At Damerham he obtained from John de Aula an acknowledgement resigning his claim to rights to six and a half acres within the new close, below Damerham Park, and to rights of common pasture in the abbot's closes, which had been alienated by Robert, the Friar of Bath.[76] This anxiety to retain control of pasture, which is a common feature of this period, evidences the increasing interest in dominical sheep farming.

Soon after the succession of Robert of Petherton (1261–74) difficulties arose with the Bishop of Bath and Wells regarding the return of writs. Hitherto they had been returnable to the abbot's bailiff at Damerham from the Glastonbury manors throughout the county, except from Idmiston, which owed suit to Alderbury. The effect was that writs were receivable at Damerham, not only from the south hundred, but from the north hundred also, for example, from manors so remote as Grittleton and Nettleton on the Gloucestershire border, and the importance of Damerham was thereby much enhanced. By this procedure the king's sheriff was excluded from the manors, hundreds and fiefs of the Abbey. Such had been the custom from a time of which there was no memory, both before and since the alienation of patronage of the Abbey by Savaric until the year 1265.[77]

---

72 It may perhaps be identified with Grange Ground, 4 acres and 24 perches.

73 John of G., p. 223.

74 Moorman, *Church Life in the 13th Cent.*, p. 267.

75 A part is annexed to the *Rentalia*, vol. V. Owing to the insufficiency of subscribers from Wiltshire, the manors in that county have not been published.

76 Adam, p. 530; John of G., p. 236.

77 *G.C.*, I, p. 223.

In that year Walter Gifford, Bishop of Bath and Wells, appropriated to himself and his own bailiffs the return of writs and established his own official at Damerham to receive writs from the Abbey's manors in Wiltshire.[78] It was not until 1275 that a royal Inquisition finally determined the dispute in favour of the Abbey.

In 1266 the king conceded, at the request of the abbot, a weekly market to be held at Martin every Wednesday, and an annual fair on the vigil, the day and the morrow of the feast of Saints Peter and Paul (June 29th),[79] to whom, it has elsewhere been suggested, the church was originally dedicated.[80]

The licence to appropriate the church of Damerham and the chapel at Martin had been granted to the Abbey by a papal bull of 1255, but it was not until 1268 that the Bishop of Salisbury and the Dean and Chapter gave their consent, thereby substituting a vicarage for a rectory.[81] The course of events has been noticed in another place.[82] As part of the vicar's sustenance the Bishop of Salisbury granted the tithes of the tenement once belonging to William Peverel in the parish.[83] Among many Peverels at Damerham the name of William does not occur elsewhere. An Inquisition of 1265 disclosed that Hugh Peverel 'was in distant parts and was active whether against the king or not', the jury was not sure. 'He has in little Damerham 100 shillings, in land, rents etc.' There were no rebels in the hundred (Damerham).[84]

The lugubrious catalogue of grievances against the foresters of the Earl of Gloucester, the lord of Cranborne Chase, upon which Adam of Damerham expatiates, fell chiefly within the period of John of Taunton, who became abbot in 1274, and have found a place in another chapter.[85] But the earl's foresters were not the only persons to practise extortion. Richard Pik, the bailiff at Damerham, extorted 20/- from Peter Purs of Martin, imprisoned for robbery, 10/- from John le Bor of Martin, accused of harbouring a felon, and 6s. 8d. each from William Herbelot and Stephen Faber of the same village', both indicted for robbery, under a promise to set them at liberty.[86]

[78] Adam, p. 543. *G.C.*, I, p. 222.
[79] *Harl. Chart.* 58.i.22. Adam, II, p. 657.
[80] *v.* Ch. IX.
[81] Adam, II, p. 534; *G.C.*, I, p. 57; John of G., p. 236; *infra*, Ch. IX.
[82] *Infra*, Ch. IX
[83] *G.C.*, I, 58.
[84] *Cal. Inq. Misc.*, I, p. 281; this was during the Barons' Wars.
[85] *Supra*, Ch. II.
[86] *Rot. Hund.*, II, p. 254 (1275).

Since Henry of Blois was abbot in the previous century, there has been little record of building. Yet, at Martin the prolongation of the nave, the chancel and the tower of the church are assigned within this period.[87] At Damerham, too, the south aisle, the arcading of the north chancel chapel and the rebuilding of the tower are said to have fallen within this century. It seems probable that both churches owe their enlargement and embellishment to the zeal of the rector, Robert of Sottingdean, who held the living about the middle of the century. In 1247 he received, as a gift from the king, ten seasoned oaks from Gillingham forest for building himself a parsonage house at Damerham,[88] and in 1252 another four timber oaks from the forest of Clarendon for his church.[89]

The parsonage house must have been that building which Walter of Wylie, Bishop of Salisbury, when ordaining the church a vicarage referred to as 'the manse, which in former times had belonged to the rectory'.[90] Whether this medieval vicarage house was on the same site as the building, let by the vicar, Thomas Pope (1554–70) for the recovery of which his successor, George Kenwyn, sued in the Chancery Court[91] there is no evidence to show.

John of Taunton apparently built the great hall at the Court House at Damerham.[92] Adam of Sodbury (1322–35) makes the same claim, but the pointed windows conform better to the earlier date. Both abbots take a pride in the magnificence of their work, using the adjectives 'noble' and 'handsome' as descriptive of the fabric. The north-west windows amply merit these epithets. They may have belonged either to the great hall or to the chapel; the latter was definitely the work of Adam of Sodbury about 1330.[93] The splendid tithe barn belongs to the end of the fourteenth century. But a cowshed, thatched with straw, is specially mentioned in the last decade of the thirteenth century.[94] Nothing more is said of the Abbey's buildings until Richard Beere in 1518 left a description of the monastic establishment. It consisted of 'a hall, a chapel, a court house, a waiting room, a kitchen, a bakehouse, and a brew-house, all situated in the Inner Court. In the Outer Court were a grange, cow-stalls,

87 *Infra*, Ch. IX.

88 *Close Rolls* (1247), p. 520.

89 *Ibid.* (1252), p. 117.

90 *G.C.*, I, p. 58.

91 Chancery Proceedings, temp. Q. Elizabeth.

92 Adam, p. 573.

93 John of G., p. 267: 'Capellas et cameras apud . . . et Domerhame fecit construi speciosas'.

94 Adam, p. 536.

and the bailiff's office, besides a barton of two acres and an apple orchard.'[95]

On Michaelmas Day 1291 John of Taunton died in the Court House at Damerham. He had been summoned to Salisbury to attend the funeral obsequies of Eleanor, the mother of Edward I, who had died at Amesbury on her return from the north of England. This final effort prostrated the ageing abbot, who, instead of returning at once to Glastonbury, deflected his route to Damerham. Suffering from a disease becoming increasingly worse, he was painfully carried along the Wilton Way to Damerham, where he died. His corpse was embalmed and, when properly pickled, was despatched to Glastonbury for burial.[96]

The death of John of Taunton was the last record made by Adam of Damerham in his *Historia*, and it is assumed that he died in this year or soon afterwards. Compared with him John of Glastonbury is an inferior substitute. Although Adam has allowed no personal detail to intrude into his scrupulously veracious record, he usually noted anything that concerned the place of his birth.

Under John of Kent, the next abbot (1292–1303), William of Martin, the successor of William the son of Helya at the manor house in West Martin, was successful in an action for the recovery of land against a person named Ingram Berenger. He is shown as holding property at Stapleham as well as in Martin.[97]

In 1297 a grant was made to William Knight, of Lovecote to enclose eighteen acres in Oldelonde 'subtus La Howe' and the remainder of Oldland was declared common pasture for the tenants at Boulsbury and Stapleham, inclusive of the Howe itself.[98] Geoffrey Fromond, abbot (1303–22), visited Damerham in 1308, where he received homage from Marjorie Coty, daughter of John Coty, who afterwards married John Fraunceys, for one and a half virgates held by her in Martin.[99] Her son Stephen Fraunceys was in 1341 convicted of felony and the property escheated to the Abbey in 1345. This tenement had been granted by Roger Forde, Abbot from 1252, to William of Tidpit from whom it descended to Reginald of Tidpit,[100] who gave it to John Coty, the father of Marjorie.

Adam of Sodbury (1322–35) maintained a successful action against

[95] *Beere*, p. 41.
[96] Adam, p. 595.
[97] *F. of F. Wilts., sub anno* 1300.
[98] Hoare, H.S.D., p. 27.
[99] *Foedary*, p. 27.
[100] *I.P.M. Wilts*, p. 248.

William of Biddlesgate in 1324, when the latter renounced his claim to pasturage in Boulsbury highwood.[101] A witness to the agreement was a William Gerberd of Martin. Five years later he reappears holding pasture and downland at Lovecote, and in 1333 he made an indenture with the Abbot concerning a field named 'Eyresmede next to Elingforde' (Allenford).[102] The grant contained the following provision: that every year he shall open four entrances, one at each end and one at either side, from Michaelmas to the Day of the Purification (February 2nd) for the stock of the abbot and his tenants to depasture therein. This meadow may be the common mead between Allenford and the parish boundary. It well illustrates the practice, later called 'breaking the field', of opening the fields to the animals of the tenants for common pasture. This appears to be the earliest known mention of Allenford.[103]

In 1331 Edward III and his queen spent the three days before Christmas at Glastonbury, where they were lavishly entertained and the recipients of sumptuous presents. Christmas was passed at Wells and, on his return to Westminster early in the new year, he issued a charter granting to the Abbot a weekly market at Martin on Fridays,[104] in addition to that on Wednesdays permitted by the grant of Henry III. The most likely explanation of this apparent superfluity of markets is that the one applied to West Martin, the other to the east tithing. Alternatively one may have been for marketing stock, the other for produce. There was, however, no market at Damerham, probably because under vigilance of the Court House there was little opportunity to evade the tolls and regulations imposed on the sale of goods.

In 1330 the king granted to the abbot free warren in all his demesne lands.[105] Free warren was the right to hunt *ferae naturae*, other than beasts of the chase, in unenclosed land, and was held to embrace the hare, fox, rabbits, pheasants and sometimes also the roe.[106] The grant of free warren seriously impugned the claim of the Earls of Gloucester, that the Hundred of Damerham, according to the perambulations of the thirteenth century, was included within the Outer Bounds of Cranborne Chase.

[101] Hoare, *H.S.D.*, p. 31.

[102] *Ibid*, p. 32.

[103] *P.N.W.*, p. 400, *note*.

[104] *Charter Rolls*, IV (1332), p. 259. *G.C.*, I, p. 313 recites an extract from the Secretum which mentions ferias et nundinas (markets and fairs), words that do not occur in the Charter.

[105] *Close Rolls* (1330), p. 169. *Charter Rolls*, 4 Ed. III, p. 33.

[106] *Selden Soc.*, XIII., cxxviii (Turner, *Select Pleas of the Forest*).

The Abbots of Glastonbury from St. Dunstan
(Dugdale: *Monasticon*, I)

942	Dunstan
	Egelwardus
972	Aelfstan
984	Segebarus
995	Beorthred
	Brithwin
1027	Egelward
1053	Ailnoth
1077	Thurstan
1102	Hurlewin
1122	Sigfrid, cons. Bishop of Chichester 1125 and deposed 1145
1127	Henry of Blois, also Bishop of Winchester
1171	Robert
1178	Lapsed to the Crown
1189	Henry de Sully, transl. to Bishopric of Worcester 1193
	United with Bishopric of Bath
	Savaric
1199	(William Pike) Excommunicated
	(William Vigor – Cellarer)
1223	Robert, Prior of Bath
1235	Michael of Amesbury
1252	Roger Forde
1261	Robert Petherton
1274	John of Taunton
1290	John of Kent
1303	Geoffrey Fromond
1322	Adam of Sodbury
1335	John of Breynton
1341	Walter Monyton
1374	John Chinnock
1420	Nicholas Frome
1456	Walter More
1457	John Selwode
1492	Thomas Wason
	Richard Fox, Bishop of Bath and Wells
1493	Richard Beere
1524	Richard Whiting, murdered 1539

Note

Mrs. Elizabeth Eames writes of the tiles mentioned in this chapter as follows: 'Two pieces of tile with large scooped keys are typical of the Wessex area in the thirteenth century. The design of crosses in squares has been found on the site of Clarendon Palace and the fabric resembles that of tiles found in a waste-heap on that site in 1939. The fabric of the other thirteenth-century piece is apparently the same and both could have been made at Clarendon Palace but similar tiles are known from other places also.'

VI

THE SIXTEENTH CENTURY

When in 1539 the still animate body of that venerable octogenarian, Richard Whiting, the last Abbot of Glastonbury, was dragged at the tail of a waggon from Wells to the convent and hanged with two of his monks on the summit of Tor Hill, and his four quarters dispersed for exhibition at the principal towns of Somerset, the regime of the premier abbey in England came to a tragic and irrevocable end. The monks were pensioned with sinecures at Westminster or put in posssesion of country benefices, and the attempt to revive monasticism in the reign of Queen Mary was from the beginning abortive.[1]

Upon the monastic estate of Damerham and Martin the agents of the crown, Pollard and Moyle, descended with an expedition equalled only by their efficiency. It is due to them and their colleagues that we have that concise yet comprehensive inventory of monastic property known as the Valor Ecclesiasticus. The valuation of the abbey's property at Damerham and Martin and the assessment of its income is here reproduced.[2] Its value, £139.11.6½, was exceeded only by Glastonbury itself.

[1] *v.* Weaver in *Som. Arch. Soc. Journ.* XXXVIII, p. 327.
[2] *Valor Ecclesiasticus* (Rec. Com), I, p. 105.

Rents of Assize and Customary tenants

Rents that were always payable to the Abbot on the feasts of the Annunciation and St. Michael the Archangel	£2.15. 7
Rents of Customary tenants and Copyholders	£90.19. 5
The site of the manor and the demesnelands let out to farm	£42.14. 8
Perquisites of courts, fines, amerciaments etc.	£11. 9. 4
The woods very well fett with oakes ashes and maples now ready to be sold and worth	£514.13. 5
Timber growing within the said woods, value	£555.16. 7
Estimated yearly revenue accruing from sale of woods and timber	£26. 0.10

There were also two eyes of Fesauntes which always have bred here. The number of men ready to be called to the service of the King is forty eight.

Spiritualities

Tithes of corn and hay appertaining to the Rectory and Parsonage of Damerham, a year	£18. 0. 0
Ditto to the Chapel of Martone	£10.13. 4
The clear value of Badpytt (Tidpit) is of which the tithe is 5/2 a year.	£2.11. 8

The total revenue amounted to £205.4.10, made up of £173.19.10 from temporalities and £31.5.0 from spiritualities. Of the former the rents of the customary tenants and copyholders constituted the largest single item, perhaps over £1,000, if equated with money values about 1938.

Hitherto the village of Martin had owned but one lord, The Abbot and Convent of Glastonbury, but henceforward the land came to be divided into three divergent freeholds. Of these the oldest was that of the Horseys, whose succession to the inheritance of the Paynes, Romseys and Northlodes has been traced in a previous chapter.[3]

The vicissitudes of the Horsey family, who did so much to embellish the village in the sixteenth century, deserve a short notice. They lived at Martin from about 1477 to 1850. The last of them, George, died in 1877 at the age of 76, having survived his wife, also a septuagenarian, by a year. Their bodies were brought from Damerham, where they ended their

[3] *Supra.* Ch. IV.

lives, to be buried at Martin among their ancestors of the previous four hundred years. In the fifteenth and sixteenth centuries they had been knights and married into the best county families; in the seventeenth and eighteenth they married the daughters of yeomen farmers; in the nineteenth, their aspirations were not so high. A branch of the family whose principal seats were at Clifton Maubank, Charlton Mackerell, and Melcombe Horsey, in Dorset and Somerset, their progression down the centuries was a parallel to that of John Durbeyfield. Indeed, did not that good woman Joan Durbeyfield cite this very analogy? 'Look', she exclaimed, 'at the Anktells and Horseys and Tringhams – gone to seed a'most as much as you.'[4]

William Horsey died, within a year or so of his succeeding to the property, in 1448. His heir was his son, Thomas, who inherited at the age of eight. In the Herald's *Visitation* he is described as 'of Burport' (Bridport),[5] and he married Ann Wykes of Bindon. On his death in 1477 he was succeeded by his son John, who was afterwards knighted. He must have inherited at a tender and lived to a ripe age, for he survived until 1550. It has been suggested that he may have been a brother of Thomas,[6] but the Herald's *Visitation* shows him to have been a son, and no pedigree furnishes a second life interposed between his father Thomas and his son William.

In two *Visitations* of the sixteenth century Sir John is styled as 'of Marton, Wiltsh'[7] and he was, presumably, the first of the family to occupy the manor house. In the 1518 *Terrier* he is Johannes Horseye, Armiger, and holds six virgates of land. He also held property in Damerham Parva, where Walter Servington had the manor.[8] He was married three times, first to Isobel Hussey, of Shapwick, Dorset, secondly to Ann Payne, and thirdly to Edith Lyte of Lyte's Carey, Somerset. By his first wife he had – besides William, his son and heir – a daughter, Edith, who in 1521 married her cousin John Lyte the son of Thomas, the brother of Edith, Sir John Horsey's third wife. On her marriage Sir John made a settlement on his daughter of 100 marks, undertook to maintain the married couple for five years, and transferred to his son-in-law some landed property as well.[9] A window of stained glass, formerly to be seen in the

[4] Thomas Hardy, *Tess of the d'Urbervilles*, Ch. IV.
[5] *Visitation of Wilts*, 1565, in *Genealogist* (new series) XII. 94.
[6] *V.C.H. Hants.*, IV, p. 588.
[7] Visitations of 1532 (Benoit's) and 1565.
[8] *Beere*, pp. 42: 'Johannes Horcy et Walter Servington tenent hamlettam vocatam Damerham Parva', and 56.

chapel at Lyte's Carey, depicts her, almost nude, with tresses of hair falling below her waist, kneeling at prayer with her husband. The figures are surrounded by the text 'Orate pro bono statu Johannis Lyte et Edithae uxoris ejus.'[10] She lived a virtuous life until her death in 1556, and was buried at Charlton Mackerell.

The marriage had interesting consequences; for, by the marriage of their daughter, Dorothy, to Anthony Ashley of Damerham[11] the two principal proprietors of land at Damerham and Martin in the following centuries, the Earls of Shaftesbury and the Dukes of Newcastle, came to be connected through the female line with Sir John Horsey.

By his second marriage with Ann Payne Sir John Horsey had a son, Peter, who in 1535 became vicar of Damerham and Martin, being the last incumbent to be presented by the convent of Glastonbury. Some biographical details of this opportunist priest, who, having embraced the reformed church with reluctance, lived to accept its bounties with gratitude, is given in another place.[12]

An encaustic tile, displaying the Lyte Arms, a chevron between three swans, which Sir John, by virtue of his union with his third wife, was entitled to impale with his own, was removed (and regrettably discarded with other *membra disjecta*) from the paving of the church at the Victorian restoration. It is tolerably certain that both Sir John and his wife Edith are interred there.

John Horsey died in 1550.[13] To him is attributed the transformation of the north transept of the church into an aisle, terminating in a chapel, in which he and his successors lie buried. This was an era of building, and Sir John shared with his relations by blood and his connections by marriage a predeliction for domestic architecture, pursued in a spirit of keen emulation. It is a reasonable assumption that he inspired, designed and largely built the manor house at West Martin. Abridged by subsequent demolition to a single wing it now exhibits little trace of its former magnificence. Aubrey, whose curiosity for the interior embellishment of

---

[9] *Som. Arch. Soc. Journ.* XXXVIII (new series), p. 43: Maxwell Lyte, 'The Lytes of Lytes Carey'.

[10] *Ibid.*, p. 38, with an illustration.

[11] *Ibid.*, p. 43, on the authority of the Heralds' visitation of Dorset, in which he is described as 'of Damerham'. *v.* also *Pemb. S.*, p. 312. John Lyte's brother William married Dorothy, daughter of Sir John Keilway, Lord of the Manor of Rockbourne.

[12] *Infra*, Ch. IX. *Pemb. S.*, p. 312.

[13] *Wilts N.* & *Q.* II, p. 113.

churches was insatiable, and his observations thereon more reliable than many others, ascribed the chapel (or more correctly the oratory) in the house to not later than the reign of Edward VI. It was paved and enamelled, he observed, with tiles emblazoning the arms of Horsey, and such enamelled bricks fell into obsolescence after the reign of that king.[14] He was connected with nearly every family of consequence in the counties of Wiltshire, Dorset and Somerset. He was the owner of property in New Sarum worth £100,[15] and his endowment of his daughter on marriage shows him to have been a man of opulence.

Sir John Horsey brought the fortunes of his family to their plenitude. A sculptured stone bearing the Horsey arms – three horse's heads, bitted, couped and bridled – was formerly to be seen, incorporated in the masonry of a wall in the cellar of the vicarage house at Damerham, to which it must at some period have been transferred. It is characteristic of domestic rather than ecclesiastical architecture. It now rests in the church. It may probably be attributed to a date between 1520 and 1550, for at this period county families were proud to boast their connection with him. In numerous country houses in Somerset and Dorset the Horsey arms may be seen glazed in stained window glass, enamelled on tiles, engraved on tombs, frescoed on interior walls and as finials to gables or other projections.[16] But since the Horseys are not known ever to have resided at Damerham, the provenance of the Damerham shield remains a problem still unsolved. The most obvious explanation is that at the time when a great part of the manor house at West Martin was demolished, it was removed by some antiquarian vicar, who, for its preservation, had it immured in the wall of his cellar. But its provenance from the manor house at Damerham, occupied at the relevant time by Anthony Ashley who married a granddaughter of Sir John Horsey, should not be ignored, and, indeed, may be the more probable source.

[14] Aubrey, *N.H. Wilts.*, p. 101. Four pieces of these tiles have been seen by Mrs. Elizabeth Eames who writes: 'The four pieces decorated with arms identified by Hugh Shortt as those of Lyte and Horsey, dating from about 1530, bear a superficial resemblance to sixteenth century tiles from Fordington St. George and other sites in Dorset and to tiles from Lacock Abbey dating from about 1550. The size and method of keying the backs differ from group to group and there is no known centre of manufacture. It is probable that each set was made at the place where it was used.'

[15] *Wilts N. & Q.* III, p. 21.

[16] *Som. Arch. Soc. Journ., loc. cit.* pp. 36, 37, 106–108. At Lytes Carey the Horsey shield might be seen in stained glass, in stone supported by a griffin, surmounting a gable, and as a fresco on the plaster ceiling of an upper room. Examples of the shield on the side of altar tombs may be seen at Sherborne and Hill Deverill.

Sir John was followed by his eldest son William, who married Dorothy, the daughter of John Ludlowe of Hill Deverill. He died in 1571.

William's elder son, Bartholomew, described as of Tarrant Gunville – probably another Horsey manor – succeeded. He had inherited some woodland property at Rockbourne, which involved him in litigation with Sir John Keilway, the lord of that manor, from which he emerged successful.[17] He rose to be a man of some eminence in his county: when England was threatened by the Spanish Armada, Bartholomew was appointed to take charge of the southern division of Wiltshire, which, besides the Hundred of South Damerham, included also Mere, Heytesbury, Hindon, Knoyle, the Deverills and other places.[18] Among his many other tasks was the responsibility for the erection and maintenance of the beacons, designed to signal across the country from village to village intelligence of the sighting of the Armada. One would have been kindled near Knighton Ashes, which, accordinig to Aubrey, was a 'sea marke. The Needles beare from it south by east,'[19] and another, perhaps, on Pembury Hill, where there was a beacon during the Napoleonic wars.[20]

Sir Bartholomew died in 1596 and was buried in the Horsey chapel in Martin church. His interment is among the earliest to be recorded in the parish registers. By his wife, Elizabeth Devenish, he had a son, Thomas, who inherited the manor and the property. His name appears, together with that of Sir Anthony Ashley, as a freeholder of the manor in the year 1607.[21] About 1621 he sold his Martin estate and in 1624 his property in Damerham to Sir John Cooper, from whom it passed to his son, Anthony Ashley, afterwards Earl of Shaftesbury. Thereafter, the Horseys retired to a less pretentious abode, apparently to Tidpit, but still retained a number of copyholds in Martin. In successive centuries they took a useful part in the service of their village, as constables, tithingmen, haywards and waywardens. Two members of the family took orders and became curates of Martin: Oliver, curate from 1682 to 1689, when he was preferred to the rectory of Wimborne St. Giles, and William from 1769 to 1772.

The whole of Damerham, except Damerham Parva and the former demesne lands of Glastonbury Abbey, all West Martin, except the Horsey

[17] *Chancery Proceedings, Q. Elizabeth* (Rec. Com., 1836), III.

[18] *W.A.M.* 14, p. 241, from the Longleat Papers.

[19] Aubrey, *N.H. Wilts.*, p. 125.

[20] *A Chronicle of Cranborne*, p. 302. And also see an interesting map, in the library of the Dorchester Museum, on which the beacons in Dorset are plotted.

[21] Court Rolls, 1607–1609.

freehold, and all East Martin and Tidpit, except what had been held in demesne by the Abbey, were granted in 1544 by Henry VIII to his sixth wife. Catherine Parr, whom he had married the previous year. Catherine enjoyed her rents during the lifetime of the king, but on her re-marriage with Sir Thomas Seymour, her property was escheated to the Crown, with which it remained until the year 1574. In that year Edmund Gheast, Bishop of Salisbury (1571–76), negotiated with Queen Elizabeth an exchange of his manor of Sonning with Eye in Berkshire for the manors of Damerham and Martin in Wilts, the manor of Loders in Dorset and the manor of Keyhaven in Hampshire.[22]

The Bishops of Salisbury had held the manor of Sonning from very early times. In size it was one of the largest manors in England, and it was the centre from which much of the administrative work of the diocese was conducted. In the tenth century the bishops were styled, according to Florence of Worcester, Episcopi Sonningenses, a passage that has given colour to the claim the Sonning was once an Episcopal see,[23] and in the twelfth and thirteenth centuries the term Praesuli Sunningenses frequently occurs.[24] When Herman transferred the see from Sherborne to Old Sarum, Sonning became a peculiar of the Dean and Chapter, a jurisdiction confirmed by Osmund.

It is, therefore, not easy to understand why a manor with such ancient traditions and associations should have been so lightly relinquished. It may be that differences between episcopal and capitular authority influenced the bishop in disposing of his principal manor. The propinquity of Damerham and Martin to his own palace was no doubt an influential factor. At the time of the dissolution of the monasteries the manor of Sonning was valued at £154.15.9 and the Wiltshire manors at £205.4.10, but owing to alienations the latter had depreciated to £146.0.11 at this date.[25] The grant refers only to Damerham and Stapleton, but there is no doubt that Martin was included. The grant does not inform us of the area transferred to the bishop, but in course of time it was substantially augmented. The demesne farms at East Martin, Tidpit, Toyd and Allenford, as they came on to the market, were added to the original property. At a survey made during the Commonwealth the bishop owned in the two parishes 3,855 acres,[26] which by 1818 had been increased to 5,750

[22] Close Rolls, 16 Q. Elizabeth, pt. XXXVI, P.R.O. Ref. C.54/961. Stephens, *Memorials of the Church of Sonning*, p. 165, gives part of the text.

[23] Florance of Worcester's *Chronicle*, I, p. 146.

[24] *Register of St. Osmund*, I, p. 335 et *passim*.

[25] *Close Rolls*, 16 Q. Elizabeth, pt. XXXVI.

acres of which the larger part, 3,576 acres, lay in the parish of Martin.

In pursuance of the policy of the Long Parliament in the Civil War of sequestrating ecclesiastical property, the manors of Damerham and Martin passed by a deed of conveyance dated 1648 to Sir William Litton for the price of £2,335.14.0½,[27] or about 12/- an acre. On the accession to the throne of Charles II they were restored to the Bishops of Salisbury, who thereafter leased them first to Denzil Holles, then to successive Dukes of Newcastle until General Sir Eyre Coote purchased the Damerham property in 1762 and his successors the Martin copyholds in 1863, having held the leases since 1810.

Lord Holles and the Dukes of Newcastle were granted leases for three lives by Bishop Seth Ward, which about 1700 were extended to five lives by Bishop Burnet, with a substantial fine on the admission of the last two. The rent paid annually to the bishops was £74.1.0 and a corn rent of twenty bushels, which in the time of Bishop Seth Ward was paid in kind.[28] The immediate leaseholder again sublet his copyholds on lives, as, for instance, to George Reade, who defied the expectations of landlords and lawyers alike by living through the reigns of six sovereigns and the Commonwealth, to die at the age of ninety-six in 1726.

The presentment of the jury at the court leet, which was annually repeated until 1920, may be earlier than 1684, previous to which date there is a lacuna in the Court Rolls. It runs: 'We present that it is our custom to have three lives and a widow's estate to every life that dieth possessed.' In the Court Rolls copyholds were inscribed 'for three lives and the life of the longest liver of them successively one after another.' The nomination of 'lives' passed through an evolution illustrative of the copyholder's determination at all costs to prolong his tenancy. At first, it was usual to enter, besides the wife, a close relation, a son or brother. Later grandsons or minors frequently occur. In the eighteenth century the choice of persons, quite unconnected with the family, seems to have been an innovation; thus, George Reade, the largest copyholder in Martin, nominated the two sons of his gardener, aged five and seven. Finally, when most of the copyholds fell into the hands of M. T. Hodding in 1855 they were taken on the lives of H.R.H. Princess Helena Augusta, aged nine, and H.R.H. Princess Louise, aged thirteen, the daughters of Queen Victoria, and a third person.

---

[26] Extract from the Diocesan Registry, furnished by Miss Whiteman.
[27] Brit. Mus. Add. 9049, in *Collecteanea Topographica et Genealogica*, I. p. 284.
[28] *ex. inf.* Miss Whiteman, from MSS in Diocesan Registry.

The introduction of 'lifehold' in copyhold tenure seems to have been an innovation of the Bishops of Salisbury. At the suppression of the Abbey customary tenants and copyholders are bracketed together, as rentpayers, implying little distinction between the two. Thirty years later a tenant held his lease for his own life and that of his wife, and the same phrase is used in the Court Rolls for the reign of James I. The widow's estate (*pro vidualitate*), an essential feature of lifehold tenure, was at this date fully recognised. But, at their former manor at Sonning, the bishops granted leases for three successive lives.[29]

Lifehold tenure, or tenure *pur autre vie*, for three concurrent, not consecutive lives, appears to have developed during the seventeenth century. It was especially common in the West of England, and was intended to provide against the contingency of the tenement falling in through the premature decease of the tenant. In theory a lease for three lives was the equivalent of fourteen years purchase of the rental value.[30] On the death of a 'life' the tenant might intrude another, which the landlord could not normally refuse, but such admission was accompanied by a fine, which theoretically was the value of eight years' purchase, but could be, and often was, much in excess of this. In the seventeenth and early eighteenth century heriots, the best horse or cow, were exacted in kind on the death of a tenant, and sometimes also on the death of a 'life'. Later, the heriot was commuted for £5.5.0.

'Damerham, Bollesborough, Alyngford, Twoyd, Tytpyt and Estmarten with the farm called Tulkes, all of which the lord acquired from the Duke of Northumberland' is the preamble prefixed to the survey of Lord Pembroke's property made in 1569,[31] the year before his death. It had been granted in 1551 to John Dudley, Earl of Warwick, created Duke of Northumberland, and, before he lost his head for his assertion of the claims to the throne of Lady Jane Grey, he found time to dispose of this property to William, first Earl of Pembroke. The date is probably 1553 when the earl obtained the advowson of the church; it cannot have been later, because the duke was executed in that year and his estates escheated. The Earl of Pembroke had already been granted by Henry VIII the estates belonging to the Abbess of Wilton, before the suppression of the monasteries, and as he had succeeded in augmenting these by the

[29] Stephens, *Church of Sonning*, p. 182.

[30] Prothero, *Hist. of British Farming*, p. 201.

[31] *Pembroke S.*, I, p. 309; *v.* also Straton in *W.A.M.* XXXV, p. 291, on the general aspects of the Survey.

immense property in North Wiltshire formerly owned by the Protector Somerset, he became one of the largest landowners in England. By his marriage with Ann, sister of Catherine Parr, sixth wife of the king, he also became an influential personage at Court.

Black Will Herbert, as Aubrey anecdotally calls him, though his portrait depicts a rather florid countenance and red hair, was a typical Tudor. His attitude towards the Reformation was opportunist; while, on the one hand, he is reputed to have been instrumental in preserving St. Nicholas's Hospital at Salisbury (the Hiram's Hospital of Trollope's Barchester novels), on the other he is said to have expelled the nuns from Wilton with shouts of 'Out ye whores, to worke, to worke, ye whores, go spinne',[32] and enclosed the precincts of their nunnery as his private park. Since the previous abbess, Isobel Jourdain, on the authority of Henry VIII himself was alleged to 'have had two children by two different priests and has since been kept by a servant of Lord Broke',[33] he had some justification for the pungency of his language.

Whatever may have been his failings, he has this claim upon our gratitude, that shortly before his death he caused a survey to be made of the vast estates he had accumulated out of monastic property. This survey was of a different character from those which preceded it in the Middle Ages. They had been drafted by the efficient staff at Glastonbury Abbey with the statistical precision of a Blue Book. This was written rather with the detached outlook of the benevolent owner of ample acres. It was undertaken by two agents, Robert Grove and Thomas Vaughan, one of whom had some aptitude as an artist, for the survey of this parish is prefaced by a thumbnail sketch of Martin church[34] and concludes with another, which cannot be identified with any existing building at Damerham or Martin.

The property now acquired by the earl consisted of the former demesne lands of Glastonbury Abbey only – the court farm at Damerham, the dominical farms at Toyd, Allenford and Boulsbury, the manor farm house at East Martin and such demesne arable there and at Tidpit, which lay in the open fields, distributed among the strips of the tenants. Anthony Ashley '*generosus*' held the chief farm at Damerham by a deed dated 1560, and was exempt from payment of tithe. At Tidpit there was a croft

[32] Aubrey, *Brief Lives* (Clark) I, p. 316.

[33] Dugdale, II, p. 318. Extract from an undated letter from Henry VIII to Ann Boleyn.

[34] *Infra*, Ch. IX.

'where the lord's wethers graze and are folded, about six acres, which in any year may be sown by Robert Swetaple and for which he pays a rent of twelve shillings'.[35] This enclosure is undoubtedly that referred to in the *Terrier* of 1518 as Lordiscrofte, then surveyed as seven acres, and reserved for the abbot's flocks.[36]

Toyd was farmed by a syndicate of Martin farmers, Richard Compton, Thomas Prince, John Prince and Robert King. Compton and Prince had both been tenants under the Glastonbury regime, but King was a new arrival. Their arable consisted of 120 acres at Toyd and 60 at Allenford, which they were allowed to sow, in accordance with the medieval practice of the three field system, with 60 acres of winter and 60 acres of spring corn. Moreover they had the use of the lord's sheep fold for which they had to find the hurdles. The rent was eight pounds and twenty-four capons annually.[37]

On the downs were 240 acres of grazing, of which 80 acres lay in Toyd and 160 acres in Allenford, capable together of supporting 720 sheep, 'with the help of the arable after the shearing'.[38] The value of downland is assessed at one shilling an acre, and of pasture for one sheep at four pence. But a croft of four acres 'where the lord's wethers are folded in stormy seasons' was worth ten shillings a year.[39] The history of this croft goes back to before the middle of the thirteenth century when Roger Petevyn gave to the Abbey of Glastonbury four acres in a field called 'Tohyde'.[40] A meadow at Toyd is also mentioned of fourteen acres from which 'by ancient custom the lord shall have only the first crop, and after the feast of St. Peter ad Vincula (August 1st) it shall remain to the tenants of the Queen at Damerham and Tidpit until the feast of the Annunciation (March 25th) and the said crop is worth seventy shillings'.[41]

Toyd next appears in the possession of John Lowe, a citizen of New Sarum, who had amassed large estates in Wiltshire on the dispersal of the property of Henry Brounker of Melksham. John Lowe died in 1632 'seized of a farm at Martyn and Tidpitt, commonly called Twyde, a pasture there called Sheepsleight, occupied with the farm and all the

[35] *Pemb. S.*, I, p. 311.
[36] *Beere*, 62. Probably Sheephill, Tithe Map No. 565, 6 ac. 1 r. 34 p.
[37] *Pemb. S.*, I, p. 311.
[38] *Ibid.* p. 312.
[39] *Ibid.*, p. 311.
[40] *Supra,* Ch. V.
[41] *Pemb. S.*, p. 312.

tithes of the farm and pasture'. In 1629 he had conveyed the farm to Anthony Weekes and William Kente for twenty-one years, who paid John Lowe or his heirs fourpence yearly and to William, Earl of Pembroke, and his heirs the rent paid by John Lowe, viz £3.15.0, on the account day at Wilton. The *Inquisition* concludes that Toyd was 'held of the King as of his manor of Bulford, in free and common socage, by fealty only; they are worth per annum clear during the said term of 21 years, four pence and afterwards they will be worth five pounds'.[42]

The farm called Tulkes in East Martin at the time of the survey was occupied by Edmund Somerset and his wife Alice for the term of their lives by an indenture dated 1566. The farm is described as containing all arable, meadow and pasture abutting upon and adjacent to the farm, both enclosed and unenclosed. Belonging to the farm were a house and stabling, with a barn for storing grain,[43] a stable and other farm buildings; a garden of an acre, a meadow called Myllclose of one acre and another called Barnclose of two acres; a meadow of three acres, and 140 acres of arable in three fields and 140 acres on the downs where he may graze 500 sheep. The rent was seven pounds a year.

The similarity of the names Tulkes and Talks has led to some confusion and has even (in our opinion) misled our best authority on place-names, which identifies the one with the other.[44] The history of the former goes back to at least before 1493, when John Selwood, Abbot of Glastonbury (1457–93) ordained as his obit that every year on the anniversary of his death there should be distributed to the poorest of the paupers fortyshillingsworth of bread, and that the convent should on the same day make wine and wassail, the cost to be born from his own revenues, namely from the land and tenements recently occupied by William Christmas, and of Rading and of John Touke.[45] A marginal note gives the variant spelling Tooke. In 1518 the Medarius of Glastonbury was holding this property as a freeholder. It was then described as comprising two virgates of arable, once belonging to Agnes Attewelle and Ada Coffyne and lately to John Tooke for an annual rent of 16s. 8d.[46]

[42] *I.P.M.*, 18 Chas. I, (1642), No. 26.

[43] *Pemb. S.* p. 311. The 'horreum' of the text may refer to the tithe barn, of which vestiges still remain. In *Beere*, p. 54, it is called a grange in the phrase 'grangeam et bertonam'. It was situated in a field still known as Vicarage Lawn or Mead, and is an extra-parochial island.

[44] *P.N.W.*, p. 403.

[45] John of G., I, p. 281.

[46] *Beere*, p. 54.

Although in the preamble the farm is named Tulkes, in the text it is significantly called Towkes, thus proving its direct descent from the obit of Abbot Selwode. There can be little doubt that this is the farm now known as Bustard Manor farm, the grange of Glastonbury Abbey, from which the management of its large demesne in East Martin was conducted. When the third earl disposed of his property, Bustard manor farm was sold with Toyd and other estates to Lawrence Hyde[47] and thereafter acquired by the Bishops of Salisbury. In the seventeenth century it was leased to the Duke of Newcastle, together with the rest of the episcopal estate, and held of him by George Reade and his descendants.[48] In 1864 it was bought by T. M. Hodding, and about 1889 acquired by Charles Bentink, who transformed a farm house into a residential villa. At the beginning of the present century, in 1901, it was occupied by Cistercian monks of Our Lady of Paradise, until they returned to the Continent after the First World War.

As far as can be ascertained, the name Bustard House first occurs in 1739, Bustard Pond in 1754,[49] and Bustard Down in 1846, when it was separately enclosed as Paradise Farm. In the first half of the eighteenth century bustards were not an uncommon species in Wiltshire, though infrequent after the turn of the century, and became extinct, except for sporadic migrants, about 1820.[50] Aubrey observed that they seldom came so far south as the Chalke Valley,[51] and they must have been *rarae aves* indeed at Martin.

[47] *V.C.H. Hants*, IV, p. 589.
[48] *ex inf.* Miss Whiteman, from the Diocesan Registry.
[49] Court Rolls *sub annis.*
[50] A. C. Smith, *Birds of Wiltshire*, p. 356.
[51] Aubrey, *N.H. Wilts*, p. 64.

VII
THE SEVENTEENTH CENTURY

For nearly two hundred and fifty years the manor houses of West Martin and Damerham Parva were owned in fee simple by the Earls of Shaftesbury, who were also the lay rectors or impropriators of the tithes. About 1621 Sir John Cooper, lord of the manor of Rockbourne, the father of the first earl, bought the Martin estate from Thomas Horsey. The manor, which under the Horseys had been six virgates,[1] was sold intact in 1856 as 206 acres to Amelia Street. In 1685 Sir John acquired, also, the manor of Damerham Parva from the Servingtons, and it remained in the family of the Earls of Shaftesbury until 1856, when it was sold to John Egremont.

The first earl's mother belonged to a family which originated from the manor of Ashley in Wiltshire, and had been connected with Damerham for at least a century before: John Aysshly held sixty-four acres there in 1518, when the two villages were held by the Abbey of Glastonbury, and Anthony Ashley, great-grandfather of the earl, held the *capitale messuagium* there from 1560/61 by a deed from Queen Elizabeth,[2] and is expressly mentioned as being exempt from the payment of tithes on this manor; but in 1567 he was required by the Exchequer to show by what

[1] *Beere*, p. 56, 'Johannes Horseye tenet sex virgates terrae'.
[2] *Pemb. S.* I, p. 309.

right he held his manor at Damerham.[3] He married Dorothy, daughter of John Lyte of Lytes Carey, Somerset and his wife Edith, the daughter of John Horsey of the manor house at Martin.[4] The Ashleys therefore had on the maternal side an hereditary connection with Martin sometime before its acquisition by Sir John Cooper. It was Sir Anthony Ashley who is reputed to have first introduced the cabbage into England from Holland, and to have planted it extensively at St. Giles.[5] The venture, according to Aubrey, was not a lucrative one. Alluding to his appointment as commissioner for the embarkation of troops in 1596, when he accumulated much plunder, Aubrey says 'there goes a Dorsetshire jest that Sir Anthony got more by Calais than he ever did by cabbage'.[6]

In 1607 he is shown as a freeholder of Damerham together with his contemporary, Thomas Horsey of Martin,[7] and in 1610 retired from the office of clerk to the Privy Council with an annuity of £50.[8] When close on eighty he married Philippa Sheldon, a bride under twenty, in the hope of a son and heir. But, as his grandson subsequently observed, 'he failed of his expectation, by reason of his age and the virtue of the young lady'.[9] He left an only daughter, Anne, who, by her marriage with Sir John Cooper of the manor of Rockbourne, became the mother of the future earl.

The future earl was born shortly after three o'clock in the morning of 2 July 1621,[10] heir to £8,000 a year. The young Anthony's childhood was spent at Wimborne St. Giles until his father's death from smallpox in 1626, a fate shared by his mother in the next year at Rockbourne, where the family had gone to evade the epidemic. A further migration to one of the Cooper properties at Whitsbury[11] enabled the young heir to escape the disease, but at the age of eight he was left an orphan.

[3] Hoare, *H.S.D.*, p. 11.

[4] *Som. Arch. Soc. Journ.* LXXXVIII, p. 43: Maxwell Lyte, 'The Lytes of Lytes Carey'.

[5] Cf. Evelyn, *Acoeteria, a discourse on sullets* (1699) 'Tis scarce a hundred years since we first had cabbage out of Holland, Sir Anthony Ashley of Wiberg (*sic*) St. Giles, Dorset, being the first who planted them in England'.

[6] Aubrey, Mon. Brit. But Aubrey was mistaken as to the place, which was Cadiz, not Calais. Cf. his tablet in the church of Wimborne St. Giles: 'in Gadium expugnatione militari balteo donatus est'.

[7] Court Rolls, 1608; *W.A.M.* XIX, p. 258.

[8] *Cal. S. P. Dom.* 1603–1610.

[9] Christie, *Life of the first Earl of Shaftesbury*, (hereafter cited as Christie) App. I, p. iii ('Fragment of autobiography').

[10] Inscription on tablet in church at St. Giles, 'paulo post tertium horam matutinam'.

Sir John Cooper, a whiskered and bearded man,[12] who with Sir Anthony Ashley had been created a baronet in 1622, had died encumbered with debts contracted by gambling at cards. He had acquired Rockbourne from Thomas Keilway in 1608, but it had already been mortgaged to Anthony Ashley since about the year 1580.[13] On his death he died 'possessed, inter alia, of the manors of Rockbourne and Fordingbridge; the manor of Whitsbury, the manor of Martyn and the land thereto belonging with the rectory and the tithes thereof; the rectory and the tithes of Damerham, the tithes of Tadpyt [*sic*] . . . lands at Downton . . . Damerham South . . . the manor of Wimborne St. Giles, Wimborne French and Wimborne Allhallows. To all of which Anthony Ashley Cooper was son and heir'.[14]

In order to defray the debts, his creditors, at the instigation of his uncle, Sir Francis Ashley of Dorchester, moved in the court of wards (the heir being a minor) without consulting the executors, for the conveyance of these estates to themselves. Thomas Tregonwell was to have Rockbourne and Sir Francis Ashley Damerham and Martin. When the executors refused to comply, they were promptly committed to prison in the Fleet, and only released on their promise to obey. Litigation continued until 1635, when Sir Francis from the witness box emitted one gape and never spoke again. Although Sir Francis had been trained in the law and had been a Recorder of Dorchester, his designs were cleverly frustrated by the defendants. He failed to recover Rockbourne because a scrutiny of the title deeds proved it to be entailed, and therefore incapable of being sequestrated for debt. The property at Martin was secured from the avidity of the creditors by a subterfuge of the executors who privately sold it to friends to be held in trust for the heir when he came of age. Of Damerham, indeed, Sir Anthony was deprived, for Sir Francis bequeathed it to his son-in-law Denzill Holles,[15] who had married his daughter Dorothy. Sir Francis had given his verbal promise to restore the property on Sir Anthony's reaching his majority, but the court held it not to be binding. It has been said that Damerham was restored to Sir Anthony at the Restoration, when the court of wards was abolished, but in a survey of Seth Ward, Bishop of Salisbury in 1668, the estate of 3,855

---

[11] Probably the house called Templemans.

[12] See his portrait by Cornelius Jansen in the house at St. Giles.

[13] *V.C.H. Hants, sub* Rockbourne.

[14] *I.P.M.* 7. Ch. I; *Collins's Peerage* (Brydges) p. 393 or iii p. 546.

[15] Denzil Holles, 1599–1680, cr. 1661 Baron Holles of Ifield, Sussex, m. Dorothy, only d. of Sir Francis Ashley, of Dorchester; *v. supra.* Ch. VI for pedigree.

acres is granted to Denzil, Lord Holles, for three lives, from 1660.[16] Among the gentry at Damerham in 1670 Denzil Holles is again mentioned, and a letter from Holles to Shaftesbury in 1680 shows that the house was then occupied by a Mr. Bulkely on a lease from Holles.[17] Holles appears to have resided there at the beginning of the Civil War, when he was a companion of Sir Anthony at some of the local field sports. But while Sir Anthony was deprived of his property, the lordship of the manor was still vested in him, and between 1646 and 1648, according to that portion of his diary that has been preserved, he frequently presided over the manorial court.[18] In 1684, Baron Holles of Ifield held this court, followed later by the Duke of Newcastle. 'Baronett Cooper' had two farms at Damerham in 1646, according to the Subsidy Rolls, one of which was the manor farm.[19]

There is no record of Sir Anthony ever having lived at Martin. It was, indeed, his intention to have done so in 1677, as appears from a letter written by his secretary, Stringer, to John Locke, the philosopher and the intimate friend of Sir Anthony. 'My lord and lady Ashley' he writes in 1676, 'are gone to Haddon to spend the remainder of the summer and ensuing winter, there to save charges and gather a good stock that the next spring they may begin housekeeping at Martin.'[20] His intention was frustrated by his being committed a prisoner to the Tower during the king's pleasure. Further displeasure was incurred by his demanding his cook to wait upon him there,[21] with the result that he spent rather longer in prison than he need have done. To the earl's reiterated petitions for release the king replied with the Scottish proverb, 'At Domesday we shall see whose arse is blackest'. In the following century the house at Martin seems to have been used either as a dower house or to have been let. But the Lady Ashlie [*sic*] whose name appears in the Subsidy Rolls for Martin between 1640 and 1649[22] can have been no other than Sir Francis's widow, Anne, the daughter of Bernard Samways of Toller Fratrum in Dorset, who survived until the latter year.

Ashley Cooper was first elected for Parliament as burgess for Tewkes-

[16] Memorandum from the Dioceson Registry, kindly furnished to me by Miss Whiteman.

[17] Christie, II, p. 365.

[18] *Ibid.*, App. II, XXXIV.

[19] *W.A.M.* 38, p. 615.

[20] *Christie*, II, p. 224.

[21] Burnet, *History of his own Times*, II, p. 118.

[22] *W.A.M.* 37, p. 354; 38, p. 615.

bury in the Short Parliament of 1640, when staying with his father-in-law, Sir William Coventry, at Croome Court. Next he was returned as one of two candidates on a double return at Downton for the Long Parliament, for which, owing to the omission of the Committee of Privileges to report its adjudication in his favour, he never took his seat. In 1653 he was elected for Wiltshire in the Barebones Parliament, and under the Instrument of Government was re-elected the following year at that memorable election when the crowds were so thick in Salisbury that the poll was adjourned to Stonehenge 'where there was room enough'.[23] He sat for this constituency until his elevation to a barony in 1661, as Baron Ashley of Wimborne St. Giles and Lord Cooper of Pawlett in the county of Somerset. He was created first Earl of Shaftesbury in 1672.

If the tenantry assumed the politics of their landlords, then both Damerham and Martin must have sided with Parliament against the king during the Civil War. At Damerham, Denzill Holles, who had achieved notoriety by being one of the five members whom Charles I impeached, and, disappointed of an arrest in the House of Commons, immortalised by the interjection 'I see my birds are flown', was a consistent parliamentarian. Ashley Cooper, after being commissioned Governor of Weymouth in the royalist cause for a few months, from 1643 to the Restoration, never wavered from his opposition to the king. This did not, however, prevent him working for the restoration of Charles II, or from being among the first to claim a pardon in accordance with the king's declaration at Breda. Although actuated by a profound conviction in favour of a constitutional parliament and a detestation of popery, which impelled him to scheme for the exclusion from the succession of James II and the legitimation of the Duke of Monmouth, his political versatility gave some justification for the contemporary lampoon:

> Ashley Cooper knew a reason
> That treachery was in season,
> When at first he changed his coat
> From loyalty to treason.[24]

After being commended for his direction of the assault on Abbotsbury in 1644, Ashley Cooper spent the critical years of the war in the leisured preoccupations of a country gentleman. He paid visits to his neighbours and kept his court at Damerham; about once a week he rode from his

[23] Ludlow's *Memoirs*, quoted by Christie, App. III., p. lvii.
[24] Lampoon on the Rump, from a collection of Loyal Songs (1731).

home at St. Giles (he was at this time actually living at All Hallows) to his house in the Close at Salisbury, and three or four times a year to London, where he stayed in Holborn. He hunted and coursed at Cobley, and once a week played bowls at Sixpenny Handley.[25]

In these pursuits he was joined by most of the country gentlemen within riding distance, who were as little affected by the Civil War as he. 'The eastern part of the county', he writes in his autobiography, 'had a bowling green at Handley, where gentlemen went constantly once a week. . . . It was well placed to continue the correspondence of the gentry of those parts'.[26] Among those who resorted thither were Sir William Uvedall of Horton,[27] 'whose good qualities were drowned in covetousness', Denzill Holles of Damerham, Edward Hooper of Boveridge, Carent of Woodyates, Hussey of Edmonsham, William Chaffin of Chettle, Henry Hastings of Woodlands, and John Tregonwell of Verditch Lodge who 'enjoyed his nightcaps, his poached eggs, his chamber pleasures and thought no further of the world'. Hastings, besides being a close neighbour, had stood godfather at Ashley Cooper's baptism. The latter may, therefore, be presumed to have had some acquaintance with the habits of his godparent when he wrote his much-quoted character of the old man (he died at the age of ninety-nine) 'in whose walks there was not a woman of the degree of a yeoman's wife or under, and under the age of forty, but it was her own fault if he was not intimately acquainted with her, . . . and in whose chapel, not used for devotion, the pulpit as the safest place was never wanting of a cold chine of beef, pasty of venison, gammon of bacon, or great apple pie, with thick crust, extremely baked'.[28] The passage exhibits an autobiographical style as racy and refreshing as later his oratorical style was classical and incisive.

But even before the outbreak of war a lively activity was noticeable in the country. Press gangs and recruiting officers had a busy time in the remoter villages, and the freshly impressed labourer quickly arrogated to himself the licence of veteran soldiery. As early as 1640 John Nicholas wrote to his son[29] in London: 'I am glad to hear you are all so quiet in

[25] English Bowling Greens were famous; 'so even that they bowl them as easily as on a great billiard table. And as this is the usual diversion of gentlemen in the country they have thick rowling-stones to keep the greens smoothe.' (Trevelyan, *Eng. Soc. Hist.*, p. 316).

[26] Christie, App. I, p. xiv.

[27] The Subsidy Rolls for these years show Sir William Uvedall to have held property in Martin.

[28] Christie, App. I, p. xviii.

[29] Sir Edward Nicholas, Clerk of the Council.

London. It begins to be bad enough here. Yesterday (being Sunday) a company of soldiers, which were pressed about Martin and Damerham in Wilts, passing through our parish towards Marlborough where the rendezvous is appointed, took all they could catch on their way, and being resisted by the owners of such poultry and other provisions as they took, they beat many very sorely and at Idmiston cut off the hand of one Nott and hurt another very dangerously, so that this morning they were all sent to gaol by the constable, as I think, for there is not a Justice of the Peace nearer than Salisbury. There were but five soldiers.'[30]

But the Civil War probably impinged as little upon the villagers as it did upon the gentry. They may have evinced bewilderment at the frequency and facility with which Salisbury changed its allegiance, their market town and the see of their bishop, who was also their landlord. Stories must have reached them of the tenacity with which Wardour Castle, no great distance from them, was defended for the royalists by Lady Arundel and her courageous garrison, 'until the hand that endeavoured to administer food, surprised with sleep forgat its employment, the morsel falling from their hands while they were about to eat, deluding their appetite'.[31] They must have got accustomed to the constant passage of troops from Blandford to Salisbury, marching through Martin Woods, Tidpit Hollow and across Toyd Down. Some may have recognised their sovereign, not, as romantic fancy so often depicts him, mounted upon a prancing charger, but 'as he marched before the foot on foot across the downs from Bryanstone to Cranbourne',[32] when in 1644 he returned from the west to Salisbury before opposing the forces of Parliament at the second battle of Newbury. Shepherds would have furtively withdrawn their flocks nearer to the farmsteads, when Lord Goring's horse, quartered at Salisbury in 1645 'commited horrid outrages and barbarities', plundering the countryside of livestock.[33] Nearest of all to Martin was the parliamentary garrison at Falston House, a tithing of Bishopstone, under the command of Major (as he then was) Ludlow, who, as he wrote to Fairfax, 'with his troop somewhat restrained the excursions of the King's garrisons thereabouts'.[34] Some indeed may have mustered with the Clubmen of Dorset and Wiltshire, that organisation whose origin has been attributed to a fortuitous meeting of Ashley Cooper with

[30] *Cal. S. P. Dom.* 1640, p. 258.
[31] C. H. Firth, *Civil War in Wiltshire*, p. 12, quoting *Mercurius Rusticus*, No. 5.
[32] Nicholas, *Progresses of James I*, quoted in Hutchins, III, p. 380.
[33] Clarendon, *Hist. of the Rebellion*, IX, p. 8.
[34] Ludlow's *Memoirs*, I, p. 148.

Serjeant Fountain at an inn at Hungerford.[35] Brought into being, according to Clarendon, by 'the intolerable oppression, rapine, and violence of Lord Goring's cavalry',[36] the Clubmen had for their object the termination of hostilities by a profession of neutrality. At Salisbury Fairfax reported to parliament that they 'will not suffer them to fight, but make them drink together and so make them depart to their several garrisons'.[37] In Dorset they assembled on Hod Hill with such obstinacy as to require the presence of Cromwell himself to dislodge them. Denzill Holles, who at this time was living in Salisbury, was reputed to be at their head, and, 'wearing a badge of white ribbon, and armed with fowling pieces, pikes, halberts and clubs, they rendezvoused at Grovely, Warminster, Stonehenge and Whiteparish to the number of 4,000 men'.[38]

Even after the execution of the king, Wiltshire continued to be the scene of many of the chief episodes of the aftermath of war. The vicissitudes of Charles II, on his escape from the battle of Worcester, brought him on 3 October 1651 to Mere, where he drank his own health with the landlord of the George Inn.[39] A long afternoon was spent journeying by way of Hindon, Fonthill and Wilton to Hele House near Clarendon.

The principal character in the Royalist Rising of 1655 was John Penruddocke, of Compton Chamberlayne, then a detached portion of the Hundred of South Damerham. The prelude to the surprise assault upon the two judges of the westeren circuit presiding over the Salisbury assize on St. Valentine's day, were the 'meetings of foxhunters', which took place at Ludgershall, West Knoyle, and elsewhere. The failure of promised support caused Penruddocke to evacuate Salisbury; with his loyal troop of horsemen he rode to Downton, and then along that road, made familiar by so many movements in the civil wars, by Tidpit, Martin Wood and Cranborne to the west,[40] where later he met his end on the scaffold at Exeter. A Mr. Kitson in the adjoining parish of Bishopstone was a principal witness against the participants, but the assize calendars reveal no name of any parishioner of Martin. By their abstention they escaped making the acquaintance of the Barbadoes, whither so many prisoners were transported, or of being shot against the south wall of Bishopstone church. The impact of the bullets, where they have splintered the masonry

[35] Locke (12th Edition) VIII, p. 268.

[36] Clarendon, *Rebellion*, IX, p. 49 or IV, p. 695.

[37] Firth, *Civil War in Wilts.*, p. 37.

[38] *House of Lords Journals*, VIII, p. 484.

[39] *Boscobel Tracts* (Bohn), p. 495. Now the Talbot Hotel.

[40] *W.A.M.* 13, 14, 15 and 55. Extracts from Thurloe State Papers.

of the chancel wall, at exactly the height of a man's head, may still be seen.

When at about 7.0 p.m. on the evening of 11 February 1660 George Monk rode out of the Draper's Hall and told the crowds that thronged Threadneedle Street that they should have a free parliament – that night when Pepys saw nothing but roasting rumps from King Street to Ludgate Hill and from Ludgate Hill to the Strand[41] – the good news reached Salisbury the following night, and the villagers of Broad Chalke lit a great bonfire on the top of the hill.[42] It must have been clearly visible from Martin; but our village, lying as it did so close to the main road from London to the west, would not have been behind hand in learning the news, and we may imagine another bonfire, kindled, perhaps, at Blagdon Gap.

Indeed, bells and bonfires epitomised the spirit of the Restoration era. The former pealed, the latter blazed on the smallest pretext throughout the reign. Bell foundries flourished at Salisbury, where Francis Foster, Nathaniel Boulter and William Purdue enjoyed, in Wiltshire, Dorset and Hampshire, an unrivalled reputation. Two bells at Martin and three at Damerham were cast or recast in this period. When Foster inscribed the Damerham bell in 1666 with the caption 'cast in the yeare of plague, warre and fire', he echoed only half the phenomena noted by the diarist, John Evelyn: 'Great frosts, snow and winds, prodigious at the vernal equinox; indeede it hath been a yeare of prodigies in this nation, plague, warr, fire, rains, tempest and commet.'[43]

The plague reached its climax in London in 1665, and most people who could afford to do so, migrated from the capital. The king went first to Hampton Court, and afterwards to Salisbury. While staying there he paid a visit to Ashley Cooper, now a baron, at St. Giles. To this visit belongs the episode in which Edward Hooper of Boveridge was invested with the order of knighthood. St. Giles was noted for its cellars, and on the suggestion of the king, the company (of whom Hooper was one) repaired there to drink the wines, as the King phrased it, 'in their highest perfection'. The king, we are told, 'paid obeisance to the centre cask', and, it being a hot day, the whole party was very soon in a condition of maudlin intoxication. Edward Hooper, more jovial than the rest, was

41 Pepys, *Diary* (Bohn) I, p. 51.

42 Aubrey, *Brief Lives*, II, p. 76.

43 Evelyn, *Diary*, II, p. 215; *v.* also Anthony Wood, *Athenae Oxonienses*, (Eccles. Hist. Soc.) p. 141. 'A great plague in England, prodigeous births, great inundations and frosts, warr with the Dutch, sudden deaths, praticularly in Oxon', etc.

sprawling crapulously on the floor, when the King bade him arise 'Sir Edward'.[44]

The Hoopers played a not unworthy part in their county and country for some three centuries, but they also have a direct connection with this parish. As part of the Boveridge estate they owned Blagdon, which also comprised Kite's Nest farm and a large part of Martin Wood, subequently sold to Henry Brounker. We have had occasion to notice the last of the Hoopers of Boveridge in another chapter.[45]

The foundation stone of the great house at St. Giles was laid on 19 March 1650/51. Ashley Cooper lived in the magnificent style of the period. In 1672, after he had been created an earl, between fifty and sixty servants sat down to meals in the great hall, exclusive of the servants and grooms of the visitors. A fragment has been preserved showing the seating arrangements; five tables were set, in order of precedence, the steward's table, the gentlemen waiters' table, the grooms', the maids' and the last table at which were accommodated the huntsman, postillions, the under brewer and stable boys.[46] That part of the house described as 'below-stairs' was accounted the best in all England, and it needed to be.[47]

In his younger days Ashley Cooper travelled usually on horseback. On his journeys to London he seldom spent more than three days on the road, and when he entered Salisbury for the assize he would ride at the head of mounted retainers. At the Oxford Parliament of 1680–81 one of the difficulties John Locke had to contend with when making arrangements for the earl's reception was to find adequate stabling. At about this date he kept at St. Giles twelve riding horses, five brood mares, the majority having a foal at foot, and an arab stallion.[48] Since the first introduction of arabs and barbs belongs to this reign, Shaftesbury must be regarded as a pioneer in the breeding of bloodstock.

In London, where he lived at this time at Thannet House in Aldersgate, he invariably travelled by coach, and his second wife was acquainted with the inconveniences of a glass coach, that is, one with glass windows, then a recent innovation.[49]

[44] Hutchins, III, p. 384.

[45] *Supra*, Ch. III.

[46] Christie, II, p. 211.

[47] Paterson's Roads (18th Edition), p. 59. Hutchins, III, p. 598. In *Country Life*, June 6 1952, Mr. Howard Colvin suggests that the house at Wimborne St. Giles may have been designed by Peter Mills.

[48] Christie, II, p. 418.

[49] Pepys, VII, p. 114. (1667). *Memoirs of Count Grammont* (Bohn) p. 148, note, dates their introduction to 1663.

Shortly after absconding to Holland, he died at Amsterdam in 1682. His embalmed corpse was shipped to Poole harbour and followed to its interment at St. Giles by a throng of Dorsetshire gentlemen. Nor was his popularity confined to his own county; after his impeachment for treason, when Edward Papillon, foreman of the jury, brought in a bill of ignoramus, the acclamation, according to Macaulay, lasted for over an hour.[50] The words, attributed to Charles II, are his finest epitaph: 'He was master of more law than all his judges, and possessed more divinity than all his bishops.'[51]

Between the Earl of Shaftesbury and the Duke of Monmouth there had been a close friendship and much political sympathy. The earl had ever been an assiduous advocate of the exclusion from the succession of the Duke of York and the legitimation of Monmouth. Although the Earl had been dead three years, Monmouth may have remembered this, when on a hot day in July 1685 he made his escape from the field of Sedgemoor to the countryside of Wimborne St. Giles. It was an event which, no doubt, excited considerable commotion in the village of Martin, through whose single street, we may suppose, troopers galloped, searching the barns and the granaries for the fugutive. Macaulay's account that Monmouth and his companion, Lord Grey, turned their horses loose in Cranborne Chase and concealed their bridles in a ditch,[52] is given greater precision in the *History of Dorset*. Hutchins, who based his account on the evidence of the tradition of 'several persons lately living who remembered the facts'[53] is now generally accepted. The horses, he says, were abandoned at Woodyates on the confines, that is, of the parish of Martin. Here the duke assumed a disguise, 'changing his habit for a poor coat . . . so might have passed for some countryman, his beard being grown so long and so grey as hardly to be known, had not his George discovered him which was found in his pocket'.[54] Farmer Kerley's grandmother, however, told the author of the *History of Dorset* that he was tall, black and genteel. His gold snuff-box, dropped in a field of peas, was taken to Mrs. Uvedall of Horton.

Monmouth was captured 'in a dry ditch covered with fernbrakes'[55] in a field, now called Monmouth's Close, at the extreme northeast end

[50] Macaulay, *Hist. of England*, VI, p. 414.
[51] Collins, *Peerage*, III, p. 424.
[52] Macaulay, II, p. 606.
[53] Hutchins, III, p. 156.
[54] Evelyn, II, p. 468. The George was the insignia of the Garter.
[55] *Ibid.*

of a strip of land known as the Island, on Shag's Heath, between the two roads leading, the one to Ringwood, the other to Fordingbridge, about a mile or so from Woodlands.[56] The place is now known as Monmouth Ash Farm, and an old ash tree on the property is said to have borne a brass plate with the inscription: 'After the battle of Sedgemoor the Duke of Monmouth lay hidden beneath this tree and was found and taken prisoner by Sir William Portman and his militia A.D. 1685.'[57] The event was of sufficient interest for a note to be recorded in the church register at Cranborne, at the burying of one Anne Harris; under the date 8th July: 'Then was Monmouth taken.' Such was the end to the career of James Scott, Duke of Monmouth, England's darling, the putative son of Charles II and that 'beautiful strumpet', as Evelyn calls her, Mrs. Barlow.[58]

When Judge Jeffries went on the western circuit to preside over the trials of those implicated in the rebellion, he forgot the advice given him by Charles II the previous year. The king had said 'it was a hot summer and he was going the circuit; he therefore desired he would not drink too much'.[59] He came to Salisbury from Winchester where his furious vociferations against the septuagenarian widow, Alice Lisle of Moyles Court, had been a foretaste of his conduct for the rest of the circuit. His meekness and moderation at Salisbury came, therefore, as a surprise. A recent biographer has ascribed his fury at Winchester to the twinges from a stone in the bladder, the timely abatement of which, at Salisbury, was the cause of his clemency. But the calendar was neither long nor serious, and he may well have thought it imprudent to have made himself unpopular in South Wiltshire at a time when his son was courting the daughter of the Earl of Pembroke. There lay no indictments for high treason, and only six persons, convicted of speaking seditious words, were sentenced either to a fine or flogging.[60] In comparison with the three hundred, or thereabouts, who were condemned on this circuit to be hanged, the penalties at Salisbury were lenient.[61]

[56] Hutchins, *loc. cit.*

[57] *Western Gazette*, 15th November 1946. The property, consisting of about 17 acres, was sold to the sitting tenant. The ash tree has been cut down.

[58] Evelyn, II, p. 472, where the possibility of his having been the son of Col. Sidney is also discussed.

[59] Burnet, History, I, p. 416.

[60] *Account of the proceedings against the rebels in the West of England in* 1685.

[61] Burnet's estimate of 600 is an obvious exaggeration; Locke's 331 is nearer the truth.

VIII
THE EIGHTEENTH CENTURY
With a note on Sir Eyre Coote

COMPARED with the political commotions of the previous century, the era of Queen Anne and the early Georges passed in almost undisturbed tranquillity. The Sweetapples planted elm trees in the certain expectation of their progeny enjoying their shade; houses were built in grander proportion, with rooms of greater size; the population multiplied with a regularity scarcely exceeded by the animals they cared for; the White Hart kept open all day and all night, and farmers and labourers alike flocked to church on Sundays to listen for an hour to the often uninspired sermon of their parson. During the first half of the century there was a phenomenal succession of good harvests; corn fluctuated little in price, and rents in consequence remained stable. It has been described as the golden age of the farm worker, and was, indeed, the Indian summer of Merrie England.

There was no change in the capital ownership of land, which at Martin was divided between the Bishops of Salisbury and the Earls of Shaftesbury. For though Sir Eyre Coote, fresh from his victories at Wandiwash and Pondicherry, built his mansion at West Park in 1762 and acquired vast property at Damerham and its neighbourhood, he did not obtain the leases of the Bishops' copyholds at Martin until 1810, nor their freeholds until 1863. Old names disappear from the village, Ffolliott, Yelf, Prince and Compton; and others take their place, Lush and Bagus, Waters and Talk.

Although at this time Wiltshire sent over thirty members to Parliament, no one in the parish was qualified to vote at the General Election of 1705 and a century later there were but three on the electoral register. But distinction was conferred on the village by the residence at Tidpit for the first three decades of the century of Thomas Grove, sometime Member for Shaftesbury. Cranborne Chase (apart from Vernditch) remained throughout the century in the possession of Pitt, afterwards created Baron Rivers. In the early years it acquired some notoriety from the diversions of the local gentry, who under the euphemism of gentlemen hunters – 'Deer-hunters now called deer-stealers'[1] – and attired in the picturesque habit and beehive helmets depicted in the Pitt-Rivers Museum at Farnham, usurped from the countryman his particular sport of poaching deer in the Chase, until the making a second offence a felony[2] in 1736 put a period to their pastime.

In the latter part of the century Woodyates was the venue of those committees of local proprietors of land which bargained with the baron for the disfranchisement of the Chase and succeeded only in effecting the prohibition of their favourite annual hunts at Tollard (1788) and Handley (1817).

Like their successors of later generations, the people of Martin no doubt deplored the passing of the 'good old days' when they saw the 'navigators' laying the turnpike road through their own fields and down pastures, yet they would have had a loyal cheer for their sovereign, George III and his queen, rumbling uncomfortably in their coach to take their recreation at Gloucester Lodge[3] in Weymouth. Occasionally the rural routine might be enlivened if the king came down to review his troops, as he did in 1776, on Tidpit Common:[4] then, we may suppose, the young men and their maids would make a holiday of the occasion. For the western progress of earlier sovereigns, interrupted by hunting parties at Clarendon, Cranborne or Wilton were now substituted those visits to watering places which did so much to make them fashionable.

[1] *W.A.M.* 33 (June 1904), p. 289. quoting a letter from Dr. Goode of Broadchalke, dated 1791.

[2] Chafin, *Anecdotes and History of Cranborne Chase* (1818), p. 13. The original of the picture in the Farnham Museum is attributed to Byng and hangs in Cranborne Manor.

[3] Now the Gloucester Hotel, Weymouth.

But seldom can the village have gained greater publicity in the London clubs and broadsheets than when the innocent offer by farmer Thain of a barn at the back of his house in East Martin to some vagrant gypsies on a chilly winter's night of 14 January 1753 brought him the notoriety of having harboured the abductress of Elizabeth Canning.[5]

Agriculture, as in the past, was the only preoccupation of the villagers: everyone took a part in it, or, like the saddler and farrier, were dependent upon it. Since the last survey in 1518, the area under cultivation expanded at Martin by 1,688 acres. This did not imply that sheep farming for wool was superseded by the production of cereals. Wool still remained of first importance and especially in Wiltshire. It was rather a manifestation of the fact that by the eighteenth century, corn was produced, not only for subsistence, but also for export. Loaded on Wiltshire-raved waggons and drawn by six horses it was conveyed to Poole or Southampton for shipment to Bristol returning, as has been mentioned, often with ship's timber from the demolition yards, of which much was used in the building of farm houses, cottages and barns.

In the eighteenth century seed was still broadcast, and at no time in the history of farming was so large a quantity of seed sown to the acre. On the other hand since the Middle Ages the yield had more than doubled, and the maxima in the eighteenth century were not far below the average yields of today. But the economic situation created by the Napoleonic wars was accentuated by a succession of wicked harvests, when wheat fetched phenomenal prices, towering in 1812 to 126s. 6d. per quarter. Necessity then, as in recent wars, compelled the maximum cultivation.

The expansion of farming under the Tudors and Stuarts led to the reclamation from waste of new land, and its enclosure under individual ownership provided additional acreage for corn production. Early instances of enclosure of common land had occurred in the Middle Ages, but the process was accelerated in the sixteenth, seventeenth and eighteenth centuries. The enclosure of Rotherdown,[6] Lodge Down, part of Bustard Down and the Burnbake fields at Tidpit Down[7] belongs to this period, and the field names Harris Down, Bachelor's Down, Compton's

---

[4] Lord Herbert, Henry, Elizabeth & George Letters & Diaries of the 10th Earl, 140.

[5] Harvey Darton, *Alibi Pilgrimage*, p. 189.

[6] The enclosure of the Chase farms by Lord Pembroke has been ascribed to 1793; Rotherdown, the old Cow Down, was enclosed somewhat earlier.

[7] The Court Rolls are evidence that the Burnbake fields were reclaimed from Tidpit Common before 1754.

and Moody's Down[8] are reminders of downland enclosed by individual farmers.

For grubbing up much of the downs, where furze, thorns and undergrowth were rampant, the practice of burnbaking (more properly burnbeaking) introduced in the previous century was very generally employed. Davis, the Wiltshire authority on eighteenth century agriculture, writing in 1794, was undoubtedly right in saying that it was a very ancient custom, for in its essentials it is the method of bringing waste lands under cultivation employed by many primitive peoples, as for instance the Bantu of Central Africa. But as a systematic process of reclaiming land, it was not practised in Wiltshire before the seventeenth century.[9] It was said by Aubrey to have been introduced into South Wiltshire by a Mr. Bishop of Merton who had learnt it in Flanders about the year 1639.[10] It is possible that this Mr. Bishop was the curate who did duty at Martin from 1625 to his death in 1638.[11] Burnbaking is defined as meaning 'to chop up with a mattock the rough surface of the land to be reclaimed, afterwards burning the parings'.[12] The turf was broken and cut with a breast, usually called a burnbaking, plough sprinkled with ashes and burnt. ' 'Tis good for the father' comments Aubrey, 'but nought for the son by reason it does so wear the heart out of the land.'[13] Experience approved this judgment for by the nineteenth century burnbaking was often prohibited by covenants dealing with conveyance of land.

Simultaneously with the reclamation and enclosure of the common lands, a number of factors had contributed to the enclosure of the open fields. The acquisition by a single individual of a number of contiguous strips in a particular furlong of the open field had become apparent even under the Glastonbury regime. For example, out of twenty acres in Curtelawe, John Strete held ten, out of twenty-eight acres in Yseworthdene, John Garret had nine, and out of sixteen acres in Smalelonde John Curteys had five.[14] The opportunity to acquire an aggregation of strips in a particular field must often have occurred by inheritance from a brother or near relation, by exchange with another for the sake of convenience,

[8] The enclosure of these fields dates from Tudor or Stuart times.

[9] *P.N.W.*, p. 450.

[10] Aubrey, *N.H. Wilts.*, p. 103.

[11] *Infra*, Ch. IX. An error of a few years would not be inconsistent with Aubrey's unmethodical memoranda. Prothero, *Hist. of British Farming*, says the practice was first introduced at Thorney by Walloon immigrants in the seventeenth century.

[12] Dartnell and Goddard, *Glossary of words used in Wiltshire.*

[13] Aubrey, *N.H. Wilts.*, p. 103.

[14] *Beere, passim.*

and especially by the acquisition of the lifehold interest and in many other ways. The convenience and economy of cultivating ten contiguous acres in one field compared with twenty half-acre strips widely dispersed must have been obvious to the farmer and operated as a stimulus to the acquisition of adjacent strips. The parson, for instance, must have walked (or more likely rode) not less than five miles to inspect the whole of his scattered glebe, extending from the turnpike to Tidpit. Glastonbury Abbey, as lord of the manor, had set an example with its demesne lands which copyhold farmers were not slow to follow.

That many of the open fields were even at the end of the Middle Ages enclosed in the sense that they were fenced or hedged is evident from the field names of early Tudor terriers. In the parish of Martin Myllehegge, Mearshegge, Shylfehegge, Longhegge, Yongeshegge and Colperyhegge indicate the existence of numerous hedges, although some may have demarcated boundaries rather than circumscribed fields. In addition to tofts and crofts, closes and parrocks, many field names denote enclosures: Yseworthdene, Les Tynengs, Stanecraft and others.[15] An estate picture depicting a panoramic view of an open field in the early decades of the eighteenth century, though not in this county, shews fields divided by helges which bear a striking resemblance to the ordinance map of today.[16] It may well be that further evidence will show that at this time the open field was already subdivided by hedges to an extent that is not generally appreciated. Conditions, therefore, were already prepared for enclosure: the subdivided field and the motive to cultivate it in severalty.

In the Middle Ages the traditional rotations had been determined by the two or three field system: autumn sown wheat, followed by spring sown barley or oats, followed by a year's fallow before wheat was again sown. Although leguminous crops were known as early as the thirteenth century, they are not mentioned in any of the surveys of Martin and were considered to be unsuitable to chalk soils. The medieval rotation was followed in the Elizabethan period; in the Pembroke survey of 1569, for example, we read: 'There are 120 acres of arable at Toyd and 60 acres at Allenford, of which they may sow 60 acres with winter seed and 60 acres with spring seed in any one year.'[17] In the open fields this rotation persisted until the middle of the eighteenth century, a year's fallow always being given before a crop of wheat, as was expressed in the

[15] *P.N.W.* pp. 450, 449, 427.
[16] *Country Life*, June 27, 1947.
[17] *Pemb. S.* (1569).

Wiltshire saying, 'Two years rest for wheat is equal to the best coat of dung,'[18] Arthur Young in 1769 found this to be the prevailing practice on Salisbury Plain. There is no record of his ever having visited Martin, but he enlarges upon the agricultural conditions in the adjacent parish of Broad Chalke, which may be assumed to be descriptive also of Martin. There he found the following rotation: I fallow, II wheat, III barley, IV oats or beans or vetches, followed again by a year's fallow. In the fourth year a variation was sometimes made by the substitution of a crop of hops or of clover, the latter sown for two years,[19] the first crop being mown and the second eaten off by sheep.[20] But as previously, there was always a year's fallow before wheat. The conclusion of Arthur Young, after his examination of this area, was that the traditional year's fallow preceding the wheat crop was wasteful of the soil, and he used all his advocacy for the clover crop.[21] At Tidpit, however, clover was sown as a catch-crop some years before Young interested himself in agriculture.[22]

The inspiration of Charles Townsend to transplant the turnip from the kitchen garden to the open field created a minor revolution in agricultural and pastoral economics. If he did not originate the idea from his leisured experiments at Rainham, he, at any rate, stimulated the practice and his nickname 'turnip' Townsend did more than his secretaryship of State to perpetuate his memory. His intention was two-fold; one, by the provision of winter fodder to put an end to the autumnal decimation of the flocks of sheep and the conversion of their carcases into salted mutton; the other, to substitute for the invariable fallow a fourth crop in the rotational course. In this latter purpose, it constituted a potent factor in the dislocation of the then accepted rotation, and consequently in the disruption of the strip system in the open field. But into Wiltshire his ideas penetrated only slowly. Arthur Young, again referring to the neighbourhood of Broad Chalke, deplored the indolence with which after the wheat stubble had been ploughed, turnip seed was harrowed in without previous preparation of the soil or subsequent cultivation by the hoe.[23] But as

[18] Davis, *op. cit.* 43.

[19] Young, *A six weeks tour through the Southern Counties*, (1769), p. 203; *W.A.M.* 54 (1951), p. 90.

[20] Marshall, *Rural Economy of the Southern Counties*, (1798), p. 345.

[21] Young, *op. cit.*, p. 268. The fallow field, also called the Summer field, usually at this time the fourth in the rotational cycle, was often called locally Old land, and was regularly folded and trodden by sheep. Also called the Clover field (e.g. at Tidpit).

[22] Court Rolls, 1754.

[23] Young, *op. cit.*, p. 204.

late as the last decade of the century turnips are not mentioned as a regular rotational crop and even in the first half of the nineteenth century a field of turnips was sufficiently rare to arouse Cobbett to ecstatic excitement.

Probably too much credit has been given to Charles Townsend. There are plenty of references to the turnip before his day, and, to quote a local one, at Burbage near Savernake Forest, of which Aubrey about 1685 wrote 'they are the best that ever I did eate. They are sent for far and near. They are not tough and stringy, like other turnips, but cutt like marmalad.'[24] But Townsend's enthusiasm certainly did much to popularise the crop.

The inclusion of turnips and clover in the regular rotational course, involved the conversion of the old two- or three-field system into a four-field course of husbandry. This change was made at Tidpit about 1757 and at Damerham about 1761.[25] The fields at Tidpit at this time were called (i) the wheat field, (ii) the barley field, (iii) the clover field, and (iv) the summer (or fallow) field. The new system enabled more food and more fodder to be grown.

Sheep folded on arable supplied the necessary manure. It was estimated that 500 ewes would adequately manure an acre in a single night. Indeed, the only competitor to muck was marl. Marling as an antidote to sourness of the soil had been known from early times.[26] At Martin, the survival of the field names La Crondelle[27] and Marlynputte (twice) and at Damerham of Pyttelonde is evidence of its use here in the Middle Ages. The practice appears to have fallen into abeyance under the Tudors. Thus, Aubrey noticing the chalk pits 'of great antiquity' round Tidpit, had to confess his ignorance as to their purpose.[28] Charles Townsend has been given the credit for the rediscovery of the value of marl. But its application must have been an onerous business. According to Young twenty waggon loads to the acre would last twenty years at a cost of 3/- an acre.[29] The method of marling at the beginning of the nineteenth century has been described by the late Mr. E. A. Rawlence as follows:

[24] Aubrey, *N.H. Wilts.*, p. 36. An early use of the word marmalade.

[25] Court Rolls, 1757 & 1761.

[26] In. Inq. 1189 the expression 'marliavit et coluit' occurs and Walter of Henley, p. 19, tells of strewing straw and marl in the folds.

[27] *P.N.W.*, p. 428. O. E. *Crundel*, a hollow, often a chalk-pit; see *The Chief Elements used in English Place-Names* (E.P.-N. Soc.), p. 19, with special reference to Hants. and Sussex dialect.

[28] Aubrey, *Mon. Brit.* pt. V. Fitzherbert's *Book of Husbandry* (1523) deplored the fact that marling had fallen into disuse; *v.* Prothero, *op. cit.* 94.

[29] Young, *op. cit.*, p. 204.

'He remembered his father telling him that in his early days gangs of gypsies used to go about with teams of donkeys, to which large wicker panniers were attached with flap-board bottoms. These gypsies would then sink shallow wells in the centre of the field to be chalked, fill the panniers, and then lead the donkey out and drop the flap. The heaps of chalk would be deposited all over the field at intervals. . . .'[30] The revived use of marl may have been a consequence of the introduction of turnips into the rotationary course, for it was the belief of the Wiltshire Down farmers that chalk in the soil was an essential accessory to a root crop. Nevertheless, the farmer must have been glad when agricultural lime and the mechanical distributor superseded the carting of chalk. The impoverishment of land from deficiency of manure led about this time to the insertion in agricultural leases of a clause prohibiting the removal of straw. At Martin there is an exceptionally early instance of the 'good husbandry clause', dated 1613. A sentence reads: 'As to the hay and straw and other fodder, commings of the current year, yearly growing on the premises, be spent upon the same premises . . . and the soil thereof to be made longer.'[31]

Marl was succeeded by lime; the site of the old kilns is recalled by the field-name Limekilns on the Damerham road and again near Kite's Nest Farm. But Limacre occurs at Damerham as early as 1518.

Even towards the end of the seventeenth century, Aubrey was complaining that wheat was replacing barley as the stable constituent of bread. 'When I was a boy,' he recalled 'wheate was very scarce; then was baked 20 bushells of barley to one of wheate; now they have altered the course of husbandry, how wisely, I cannot say, I something doubt – and spend 20 bushells of wheate to one of barley.'[32] This assertion he supported by observing that Charles II, when staying at Salisbury, had found both the bread and the beer unpalatable.[33] But his statement was only partly true, and such change as there was, was confined to the east of England and to the upper classes. In 1528 it was said of Wiltshire 'wc have reason to believe that in that county barley was commonly used as bread corn',[34] and corn certificates show that, in those hundreds, which are quoted, the excess of barley over wheat was 28% and in some places double.[35] Three

[30] W.A.M. 43, p. 501 (Rawlence, 'Ancient British Agriculture in the South and West).

[31] Court Rolls, 1613.

[32] Aubrey, *Top Coll.*, p. 211.

[33] Aubrey, *N.H. Wilts.*, p. 104.

[34] Ashley, *The Bread of our Forefathers*, p. 41.

years before Aubrey's birth a State Proclamation described barley as 'in times of scarcity the breadcorn of the poor';[36] at the time of his death only 38% of the bread consumed in England was made of wheat.[37] Until the nineteenth century was well advanced, the staple food of the villager and the agricultural worker was the unpalatable and indigestible barley bannock.[38] The accounts of the Overseers of the Poor at Martin contain many such entries, as that in 1800 'a bushell of barley for bread for the poor'. Of the cereals grown, barley preponderated from which was made by most cottagers that home-brew, which diluted their diet from dawn to bedtime.

The reclamation of waste, farmed in severalty, the conversion of the medieval open field into a four-field rotational course, the introduction of catch-crops, such as clover and turnips, the application of fertilizers, like marl and lime, were the harbingers all over England, that prepared the way for 'inclosure'. Yet, although all these things happened here, only at Damerham did inclosure ensue. Damerham was inclosed, on the petition of the Bishop of Salisbury, the owner of the greater part of the land, Sir Eyre Coote, who held the copyholds of the bishop, the Earl of Shaftesbury, the impropriator of the tithes, the Earl of Chichester, the patron of the living, Thomas Longland, the vicar and the freeholders, by an Act of Parliament dated 1818,[39] but it was not carried into effect until 1830. The operative clause was no. xix, which affirmed that all rights of common were extinguished over the land enclosed. Thus, the villagers lost their arable strips in the open fields, which they had cultivated from the earliest times.

Tidpit was never enclosed. In the Tithe Award of 1840 the open fields were still apportioned in strips, averaging an acre or less in extent, distributed among six copyholders and farmed by four farmers. As the century progressed the land became concentrated first in two and finally in one farm. Thereafter, the need for inclosure disappeared.

The inclosure of Martin is not so simple. It has sometimes been assumed

---

[35] Ibid., p. 187.

[36] Davies, *Early Stuarts*, p. 296. quoting Leonard, *Early History of Poor Law Relief*, p. 145.

[37] Trevelyan, *Eng. Soc. Hist.*, p. 296.

[38] Olivier & Edwards, *Moonrakings*, p. 36. *v.* also W. H. Hudson, *A Shepherd's Life*, Ch. xviii.

[39] 58 Geo. III, cap. IV. There is a copy of the Awards with a map in the Public Record Office, and another in the County Archives, Winchester, without a map.

that it was enclosed at the same time as Damerham.[40] But there is no record of it in the catalogue of inclosures at the Public Record Office, nor in the list of Wiltshire inclosure awards, compiled by Mr. W. E. Tate.[41] Had it been a statutory inclosure within the last two centuries it is inconceivable that it could have escaped notice. In default of the awards themselves, it may be possible to arrive at some conclusion from the examination of other documents. It is certain that Martin was enclosed before 1840, the date of the tithe map. In that map there is no vestige of strip cultivation or of an open field system; on the contrary, farms varying in size from 30 to 400 acres, comprising enclosed arable fields from two to forty acres in area, correspond almost to those of the present day. Moreover, whereas at Damerham any transaction concerning the copyholds in the nineteenth century, was accompanied by the clause, 'and all allotments of land allotted and awarded in respect of the said premises by the Award of the Commissioners under the Damerham Inclosure Act',[42] no such reference is made to conveyances of land at Martin.

Turning back to the eighteenth century, old title deeds of property in Martin disclose no trace of open field cultivation. The evidence from the Court Rolls is to the same effect; the description of copyholds record large holdings, attached to farms, known by the name of their owner or some predecessor, Welch's, Thane's, Loxley's or Garrett's. While there are plenty of allusions to strip farming and to an open field system at Damerham and Tidpit, there are none at Martin.

In the seventeenth century the Court Rolls have survived in two series, the first from 1606 to 1613, the second from 1683 to 1685. At both periods the jury are found legislating for the open fields at Damerham and Tidpit but never at Martin. Presentments for the repair of hedges between the Wheat and barley fields, or the barley and the summer fields, the 'bounding' or 'breaking' or 'laying up' of fields[43] are of frequent occurrence at both the former villages but find no place in the presentments from Martin. An admission to a copyhold in 1610 seems to show that considerable enclosure had already taken place; Thomas Harris is admitted to a messuage, attached to which were thirteen acres in Blackland field and twelve acres in Longbarrow.[44] But, his ancestor, William, a

[40] *V.C.H. Hants.*
[41] Tate, in W.A.M. 188 (1945).
[42] e.g. Court Rolls, 1834 *et seq.*
[43] Court Rolls, 1610, 1611, 1612.
[44] Court Rolls, 1610.

hundred years previously held only one strip of less than one acre in each of these fields. Although the evidence in this century is less definite, the indications are that Martin was already enclosed. Aubrey, it may here be mentioned, observed that in North Wiltshire fields were being rapidly enclosed between 1635 and 1695.[45]

There is, however, no doubt whatever that at the beginning of the sixteenth century Martin was under strip cultivation. The survey of 1518 was in its comprehensiveness and meticulous detail unequalled by anything the Abbey of Glastonbury had hitherto produced. Over 1,500 strips, each averaging less than an acre, were enumerated, their area stated and their situation named. From the survey of the Earl of Pembroke in 1569 nothing can be deduced.

The conclusion to be drawn from this evidence is that Martin was enclosed sometime between 1518 and 1685, and probably between 1518 and 1606, possibly by common consent of the strip-holders.[46]

When in 1762 General Sir Eyre Coote returned to England and bought the West Park estate, he established a dynasty at Damerham and Martin that was to endure until the twentieth century was well advanced. Sir Eyre Coote shares with the first Earl of Shaftesbury the distinction of being incomparably the most notable public person to have held the freeholds of these villages, and a brief account of his career and character may not, therefore, be altogether out of place.

Eyre Coote was a descendant of that Irish family which in the year of the Restoration of Charles II produced the Earl of Montrath and the Earl of Bellamont, the first Governor of New York, whose property is said to have expanded over eight Irish counties and to have amounted to nearly a million acres.[47]

It is one of the strange incongruities in human affairs that the soldier who, on the admission of historians, by his victories at Wandiwash and Pondicherry put an end to the aspirations of the French in India, and by his campaign at Porto Novo saved Madras from the domination of Hyder Ali, should have started his military career by being court-martialled for cowardice.

Born in 1726, he was commissioned as ensign to the 27th, 'our inniskilling regiment of foot' and took part in the battle of Falkirk in 1746, from the field of which he, with others, ran away with such celerity

[45] Aubrey, *N.H. Wilts.*, p. 104.
[46] For an example of this procedure, V. G. N. Clark in *E.H.R.* 87.
[47] It was Bellamont who captured Captain Kidd, the pirate.

that he arrived in Edinburgh, some twenty miles distant, well in advance of his regiment. He was suspended by the findings of the court-martial, which held him to have been not guilty of cowardice, but guilty 'of going to Edinburgh before the regiment'.[48] Either because of his explanation that he wished to prevent the colours which he bore from being captured, or because of the prevailing shortage of officers at the time, Coote was reinstated and appears to have served on the Continent with the 37th (Rothes). By 1755 he had got his company and exchanged to the 39th (Aldercron's), then about to sail for India. It had been raised in Ireland in 1701 and was known at that date by the Colonel Coote who raised it, almost certainly an ancestor of Eyre Coote, and is now the 2nd battalion Dorset Regiment, whose motto is appropriately *Primus in Indis*. He distinguished himself at Chandernagore, was present in Calcutta after the Black Hole episode, and at a council of war summoned by Lord Clive gave his vote, in opposition to his chief and the great majority of senior officers, for an immediate attack at Plassey. With a reputation much enhanced by this battle he returned to England the following year. His services were recognized by the East India Company, and when trouble broke out again was authorised to recruit 'by beat of drum or otherwise' an additional regiment which, taking rank as the 84th, was known in the army as Coote's Regiment and despatched again for India.[49]

After the victorious campaign of Wandiwash (the battle which gave us India, as one of the garrison invested within the walls wrote in his diary), the assault of the almost impregnable fortress of Permacoil, of which a prisoner detained there wrote 'nothing but devils or monkeys could take it',[50] and finally the unconditional surrender of Pondicherry, Coote returned to England in 1763. On his way home he married at St. Helena Susanna, daughter of Charles Hutchinson, governor of the island. Westrow Hulse, Coote's chaplain, later described her as a pattern of excellence[51] and when Boswell explored the highlands of Scotland she impressed him as 'that very agreeable woman'.[52] Coote was presented by the Directors of the East India Company with a diamond-hilted sword, costing £747, and with the fortune he had amassed in India he bought

[48] Wylly, *A Life of Sir Eyre Coote*, p. 12; from this biography much of what follows is borrowed. (Hereafter cited as Wyly.)

[49] *Ibid.*, p. 60.

[50] *Ibid.*, p. 86.

[51] *Ibid.*, p. 121, quoting Guise, *Letters of Warren Hastings*, p. 104.

[52] Boswell, *Tour of the Hebrides*, 28 Aug. 1773.

from General Cholmondely West Park in the parish of Rockbourne, a house built about 1720 by a Mr. Durnford, the then rector.[53] He was gazetted colonel in 1765, elected member of Parliament for Leicester in 1768 and for Poole in 1774.

In 1770 he sailed for the third time to India as commander-in-chief of the East India Company's forces, but in consequence of quarrels about powers and precedence returned in 1771, by the overland route, being one of the first to do so, and on his arrival in England was made a Knight of the Bath. As colonel of the 37th Regiment then stationed at Fort St. George, Inverness-shire, he entertained Dr. Johnson to dinner with, according to Boswell, the regimental band playing in the square before the windows.

He made his fourth and last voyage to India in 1778, as lieutenant-general and commander-in-chief in the East Indies, accompanied by his wife and other ladies and with Westrow Hulse as his brigade chaplain. The battle of Porto Novo, a decisive blow to the arms of Hyder Ali, was followed by lesser but uniformly successful engagements at Pollilore, Sholinger and Arnee, which liberated Madras. After a few months' recuperation at Calcutta he returned to the front on board the *Resolution*, which fell in with four French privateers. It was during the anxieties of the chase that the general whose constitution was exhausted with fever and the haradships of war, 'dropped on deck struk by a paralytic stroke', from which he never recovered. He died shortly after landing at Madras and was buried in the church of St. Mary. Nine months later his corpse was exhumed encased in a leaden coffin and transhipped to England. It was disembarked at Plymouth in September 1784 to the accompaniment of a salute of guns and the bands playing a dirge, and reinterred in Rockbourne church at a funeral attended by all the principal gentlemen of the district when Westrow Hulse is said to have preached 'a most pathetic sermon'.[54]

An effusive eulogy, after the fashion of the time, signed T.D. and dated from Fordingbridge contains the following lines of appreciation.

Polite, obliging, affable and free
From distant pride and dull formality,
Now did his raptured tongue with rapture dwell
on every sportive thought and mirthful tale.
He too was pleased to tread the path humane

[53] Radcliffe, *Notes on the Parish of Rockbourne*, p. 13.
[54] Wylly, p. 14.

Where charity led up her gentle train.
A generous kindness ever warmed his breast
To feed the poor and succour the distressed
To the sad orphan timely aid to bring
And teach the mournful widow's heart to sing,
Whilst all around confessed that Heaven designed
In blessing him with wealth to bless mankind.[55]

Lady Coote survived her husband until 1812, spending most of her time at West Park, until she delivered it over to her husband's heir the second General. She is the benevolent patroness, who did not disdain to visit the poor and the sick, to whom a sympathetic Curate pays a well-merited tribute, as appears hereafter.[56]

There exist three monuments to the General. One in the north transept of Westminster Abbey represents Victory suspending a medallion of Sir Eyre Coote to a palm tree, beneath the foliage of which reposes a lachrymose native of India. A second is a statue formerly in the Leadenhall Street Office of the East India Company and now in the India Office in Whitehall. The third is a monolith erected in a conspicuous position in the grounds of West Park, by Jane Bagwell, the second wife of the second General, in commemoration of the military achievements of both Generals.

It was the intention of Warren Hastings to have set up a fourth in the square at Calcutta. He had proposed that the immense column with the image of a lion on the top, a monument of prehistoric India, discovered in the province of Hajespore, Subanbahar, and locally known as Rajah Boemsing's walking stick, should be transported overland on truckles and floated down the Ganges 'on rafts of timber'.[57] The operation, not less stupendous it would seem than the transportation of the monoliths of Stonehenge, was abandoned on account of the expense and the probability of damage to the monument. In India his memory is perpetuated only by a portrait in the Exchange at Madras, where it was said no sepoy ever entered without first doing obeisance.

As a soldier he was more brilliant than orthodox. His strategy in the Wandiwash campaign was so fallible that he himself admitted that the inexplicable desertion of the French fleet alone saved him from inevitable surrender.[58] His courage was never in question as was proved by his

[55] Wylly, p. 367.
[56] *Infra*, Chap. X.
[57] Wylly, p. 370.

personal reconnaissance of the fortifications of Pondicherry under intense fire. He had a flair for detecting the most assailable point in a hostile position or the most vulnerable spot at which to effect a breach in a fortification. His favourite method of attack was an advance *en echelon* upon the enemy's flank, and he is credited with the innovation of deployment in ranks two deep, instead of the single rank formation usually adopted at this time. His forced marches under an Indian sun with discontented troops, chronically in arrears of pay, almost always short of rations and with seriously defective transport, are little short of miraculous. Yet the only mutiny he had to quell came from his European soldiers. His army was always outnumbered and he was opposed by Hyder Ali, the greatest commander ever produced by India, in command of the most formidable army ever recruited.

'Our Black troops look up to him as something more than human' wrote an officer in Coote's army, while other contemporaries indulged in such expressions as 'the soldier's friend' and 'beloved of the army in India'.[59] When his death became known the native population voluntarily imposed upon themselves a public mourning throughout Bengal.[60]

On the other side, his ambition, vanity and covetousness were a by-word in India. That he engaged in trading transactions with Indian magnates was not peculiar to him; it was the customary sideline of most employees of the East India Company at that time. His venality made it worth the while of Warren Hastings to augment his salary of £16,000 a year as commander-in-chief by an annual subsidy of £18,000, under the pretext of a field allowance, in order to secure his vote in council,[61] an action which later formed a charge at his trial. It may not be true, but it is in harmony with his conceit, that he exploited the vote which he gave before Plassey in favour of attack, to increase his reputation in England as the victor of the battle.[62]

Lord Clive thought him mercenary and prone to intrigue, and Macaulay, who was not specially prejudiced against him, described him as capricious and fretful, having more regard for his allowances that his duties.[63] Yet he retained the confidence of the East India Company in London, and, in his early career at any rate, also of the Prime Minister.

---

[58] Malleson, *Life of Warren Hastings*, p. 323.
[59] Wylly, p. 306.
[60] *Ibid.*, p. 358.
[61] Mill, *Hist. of British India*, V, p. 221.
[62] Malleson, *op. cit.*, p. 319.
[63] Macaulay, *Warren Hastings*.

'You are a tip-top favourite with Pitt', wrote Sullivan, Chairman of the Board, in curiously modern idiom.[64] But he was an embarrassment to everyone with whom he had to deal in India and got on with no one. 'He resigns or threatens to resign about once a week', wrote a colleague. Warren Hastings, a friend and loyal supporter of Coote, felt impelled to report to his Chairman, 'May honour and success attend him [Coote] in any other part of the world, but God forbid that he should return to India',[65] and again, 'My letters are all friendly to him, his to me all petulant and suspicious'.[66] Du Pre, the Governor of Madras, commented that he quarrelled continually in both presidencies where he served. None the less he was one of England's greatest generals.

The early career of his nephew who succeeded him was as distinguished as that of his uncle. Commissioned to the 37th Regiment, now the Royal Hampshires, he took part in the campaigns in America from 1776 to 1781, being present at the engagements at Brooklyn, Brandyaine, Charleston and Yorktown. In 1795 he was given the important command of the Light Brigade, then serving in the West Indies. He saw service in Holland in 1799 and with distinction in Egypt in 1800, for which he was rewarded with the Order of the Bath. When he was appointed Governor of Jamaica in 1805, his health first began to fail, undermined by that pestiferous fever, which choked the West Indian cemeteries to overflowing with the graves of so many valuable soldiers. If, as has been asserted, his brain was at this time already affected, it is an example of singular ineptitude on the part of the authorities at the War Office that he was selected to take command of the crucial operations against Flushing in the mismanaged Valcheran expedition of 1809. Contemporary diaries agree that in the early stages of that disastrous campaign he did all that was possible in appalling conditions. But he emerged from that campaign marked with 'eccentric behaviour', and he was never actually employed again in any military capacity.

He had been Member of Parliament for Queen's County since 1802, and his 'eccentricity' did not dissuade the electors from returning him at the head of the poll for Barnstaple in 1812. He was gazetted a full general in 1814.

He died in 1823. He married as his first wife Sarah Rodbard, the subject of Romney's finest portrait, in 1784.[67] She died at the early age of thirty

[64] Forest, *Life of Lord Clive*, II, p. 182.
[65] Wylly, p. 135.
[66] Forest, II, p. 152.

in 1795 and lies buried in Rockbourne church. His second wife, Jane Bagwell, erected in the grounds of West Park a monolith to commemorate the military achievements of both generals.

[67] Painted in 1784 for a fee of 80 guineas, it was sold to America in 1902 for £10,000.

IX

ALL SAINTS CHURCH, MARTIN

With a note on St. George's, Damerham

THE church at Martin is dedicated to All Saints, which, after that to the Virgin Mary, is the commonest dedication in Wiltshire, and, indeed, in the whole of England. It does not, however, necessarily follow that this was its original dedication. Dedication to All Saints, although dating from the eighth century, did not become popular until the fourteenth century, when the day was adopted to combine on one single occasion the numerous feast days and holidays of the church. While it was as common before as after the Reformation, it was also especially common as a re-dedication.[1]

There is some evidence that the church may have been originally dedicated to St. Peter and St. Paul, whose feast fell on June 29th. This dedication belongs, almost without exception, to the pre-Reformation period.[2] The occasion of the fair or revels granted to Martin by a charter of Henry III in 1266 was the vigil, the day and the morrow of the feast of St. Peter and St. Paul,[3] and fairs usually coincided with the feast day of the patron saint. Moreover, the orientation of the church is 22 degrees north

[1] Arnold-Forster, *Studies in Church Dedications*, II, p. 502.

[2] *Ibid.* I, p. 56.

[3] *Harl. Chart.* 58, i, p. 22.

of east, that is the exact declination of the sun towards the north at the summer solstice and raises a presumption that the church was orientated and the foundations set out about midsummer. If there is any substance in the theory that dedications were associated with the day of foundation, this fact suggests that at Martin the church may have been originally dedicated to St. Peter and St. Paul.[4]

The parent church at Damerham is dedicated to St. George. St. George of Cappadocia came into vogue about the reign of Richard I, but as a dedication it did not become popular until the reign of Edward III, when he was adopted as the patron saint of the Garter, displacing Edward the Confessor. A tympanum above the south door, depicting a figure on horseback, presumably St. George, accoutred in armour and spurs, charging down a prostrate Saracen, has been attributed to the time of Richard I.[5] It closely resembles the better-known tympanum at Fordington, now a suburb of Dorchester, which is ascribed to the middle of the twelfth century. The dedication of the church is not likely to be later than the tympanum, and may be earlier. St. George was a favourite saint with Glastonbury Abbey. An altar at Glastonbury was dedicated to him by Adam of Sodbury, abbot from 1322 to 1335,[6] and in the following century the Abbey's hospitium was named the George Inn.[7] The dedication to St. George as early as the end of the twelfth century is, however, sufficiently uncommon as to be worthy of record.

Notwithstanding the extensive restoration of the nineteenth century, the church at Martin preserves many of its original features and is, architecturally ,not without interest. The western part of the nave represents a complete Norman church, measuring 24 feet by 17, which may be as old as 1080 and is certainly not later than the early part of the twelfth century.[8] The eastern limit is marked by a quoin clearly visible on the exterior of the north wall, a foot or so west of the transept. The west end coincided with the archway separating the nave from the lower stage of the tower. The sanctuary may have been aspidal in form.

In addition to a south door, there was a north entrance with square

[4] Aubrey was a Churchwarden at All Saints, Broad Chalke, also probably a re-dedication.

[5] Clapham, *English Romanesque Architecture after the Conquest*, p. 138. For the original of the story of the intervention of St. George at the Battle of Antioch in 1098 *vide* William of Malmesbury II, p. 420 and Arnold-Forster II, p. 472.

[6] Dugdale, p. 6.

[7] John of G. I, p. 267.

[8] Ponting in *W.A.M.* 28, p. 17. The later date is preferred by *V.C.H. Hants* IV, p. 592.

jambs and a plain tympanum, the vestiges of which are distinct on both the interior and exterior walls. At the north-east angle of this original church is what appears to be a stoup for holy water, which, unless it has been transposed, must have served those entering by this door.[9] The north door may have been intended for the use of the residents of West Martin and particularly of the manor house, while the south door was used by the parishioners of East Martin. The windows in the nave are all of later date. The elevation of the roof can be discerned from the drip-course on the wall of the tower. If we picture a thatched roof and an earth floor, strewn perhaps with straw, we can visualise with fair accuracy this small place of worship at the time of the early Norman kings.

To the original south door a porch was added at the end of the fourteenth century, many of the original stones being incorporated in the reconstruction.

The increase in the population and the influx of strangers which followed the Norman conquest necessitated more ample accommodation in the church. Moreover the thirteenth century was an age of architectural construction and enlargement. The chancel, which in the Norman church had been little more than a recess for the altar, was now projected eastwards as far as the present chancel arch and enlarged to the width of the nave. The priest's door, west of the present position of the pulpit, now blocked, which belongs to this century gives some idea of the extent of the church at this time. The jambs of this door can be distinguished on the exterior face of the south wall. At their base lies a recumbent sculptured figure on a slab of purbeck marble ascribed to the same date. It measures only one-and-a-half feet, and may originally have been superimposed over the doorway in an erect position. In this century, then, the century in which Salisbury Cathedral was built and completed in thirty years, we may imagine a long narrow church without transepts and with a low roof extending from the tower wall to the chancel arch.

In the following century the chancel was prolonged to its present length and has, with two exceptions, the squint and the piscina, remained in its original state unaffected by subsequent restoration. The absence of cusping in the windows is worthy of note in a century during which decorative design reached its highest culmination. The north window consisting of two trefoiled lights with a trefoil and scroll label above is ascribed to the year 1310, and there are two similar windows in the south wall. At the eastern angles are some unusually large stones, which have

[9] Recent investigation by Mr. Hugh Shortt indicates that it is not a stoup.

been reset. The squint in the north wall, to which reference will be made later, belongs to the early Tudor period, and the piscina, made to appear ludicrous by the elevation of the floor level at the Victorian restoration, is an addition of the sixteenth century. The priest's door is coeval with the rest of the building.

The glass in all the chancel windows is modern, the benefaction of Thomas and Mary Waters in 1879. Whether they contained stained glass previously is not known, but Lord Shaftesbury as the lay impropriator had repaired and reglazed them as recently as 1871. One of the two chairs in the sanctuary was made and carved by the Rev. Edward Peacock, of Frome and Martin and presented in 1896. The other was the gift of his wife Eleanor in 1867. The reredos was put up in memory of the Rev. G. B. Daniell, the first vicar.

The south transept dates to the first half of the fourteenth century,[10] and was, therefore, immediately subsequent to the eastward extension of the chancel. Between the jambs of its east window was a mural depiction of a kneeling figure and a scroll bearing the words 'O beata dei mat: miserere mei', indicating its use as a Lady chapel. Some letters may still be faintly distinguished. In the south wall is a piscina wth an ogee cusped arch and square bowl with an added wooden shelf. The north-east and south-west angles are supported by diagonal buttresses and the roof by a tie-beam. Besides the transept buttress there is another supporting the chancel arch with no corresponding buttresses on the north side, a fact which may show improved building in the fifteenth century. Towards the end of the eighteenth century the Lady chapel was converted into a vault for the Talk family. William Talk, magistrate and alderman of Salisbury, mayor of that city in 1762 and high sheriff for the county in 1769 had succeeded to copyholds in Martin from ancestors who first appear in the first decade of that century. He erected a gallery over the transept arch, conveniently sited so as to be directly above the font, as it then stood, and adjacent to the pulpit which at that time occupied a position at the angle of the south transept and the nave. The parapet of the gallery, which was dismantled at the restoration in the mid-nineteenth century, can still be seen. William Talk was the last of his family to be interred in the vault on Christmas Eve, 1797.[11] The tablet to his memory

[10] *V.C.H. loc. cit.* assigns it to the year 1340; Ponting to the end of the fourteenth century.

[11] In *W.A.M.* III, p. 230, William Talk is erroneously said to have been buried at Damerham.

recites that he left to the churchwardens and overseers of the parish £3,000,[12] the interest on which was to be expended as necessary upon the repair and maintenance of the burial ground of himself and his family and of the gallery built by him and also of an adjoining window, inserted by his brother-in-law, John Woodward. The remainder was assigned for the support of six old persons of the parish, who in the terms of the original will, were to be provided with 'cloth coats and waistcoats for the men and camblet gowns and petticoats for the women' and £3 worth of faggots. For the maintenance of the burial ground the parish clerk received each year a guinea. A pension of 8/- a week has now been substituted for clothing and regular attendance at divine service is no longer insisted upon. Each year on Whit Monday the mayor and four senior aldermen drive to Martin to dispense the charity of this munificent citizen.

The stained glass in the south window of this transept was inserted in 1887 in memory of Thomas and Mary Waters, the donors of the glass in the chancel windows. Thomas Waters had throughout his life been a devoted friend and benefactor of the church. At his death he bequeathed £275, invested in consols, the interest on which he desired be distributed on St. Thomas's day among old people at Martin in the form of money, food or clothing.

The north transept was built in symmetry with the south transept early in the fifteenth century, and connected with the nave by a two-centered arch. It was lighted by the lower of the two windows in the west wall and the westernmost window in the south wall, both of which are typical of this period. With the completion of this transept about the middle of the century (and before its extension eastwards) the church became cruciform in arrangement, consisting of a nave, a chancel and two identical and symmetrical transepts.

Towards the end of the century or early in the sixteenth, the church lost this symmetry when the north transept was converted into what approximates to a north aisle. The problem confronting the builders was to transform a transept roof running north and south to an aisle roof running east and west; to replace a gable at the north end of the transept by one at the west end of the aisle. Their treatment consisted of retaining the square-headed window in the west wall, which had formerly been

[12] *Wilts Charities*, p. 521. The principal in 1800, when the charity was confirmed by the Master of the Rolls, stood at £3018.18.0, invested in 3% consols, yielding about £142 annually.

under the eaves of the roof, and adding a typical fifteenth century window above and slightly to one side of it in the centre of the new west gable. The timber transome on which the original roof rested may still be seen.

The extension eastwards involved the insertion of two new bays which with the rest of this aisle belong to the early sixteenth century. A four-centred arch gives access to the aisle from the nave. A three-light window under the eastern gable and a five-light window in the north wall are of a type more commonly associated with domestic than ecclesiastical architecture. In front of the large window is a space which may have been intended for a tomb, but has, apparently, never been filled. The north door by which the aisle is entered is of the same date. The enlargement of the transept can be distinguished by the use of regular courses of wrought masonry in the new work in the place of the undressed flints of the old. The effect of the enlargement was to create a chapel rather than an aisle, and there are good reasons for supposing that, in fact, it was erected with this object by Sir John Horsey, who at this time occupied the manor house. The cavernous aperture, inappropriately styled a squint, which was inserted in the chancel wall at this time, affords from the manorial pew beneath the great window a prospect of the altar. On the abaci of the capitals of the arch in front are two small crosses carved to avert evil influence from the occupants of the chapel.

Beneath the organ there may be a vault containing the tombs of Sir John Horsey who built the chapel, and of Sir Bartholomew Horsey, who is known to have been buried in the church in 1597. An ancient stone coffin lid was, in fact, excavated at the restoration of the church, but so mutilated by a mason that it was discarded with the debris. The only inscribed tomb that has escaped the superstructure of church furniture is one to the memory of Sir Gabriel Lapp, who died in 1668: 'depositu gabrielis lapp armigeri qui obit . . . dei February A.D. 1668.' He was a great grandson of a Mary Horsey[13] and his hatchment was recently unearthed from an old barn behind the White Hart Inn, bearing his crest and arms.[14]

In the large perpendicular window is a fragment of old amber glass, discovered among some rubbish in the second stage of the belfry. In the

[13] *Visitation of Wilts*, 1623, p. 51. He was born in 1618.

[14] A mermaid, issuing, proper, in her dexter hand a purse, gules, in her sinister hand a comb, or. It has been stated (*Country Life* July 1952) that the lozenge-shaped hatchment was introduced from Holland about the time of the Restoration. If this be so, this is an early example. There is, however, one dated 1631 at Marnhull, Dorset.

western window of this wall are the crest and arms of Henry Brounker[15] (1841–95) of the family that acquired Boveridge from the Hoopers in 1788, and with it became the owner of Kite's Nest Farm and part of Martin Woods in this parish.

The tower and the tower arch were built in the first quarter of the thirteenth century. Its history is mainly a record of buttresses. In its original form the tower had three buttresses against each exterior wall, of which only four now survive (on the west front the centre and north-west buttresses, each with one set-off; on the north face, that at the north-west corner; on the south face, the centre buttress which is almost flat and has no set-off). The early buttresses can be distinguished from those set up later by their having not more than one set-off.

In the lower stage were two small square-headed windows in the west wall, one of which was replaced by a window of two lights in the fifteenth century. In the upper stage were two lancet windows on the west and south walls, but the latter was blocked and vestiges of it are only perceptible from the inside. As originally built, like most other towers of the period, it was designed for defence and storage of goods.

The insecurity of medieval towers is proverbial, and that at Martin had no greater permanency than the majority. But though its foundations were found to be defective, it never collapsed. In the fifteenth century three new diagonal buttresses at the corners were added, and three old ones rebuilt, and about 1890, when it threatened to collapse, it was underpinned.

In the course of reconstruction the tower was raised a stage and surmounted by a low steeple. It has often been supposed that there had been no addition to the tower until the present spire was erected towards the end of the eighteenth century. But a small etching, prefixed to a survey of the estates of Damerham and Martin,[16] acquired by the first Earl of Pembroke in 1569, clearly depicts the church at Martin surmounted by a steeple. The drawing is undoubtedly intended to represent All Saints Church, in spite of the omission of the south transept, and is certainly the earliest picture of the church ever made. It was probably drawn from memory rather than sketched on the spot.

[15] Crest: Out of battlements Sable, a dexter cubit arm vested argent, charged etc.; Arms: argent 6 pellets, 3, 2 and 1, a chief embattled, sable. With the motto, DUTY. Henry Brounker married a sister of Mrs. Bentinck of Bustard House, Martin.

[16] *Pemb. S.*, II, p. 309. Straton in *W.A.M.* 32, p. 293, mistakenly identifies it with the church at Damerham, which has a bell turret superimposed upon a massive tower, where normally a south transept should have been.

The date 1787 is incised on the masonry of the string coursing at the base of the parapet. The date denotes the substitution of a plain for a crenellated parapet, and the replacement of the old low steeple by an octagonal spire. The parapet is no longer accessible owing to the recent staging of the bell frames. There is some old blue glass in the edge of the west window of the lowest stage of the tower.

The present waggon-headed roof of the nave is ascribed to the sixteenth century, when it replaced what was probably a truss and rafter construction. It is plastered, supported throughout by tie-beams, and was at one time ceiled with lead. The nave was leaded in 1805, as appears from a water colour painting made in that year,[17] but the main roof was only stripped within living memory. A story, which may contain a fragment of truth, records that the lead was given away to the contractor, who extracted from it enough silver to defray the cost of re-roofing the church with tiles. The roof of the nave was gutted by fire on the night of 26 November 1950.

The principal sepulchral memorials have already been referred to. It remains to add that in the south transept is a tablet to Elizabeth Blandford, a sister of John Talk who married into the Martin family of Blandfords and died in 1779, and another to John Woodward, who was responsible for the adjoining window. A stone on the floor records the death of John Grove, in 1772, a gentleman whose family had lived at Martin and Tidpit since the end of the sixteenth century. In the north transept there was found at the restoration an encaustic tile on which were emblazoned the arms of the Lytes of Lytes Cary, Somerset: gules a chevron between three swans argent, on either side being the letters J.L. Sir John Horsey had married as his third wife Edith, daughter of John Lyte,[18] and the north transept chapel had become for all intents and purposes dedicated to the Horsey family. In the nave are tablets to the families of Reade, Hodding and Peacock,[19] and to members of the Waters family.

The nineteenth century was devoted, at Martin as elsewhere, largely to restoration. Already as early as 1813 the churchwardens' accounts record

[17] Buckler collection of water colours 11.9, in the Devizes Museum.

[18] *Supra,* Ch. VI.

[19] The Rev. Edward Peacock of Rockford Nunnery, Frome, and of Reade's Farm, Martin (1820–1903), married Eleanor, daughter of Mathias Thomas Hodding of Fryern Court and Salisbury. M. T. Hodding had married Eleanor, daughter of George Reade, ob.1810, of Fryern Court, who owned most of the copyholds in Martin.

the purchase of four loads of stone from Sarum, two loads of sand from Boulsbury, one load of lime from Broad Chalke, and 300 tiles.[20] But it was not until 1851 that the vestry began seriously to consider restoration. Some idea of the condition of the church may be gathered from a letter written at this time by the Rev. R. Allnutt, then Vicar of Damerham. 'The church' he wrote, 'was in a state of dilapidation almost indescribable: the tail-boards of waggons used for the backs of pews.'[21] In 1831 the seating was recorded as accommodating 400 persons out of a total population of 599.[22] The case for re-pewing the church was strengthened by the estimate of the Rev. G. B. Daniell, the first vicar, that by 1857 the population had increased to 640 souls, some fifty more than the official census. In that year a faculty was obtained to 'restore the district chapelry of Martin', and the specifications included 'taking down the gallery, pews, communion table, font, pulpit and lectern, and making various alterations'. Alderman Talk's gallery was bricked in, the top of the parapet alone being left to mark the site. The carved oak woodwork of the old pews found its way to private houses, where the stairways and apartments are enriched by its panelling; the simple stone font with its capacious bowl, having been removed to form the centre-piece of an ornamental garden, was replaced by a hideous exhibit from the wares of a local monumental mason. Its position, too, was changed; formerly it had stood at the angle of the south transept and the nave, almost directly beneath the pulpit, a very unusual position, according to an authority on this subject.[23] Now it was relegated to the base of the tower. The carved Jacobean pulpit was spared, but it was moved some yards back from its previous position.[24] The old lectern having been discarded, a new one was donated by Thomas Waters of Tidpit in 1883. The varnished deal seating, calculated to promote rather than obviate the discomforts of the congregation, was supplied by the Church Seating Society, and in 1888 the private pews, allocated to the copyholders, were abolished and the seating made free.

The original estimate of £397 was raised by donations from the villagers and from such non-resident landlords as Lord Shaftesbury, Sir Eyre

[20] Churchwardens' Accounts.

[21] Extract from a letter preserved among papers in the Vestry chest.

[22] *Ecclesiastical Revenues*, p. 830.

[23] Bond, *Fonts and Font Covers*, p. 89. The single instance of this position cited is at Swymbridge, Devon.

[24] For the positions of the pulpit and font, *c.* 1830, see diagram, Hoare, *H.S.D.*, p. 17.

Coote, Henry Brounker and Thomas Hodding, as well as the Bishop of Salisbury, all of whom subscribed handsomely. It was, however, exceeded, and in 1859 the vestry, after an acrimonious discussion and against strong opposition, carried on a poll held at the White Hart Inn by 58 votes to 48 a motion for the imposition of a church rate. The entire work cost £520.

In 1871 further small improvements were made, 'to obviate present discomforts'. The windows were repaired and reglazed; curtains were suspended over the entrances and matting laid down on the floors. The intention was to stop draughts, but it was not until 1886 that a stove was installed.

Serious cracks, however, had now developed in the masonry of the tower, threatening the collapse of the spire. The tower was underpinned and the flints used in its construction recemented. At the same time the roof was stripped of its lead and replaced with tiles. The cost was £1,208, towards which the Ecclesiastical Commissioners contributed £262. The church was formally re-opened by the Bishop, Charles Wordsworth, in May 1896.

Perhaps what most altered the general appearance of the church was the raising of the floor level. Hitherto the floor level had been uniform from the tower to the sanctuary, with perhaps a single step in the chancel. By building steps at the chancel arch and again at the sanctuary the restorers not only buried the bases of the piers and concealed the lower part of the piscina, but spoilt the proportions of the building and the loveliness of the vista towards the altar.

The organ was installed in 1884 and dedicated by Dr. Wordsworth, Bishop of Salisbury. The harmonium, which had hitherto done duty, sold for £5.

The development of the church throughout the centuries may be roughly summarised as follows:

c. 1100 A small rectangular Norman church not larger than a small room in a private house.

c. 1250 A long nave with tower and chancel, but without transepts.

c. 1450 A cruciform church, with symmetrical transepts.

c. 1520 The church in its present arrangement, with two transepts and a north transept chapel.

It may be assumed that the church at Martin came into being in the same way as other village churches, in obedience to an impulse, that prevailed all over western Europe, to build a place for Christian worship. The lord of the manor was usually the person who responded to this impulse: he gave the land on which the church stands, that is the advowson, and endowed it with glebe for the sustenance of the priest. We know nothing about the manor at the time of the Norman Conquest, and Domesday Book is silent about the holders of land, except for the names of three persons the ancestors of those who later held by military service. William the son of Helye was granted the manor of West Martin not earlier than 1126 and probably a good deal later, since he was alive in 1189, while the church's original features, as has been said, are ascribed to a still earlier period. Henry of Blois, on his own admission, repaired and embellished the church at Damerham, and such building as was done at Martin in the middle of the twelfth century may with strong probability be attributed to his inspiration. Robert of Sottingdean, rector of Damerham c.1245, is the most likely architect of the thirteenth century work.[25] He succeeded in enlisting the interest of the sovereign in the building both of the vicarage house and the church at Damerham, and may be presumed not to have altogether ignored the church at Martin. Glastonbury Abbey did not owe a direct obligation to the two churches until their appropriation in 1268. From this date the Abbey, as rector, was under an obligation to repair the chancel, and its prolongation to its present length and the addition of the Lady chapel which belong to the fifty years following may be a consequence of appropriation. But the Abbey's contribution to the architecture of the church was in all probability surpassed by the voluntary effort of the parishioners. As an example of this, it may be affirmed with some assurance that the north transept chapel was the individual work of Sir John Horsey in the early sixteenth century.

In 1553 Edward VI caused an inventory to be made of church plate and bells in all churches and chapels.[26] The commissioners in Wiltshire belonged to three well-known county families, Sir Anthony Hungerford, Sir William Servington and Sir William Wroughton. The churchwardens were summoned to New Sarum and 'to bring with them such parcel of plate, jewells, metal and other ornaments (whatsoever they may be) belonging to your church, chapel, guild, brotherhood, fraternities or companies as do remain in your custody or of any other person or persons to your knowledge the uses aforesaid as you will answer upon oath. The great bells and the saunce (sanctus) bells in the steeples only excepte'.

[25] *Supra,* Ch. V.

[26] Stat. 7 Ed. VI. *v. W.A.M.* 12, p. 366.

Their report was as follows:

	Goods to be safely kepte		In plate to ye Kings use
	Chalice or cup	Bells	
Damerham	XVI	III	IIIIoz.
Martin	XI	III	XVIIoz.

The inventory reveals, rather surprisingly, that Martin was richer in plate than Damerham. But its loss was in higher proportion: seventeen out of twenty-eight ounces being appropriated by the king, while Damerham sacrificed only four out of twenty.

The chalice which the parish was allowed to keep has since disappeared. The present chalice bears no date or hallmark, but is ascribed to the late Elizabethan era about the year 1600.[27]

The earlier of the two patens is dated 1728, the later 1744. It was presented by Mrs. Reade and her donation is recorded in the Parish Registers as follows:

The communion Plate, the gift of Mrs. Martha Reade, to the parish church of Martin, was given the 28th day of January in the year of our Lord one thousand seven hundred and forty four.

Thomas Staples Curate.
James Shrimpton }
Joseph Haiter } Churchwardens.

Mrs. Reade was a member of that family which lived at Fryern Court and held property in Martin. It is, perhaps, interesting that the Curate, Thomas Staples, six years later married a Mrs. Mary Reade, widow.

A glance at the inventory of 1553, given above, shows that at that date both Martin and Damerham possessed three bells each. None have survived, though it is possible that, having become cracked, they were later recast and inscribed with the initials of their founders at the date of recasting. Bells were more easily fractured then than now, when the method of percussion was to bring the clapper on to the bell instead of rotating the bell on to the clapper. Other explanations may be found in the ire of the Puritans against bell-ringing or the need for melting down bells into ordnance. Today there are six bells, of which three were given within the last twenty years. In chronological order they are:

[27] Nightingale, *Church Plate of Wilts*, p. 52, where it is described as belonging to the Gillingham type.

1.	1606	Tenor inscribed 'Thanke God'. J. W.	8 cwt. 3qr. 22lb.
2.	1657	By Francis Foster H.P.XF.F.XO.H.XI.G.[28]	4cwt. 3qr. 16lb.
3.	1662	By Purdue, inscribed with the names of the churchwardens Richard Compton and Robert Harris.[29]	
4.	1934	By Mears and Stainbank given by Helena Augusta Read.	4cwt. 0qr. 13lb.
5.	1934	By Mears and Stainbank given by Kate Blanche Hibberd in memory of Ambrose Blandford of Tidpit.	4cwt. 3qr. 1lb.
6.	1939	By Mears and Stainbank presented by public subscription.	

The bell of 1606 was cast by John Wallis, whose initials are inscribed on it. John Wallis is thought to have cast his bells in Culver Street, Salisbury, which was formerly known as Bellfounders Street.[30] In Wiltshire alone he cast 216 bells and, among neighbouring villages, at Rockbourne and Coombe Bissett in 1617.

Francis Foster, whose bell casting period covered the years 1654–75, was in partnership with William Purdue and Nathaniel Boulter at Salisbury. Besides casting the well-known bell at Damerham recording the date 'In the year of Plague, Warre and Fire', he cast four bells at Fordingbridge.

The bell of 1662 is by William Purdue (1610–73). His main foundry was at Bristol but about the time of the Restoration he appears to have established a branch at Salisbury. In 1659 he cast bells at Broad Chalke, in 1660 at Ebbesbourne Wake, and in 1661 at Salisbury Cathedral.

The three modern bells were due to the campanological enthusiasm

[28] The initials probably stand for Henry Prince (Churchwarden), Francis Foster (Bellfounder), Oliver Horsey (Curate) and John Grove (Churchwarden). Oliver Horsey is not known to have been Curate before 1680, but the records at this time, and especially during the Commonwealth, are defective. The families of Prince and Grove produced other Churchwardens during this century.

[29] Walters, *Church Bells of Wiltshire*, II, p. 135, erroneously gives the date 1660 for this bell, a mistake perpetuated by Mears and Stainbank in a list framed in the south porch, commemorating the rehanging of the bells by that famous firm. Personal inspection, in company with the then Vicar, the Rev. Skillbeck Smith, has proved beyond doubt that 1662 is correct. Mears and Stainbank are also responsible for substituting 1616 for 1606 as the date of the tenor bell. Walters is correct in giving the date as 1606.

[30] Lukis, in *Brit. Arch. Assoc. Journ.* 1889.

of the vicar at that time, the Rev. R. Skillbeck Smith, who also rebuilt the bell stage and frames. The three old bells had last been re-hung by John Daniell about 1860.

A few sporadic entries in the accounts of the churchwardens disclose a loyal and healthy political opinion in the village. Every year until the middle of the last century on the 5th of November a peal of bells was rung 'for the preservation of the King and Parliament' and the payment of six shillings is recorded to be expended on the consumption of beer at the White Hart.[31] Again, on 12 November 1820, when news reached the village that the action for divorce by George IV against Queen Caroline had collapsed the bells rang out 'for the Queen's defeating her enemies'.[32] The ringers got six shillings on this occasion, but only three the following year for ringing on the king's coronation day. The loss of the earlier volumes of the churchwardens' accounts is much to be deplored.

To the student of horology the church affords ample material. Incised upon the walls are no less than eight scratch dials or mass clocks.[33] Some are doubtless copy dials, carved by some mischievous schoolboy; others have been demonstrably transposed. Types vary considerably; some have plain radii, other holes at the extremity of the radii for the insertion of pegs, while another is of the wheel type. Their positions are sited for the convenience of the users of the church: those on the tower buttresses for the congregation of West Martin entering by Church lane; those on the buttresses of the south transept, next the porch, for worshippers from East Martin, entering by the wicket gates; that next the priest's door for the use of the parson. All the dials are much weathered and in peril of complete obliteration.

The dials did not denote time, but were devices to indicate the hours of service. From the mass line, which is usually incised more deeply than others, it may be inferred that mass was sung, following tierce, at about 10 a.m. (allowance being made for the deflexion of the church from true orientation). This was the service at which the largest congregation might be expected to be present. Where dials are in pairs, it may be assumed that one denotes the time of service in summer, the other in

[31] This entry occurs in many parochial accounts, e.g. at Cranborne.

[32] Since the Divorce Bill was not finally disposed of in the Queen's favour until late in the afternoon of November 10th, the news reached Martin in tolerably fast time.

[33] *Hampshire Field Club*, XV, 3, p. 272 records four only, omitting two on the Tower buttresses and two on the South Transept.

winter. From such pairs it is possible to deduce that vespers were sung at about 1.30 p.m. in winter and about 2.30 p.m. in summer. That on the diagonal buttress at the south-east corner of the south transept, nearest the priest's entrance, is the only dial to mark sunrise and to indicate the hour of matins and prime at the early morning hours of 6 and 7 a.m.

The dial built into the diagonal buttress at the south-west angle of the transept, which is inverted, mutilated and obviously transposed, cannot be later than the early part of the fourteenth century, when that buttress was built, and may be much earlier. The wheel-type dial on the same buttress cannot be earlier than the middle of that century, and the dial near the Priest's door not earlier than the end of that century. But the dial on the original buttress against the centre of the south face of the tower may well belong to the previous hundred years.[34]

The church was drained in 1838 and the churchyard surrounded by a wall in 1873. The old churchyard was enlarged in 1923 by the addition of land to the east, taken partly from glebe. Two noble yew trees, the emblem of immortality, dominate the old graveyard. The most imposing of the sepulchral monuments are the tombs at the south-west of the church, of the families of Reade of Fryern Court, Garrett-Reade of Alderholt Park and Waters of Tidpit and Martin. There are less than a score bearing dates of the eighteenth centuary, among them a vault to John Hancock, Gentleman, on the slab of which his arms may be indistinctly discerned,[35] who died in 1725; that of Thomas Blandford, who died in 1724, and another of John Sweetapple, dated 1731. Up to the middle of last century there is said to have existed a spectacular monument to Hercules Stanley, who styled himself king of the gypsies. It was prostrated by the kick of a stray horse that roamed uninvited into the cemetery.[36] Admirers of Gilbert White of Selborne may recall the letter in which he writes 'we have two gangs or hordes of gypsies. . . . One of these tribes calls itself by the noble name of Stanley'.[37] Beneath the west front is a cross to William Lawes, who under the pseudonym Isaac Bawcombe has been depicted in W. H. Hudson's *A Shepherd's Life*. The village centenarian was Hannah Baker, who in 1865 died at the age of 101. For the rest, they are the graves of farmers, farm hands and shepherds.

[34] *Vide Hants. Field Club*, XVI, 3, by the author, for a detailed study of each dial. *v.* also A. R. Green, *Sundials*, pp. 163–164 and 126–129.

[35] A chevron between three cocks, impaling the arms of Goddard, a chevron between three crescents.

[36] Neville Henderson, Rector of Broad Chalke, Scrap Book of Newspaper cuttings in the Souter library, Salisbury.

By 1923 the old cemetery had become greatly congested; the tiny mounds lay in close juxtaposition and corpses were superimposed one on another. That within the confines of this little churchyard there lie the remains of some two thousand bodies is explicable only by the fact that during most of the church's history no burial acts regulated the depth of the grave, that only a proportion of the bodies were enclosed in coffins, and that the action of chalk and lime promoted rapid decay. As a worthy sexton once remarked 'We used to take one out to put another in.' Doubtless there was once an ossuary or bone hole and its position may have been in the south-west corner of the Old Cemetery.

The entry in the registers under the year 1710 of 'Buried in Woollen' may be perplexing to those unfamiliar with the statute passed by the Parliament of Charles II in 1677.[38] To promote sheep farming and encourage the use of wool, Parliament of that year enacted that all persons be buried in a woollen shroud: 'No corpse of any person shall be buried in any shirt, shift, sheet or shroud made or mingled with flax, hemp, silk, hair . . . or any other thing than what is made of sheep's wool only.' The parson was required to record this fact in the register of burials, the deceased's relatives to support the fact by affidavit, and the act had to be read publicly in church each year on the Sunday following St. Bartholomew's Day. The penalty attached to an infringement was £5, and an exception only made in the case of persons dying of the plague. It was not, however, until a generation after the enactment that the curate at Martin first recorded the fact, in 1710, against the names of six persons only. But the descendants of the families of Lush, Thain, Prince and Reade may have the satisfaction of knowing that their forebears were buried in strict compliance with the act of 1677.[39]

In 1255 a bull of Pope Alexander IV granted a licence of appropriation of the church of Damerham (which included that of Martin) to the use of the abbey.[40] Nevertheless, Abbot Roger Forde between 1255 and 1261 appointed Henry of Wyngeham rector in opposition to the wishes of the convent, and it was only on the intervention of Ottobonus, the papal

---

[37] Gilbert White, *Nat. Hist. of Selborne*, Letter XXV.

[38] Stat. 30 Chas. II, cap. 3 (1677), entitled *An Act for Burying in Woolen.*

[39] The chief offenders against the Act were among the aristocracy. In the neighbouring village of Cranborne Lady Katherine Leigh in 1681 and Lady Catherine Wyndham both paid forfeiture for infringement. (*Notes on Cranborne Church*, Rev. L. F. Addison.)

[40] Adam, II, p. 323; John of G., II, 382.

legate, that the appropriation was enforced.[41] Walter of Wylie, Bishop of Salisbury, confirmed it in 1267, while reserving to himself the assessment of the vicar's maintenance and the right of institution.[42] In 1268 the dean and chapter added their consent.[43] The scribe who recorded the appropriation of the churches in the Rentalia appends, with apparent irrelevance, the following couplet, which it would be difficult to surpass for neatness and terseness:

Si sapiens fore vis sex serva qua tibi mando
Quid dicas, et ubi, de quo, cui, quomundo, quando.[44]

In 1270 John Burnel was presented by the convent and admitted and instituted by Bishop Walter of Wylie, to the perpetual vicariate of Damerham and Martin.[45] The bishop took the opportunity afforded by the Institution to announce the provision he had made for the vicar's maintenance; the house and manse, which in former times had belonged by custom to the rectory; the arable, meadow and pasture; the homage, rents and services and all other things appertaining which the rectors of these churches had hitherto been accustomed to hold and enjoy, under the name of rectors; further, the tithes, greater and less, from the whole of the tenement once belonging to William Peverel[46] in the parish, as well as all small tithes, by whatever name they are called, and the altar dues[47] of the whole parish of the said churches with all that appends thereto, except the tithes, greater or less, derived from the demesne and the court of the said abbot and convent, which with all tithes of sheaves of the whole parish, which are not assigned for the perpetual use of the abbot and convent. The value of the vicarage in 1291 was £13.6.8.[48] By 1535, at the time of the suppression of the Abbey, it had exactly doubled, and was returned as £26.13.4, but deductions were made of £1.6.2 to the Archdeacon of Sarum and 2/- to the Abbot of Glastonbury.[49]

[41] Adam, p. 534; John of G., I, p. 236.
[42] *G.C.* I, p. 57.
[43] *Ibid.*, p. 58.
[44] *Rentalia*, p 194.
[45] *G.C.*, p. 58 *v.* also Dugdale, I, p. 33.
[46] For the Peverel property in Damerham Parva, *v. supra*, Ch. IV.
[47] *Alteragium* is defined in the glossary annexed to *Adam of Damerham* as comprehending tithes of wool, lambs, colts, calves, pigs, goslings, chickens, butter, cheese, hemp, flax, honey, fruits, herbs and such small tithes with offerings that shall be due within the parish. Cf. Ralfe Turner *versus* the Rector of West Haddon, in I. Q. Elizabeth.
[48] *Taxatio Ecclesiastica of Pope Nicholas III* (Rec. Com.) p. 181.
[49] *Valor Ecclesiasticus*, I, p. 105.

From this date vicars were substituted for rectors, and were regularly presented by the patrons, the Abbot and Convent of Glastonbury and instituted by the bishop of the diocese. The relative position of the parochial church to the abbot and the bishop also became regular; the pope had sanctioned the appropriation of the churches to the abbey; the bishop and the dean and chapter had approved it. Thenceforth the abbey became the patron of the living, received the greater or rectorial tithes, presented secular vicars and paid them a fixed stipend. By virtue of its patronage the abbey may have contributed to the building, while the parochial churches on their part devoted a portion of the parochial revenue to the support of the abbey. The chief purpose of appropriation, however, was fiscal, to derive from the parish church as much revenue as possible. The abbey's contribution to building has already been conjectured; the parish contribution to charity had been, even before appropriation, specifically ten shillings.[50] This was augmented in the time of Abbot Beere by an equivalent amount out of the rent of the abbey's *hospitium* and assigned to the maintenance of poor women below the abbot's gate.[51] A similar contribution was attached to the tenure of Lotteshame[52] at Damerham, held at this date by John Rode. These were probably the ten poor women accommodated in an alms house built in the north precincts of the abbey by that abbot.[53]

After the suppression of the monasteries the patronage of Damerham lapsed to the Crown. In 1554 it was granted to William Herbert, first Earl of Pembroke, and retained by his two successors until 1622. In that year it was acquired by William Cecil, the second Earl of Salisbury, and remained in that family until 1698, when James, the fourth earl was impeached for his adherence to the Catholic faith. The patronage was next obtained by John Holles, first Duke of Newcastle, and the Pelhams who succeeded to the dukedom retained it until 1801. It then passed to the Hyndman Trustees in whom it is still vested. The vicarage of Martin is in the gift of the vicar of Damerham.

A list of the vicars of Damerham with Martin, extracted from the episcopal registers is given in an appendix to this chapter.[54] It contains

50 *Rentalia*, p. 5.

51 *Beere*, p. 64.

52 *Beere*, *loc. cit.*

53 Dugdale, I, 7.

54 Sir Thomas Phillipps, *Wiltoniae Institutiones*, from which, however, there are several omissions. An index will be found in *W.A.M.* 28, p. 218. *v.* Appendix to this chapter.

no institutions earlier than 1315 (at Tidpit 1307), but from various sources it is possible to elicit a few names in the previous century. Robert of Sottingdean was rector since before 1247, and during the next five years would seem to have been engaged in building operations at the church of Damerham and the parsonage house there. There is also extant a grant by him of land at Damerham to Albertus de Summa, a papal deacon, in consideration of six pennies paid to the convent of Glastonbury on condition that he should neither obstruct improvements made by the abbot, nor overstock the pasture.[55]

Reference has already been made to Henry of Wyngham. John Burnell was the first vicar to be instituted, after the appropriation of the two churches, by Walter of Wylie, Bishop of Salisbury, in 1270. About 1281 he was appointed custos or master of St. Nicholas's Hospital at Salisbury.[56]

Two extant documents concern his successor to the vicarage, Richard of Chisingbury. The first is an acknowledgement that he holds no rights of pasture for cattle or pigs in any pasture, meadow or wood of the demesne, whereby the rights of the abbey or its tenants might be infringed.[57] This document, which is undated, amounts to a re-affirmation of the rights acquired by the abbey under the appropriation of the two churches.

The second deed, also undated, has some peculiarities of its own. It is a contract of manumission, whereby Ralf de Baskerville, the holder of half a knight's fee at Tidpit, sold his villein (*nativus meus*) Philip Hardyng to Richard, vicar of Damerham, for the sum of twenty shillings, 'which money was paid into his hand', thus liberating Philip Hardyng from the bonds of servitude.[58] Baskerville's motive and the vicar's participation have alike been misunderstood. Hoare stigmatises the latter's action as 'unclerical (at least unchristian)'. But sale was one of two ways only open to a master desiring the manumission of his slave. By a legal fiction, because a slave was deemed incapable of owning money, the price had to be provided by a third party,[59] in this case the benevolent vicar.

The average stipend of a vicar in the Middle Ages was £3.6.8 a year and the average value of a living to a rector about £6,[60] but these men were farmers as well as parsons, and ploughed their strips in the open

[55] Hoare, *H.S.D.*, p. 30.

[56] Wordsworth, *St. Nicholas's Hospital, Salisbury*, p. 210.

[57] *Hoare, H.S.D.*, p. 28.

[58] Ibid., '20 solidi sterlingorum quos mihi per manibus solvit unde . . . ab omni nativitate et servitudine liberavi'.

[59] A. L. Poole, *Obligations of Society*, p. 30, and Vinogradoff, *Villeinage*, p. 151.

fields with the rest of the villein tenants. It was customary for the parson's glebe to be twice that of a villein tenant or two virgates, the equivalent on this manor of about sixty acres. This, in fact, was the glebe of the Vicar of Damerham, half of it lying in Martin. The Vicar in 1341, for example, kept a bull, four cows, four bullocks (for his plough team), two draught horses, and had pasture for eight head of cattle and 250 sheep.[61] At the same date the Rector of Tidpit owned 200 sheep.

History knows little or nothing of these men who throughout the Middle Ages devoted their lives to their parish. Some idea of the qualifications of the medieval priest can be gathered from the register of Simon of Ghent, Bishop of Salisbury, concerning John of Stykelynch, rector of the hamlet of Tidpit in the parish. He was an acolyte at the time of his presentation by the Abbot and Convent of Glastonbury to the benefice at Toudeputte. On 6 October 1307 he was instituted at Sonning, then an important manor of the Bishops of Salisbury. In the following year, as a subdeacon, he was licensed to the rectory for a period of three years under the constitution of St. Boniface. In 1312 a license was issued at Ramsbury for his ordination as deacon 'by any catholic bishop in communion with the apostolic see'.[62]

After the Reformation occasionally a few details transpire. The last vicar to be appointed by Glastonbury Abbey was Peter Horsey, a son of Sir John Horsey, of the manor house at Martin. In the register of Institutions under the date 1554 the letters *p.d.* are appended to his name, indicating *per dismissionem*,[63] and he was duly succeeded by Thomas Pope, as vicar. For what scandal he was deprived of his living does not appear, but it seems probable that it was an error of doctrine. But, by the end of the following decade he emerges, his indiscretion atoned for and is reinstated in his benefice at Damerham, described as '*modernus vicarius*'.[64] Moreover, so firmly established was he in the favour of his patron that at the same time he enjoyed the rectory of Winterbourne Bassett[65] and the chaplaincy of Charlbury [66] in Dorset, both livings in the gift of the first Earl of Pembroke. Indeed, the accumulation

[60] Moorman, *Church Life in England*, p. 154, calculated from an analysis of the *Taxatio ecclesiastica*.

[61] *Nonarum Inquisitiones* (1341), p. 168(b).

[62] *Register of Simon of Ghent*, I, pp. 691, 884, 908.

[63] Phillipps, *Wilt. Inst.*

[64] *Pemb. S.* I, p. 312.

[65] *Ibid.*, I, p. 264.

[66] *Ibid.* I, p. 110.

of preferments in one person was not uncommon about this time. The predecessor of Peter Horsey, William Pickname, was instituted vicar of Damerham in 1507 and lived to sign the *Valor Ecclesiasticus* in 1535. In the interval, besides the living of Damerham, he was prebendary of Yatesbury in 1515, of Ruscombe in 1517, of Yetminster in 1518, and of North Grantham in 1519.[67] William May is not shown in the list of Sir Thomas Phillips, but as vicar of Damerham he subscribed to the Act of Uniformity in 1677 and again in 1690.

In the following century John Nourse (1723–54) was a canon of Salisbury Cathedral, holding from 1727 the prebend of Major Pars Altaris,[68] which had at one time been attached to the bishopric until it was exchanged for that of Potterne. His successor, Samuel Ogden (1754–66) was Woodwardian Professor at Cambridge, where in the cloistered precincts of his college he composed those sermons on the efficacy of prayer which elicited the approbation of Dr. Johnson, and afforded consolation to Boswell in his sickness and imminent perils of shipwreck off the Isle of Mull.[69] Thomas Longland (1822–49) combined the living of Damerham with the vicariate of Portchester. Their prolonged absences from the pastoral care of their parish evoked dismay among their overworked curates and reduced their villages, deprived of their natural champion against despotic authority, to a deplorable state of misery.[70]

The offices which it was incumbent upon a parson to perform are multifarious and numerous. It is probable that in the Middle Ages the population of Martin was not less than it is today: it is quite certain that baptisms, marriages and burials were of far more frequent occurrence. Only a resident minister could cope with the numerous offices which the post-Reformation parish registers show to have been performed every day and every month. And although the parish of Martin was not created a separate ecclesiastical district until the middle of the nineteenth century, in practice it had become largely independent of its parent church of Damerham.

The statutes of Winchester required that a chapel with an appendant graveyard be built in all villages distant more than two miles from their parish church.[71] Both Martin and Tidpit fell within this category, but,

[67] *Fasti Ecclesiae Salisburiensis*, pp. 386, 388, 415, 483.

[68] *Ibid.*, p. 401.

[69] Boswell, *Tour of the Hebrides*, Oct. 3rd, 17th and 24th, 1773.

[70] Philip Hanvil, Curate, *A brief Statement of Facts of unparalleled inhumanity, oppression, cruelty and neglect in the treatment of the poor in the parish of Damerham South*, published 1796.

though Tidpit was a rectory before the date of its ordination as a vicarage, the church at Martin was commonly denoted a chapel. It was, for instance, so described in the *Valor Ecclesiasticus* of 1535 and in ecclesiastical blue books of the last century. There can be little doubt that throughout the Middle Ages the vicars of Damerham appointed chaplains, having the cure of souls, paying them a fixed stipend of one or two pounds a year, little more, in fact, than a labourer's wage.[72] The function of the chaplain or parish priest was to repeat the mass daily in his church and to perform the necessary rites mentioned above. From 1606 ministers, styling themselves curates officiated in the church and signed the parish registers. A list of them, so far as their names can be ascertained, is subjoined to this chapter.[73]

It is possible that at Martin in the Middle Ages they lived in the fifteenth-century house, which still bears the name of 'the Priest's House'. But in later centuries, until the building of the present vicarage house, they occupied a dwelling situated on what is now the school playground, and pursued their meditations in a garden, secluded by yew trees to the south-west of the church. Three, at any rate, were buried in the churchyard, though no stone now records their graves: John Bishop, buried in 1638, Joseph Hosse, in 1739, and Thomas Staples, in 1775.

The parish of Martin was made a separate ecclesiastical district in 1847, and in 1866 the benefice was made a vicarage.[74] The first vicar, the Rev. G. B. Daniell, was admitted in 1867. The endowment in respect of the benefaction amounted to £33.6.8, to which an equivalent grant of perpetual annuity was added.[75] Both grants were increased to £39 in 1886. The stipend was £94 augmented by a grant of £40.8.4 from Queen Anne's Bounty and a provision was made safeguarding the incumbent against a loss from tithes. By 1930 the stipend had reached the value of £346 gross,[76] to which Queen Anne's Bounty contributed £76. The glebe has been reduced to a couple of acres upon which are the vicarage house and garden.

Visitations and the presentments of churchwardens had a very real and practical value in the seventeenth and eighteenth centuries. They afforded an opportunity not only for the exercise of ecclesiastical discipline, but

71 Moorman, *op. cit.*, p. 14.
72 Hamilton Thompson, *The English Clergy*, p. 122. Moorman, *op. cit.* p. 55.
73 Appendix II.
74 *London Gazette*, 31 Aug. 1866, p. 4860.
75 *Ibid.*, 1864, p. 3490.
76 *Crockford's Directory*. It has since diminished and in 1948 is shown as £288.

also for the ventilation of grievances. Those who did not attend church and others who omitted communion were regularly presented during the bishopric of Seth Ward. In the Act Book of the Consistory Court it is recorded that Robert Horsey of Tidpit was presented for being the father of a bastard child in 1683, and in the same year Edward Moon of Martin for a clandestine marriage. On the other hand, in 1668 the churchwardens of Martin are found complaining that 'Mr. Jo. Balham our vicar has not provided us with a sufficient curat as wee fformerly have had for wee have not our prayers read in church according to the cannons', and again in 1674 that the vicarage houses are much out of repair 'in so much as they are almost like to fall'.[77] In the Middle Ages communion once a year at Easter was usual, and then, since the twelfth century, only in one kind. From the vestry accounts it transpires that throughout the eighteenth and early nineteenth centuries communion was celebrated only four times a year at the cost of 12s. 6d. for wine each time. Pentecostal oblations of Whitsun farthings were rendered to the mother church of Damerham as late at 1811.

There exists no complete list of churchwardens. Some few in the seventeenth and eighteenth centuries have left their names in the registers or, as in 1660, on the tenor bell.[78] Chiefly noteworthy in the nineteenth century is the length of tenure of office by individuals wardens. *Facile princeps* was Martin Sweetapple Friend, who was vicar's warden for forty-two years without a break from 1841 to 1883. Between 1850 and 1891 George Waters was in office for twenty-eight years, and Richard Williams was warden from 1805 to 1831, and John Hewitt from 1820 to 1840.

At the manor house in West Martin there once was a private chapel of which our sole knowledge is derived from a sentence of Aubrey: 'A little chapel at Merton in the Earl of Shaftesbury's house is paved with tiles whereon are annealed or enamelled the coat and quarterings of Horsey'.[79] It was probably built about 1550 by Sir John Horsey and may have been an apartment of the manor house.

A house belonging to Dorothy Harris at Martin was licensed for Presbyterian worship in 1672.[80] This may have been Harris's farm. A

[77] Churchwardens' Presentations in the Diocesan Registry, kindly furnished to me by Miss Whiteman.

[78] *v.* list at end of chapter, Appendix IV.

[79] Aubrey, *N.H. Wilts.*, p. 101.

[80] *Cal. S. P. Dom.* 1672, p. 679.

similar licence was granted to Mary Harris, probably her sister, at Damerham in the same year.

Even during the lifetime of George Fox (1624–91) the founder of the Society of Friends or Quakers, there were at Martin disciples of the movement. Its tenets were embraced wholeheartedly by the Blandford family, which seems to have been alone in its adherence to the cause. Agnes Blandford in 1664 and Katherine in 1671 were married according to the rites of the sect.[81] John Blandford and his wife Susannah were presented before their bishop for not attending church in 1668 and excommunicated for two years.[82] Bernard Blandford lent his house for their meetings in 1669. John Blandford was their instructor, and Joan Blandford was enrolled at a monthly meeting in 1678. Martin is just the sort of place in which Fox himself might have preached on one of his itineraries up and down the country. The Blandford family accounted for half the dissenters from the combined villages recorded in the census of Bishop Compton in 1676. Thomas Blandford, however, was a churchwarden at Martin in 1683.

The date inscribed upon the Methodist chapel is 1829. A bequest of £200 was made to it in 1900 by Malachi Martin, who, at one time, had been a prominent orthodox churchman.

In 1901 Bustard Farm was occupied by the Cistercian Fathers of our Lady of Paradise. These Trappist monks were farmers on a large scale, managing not only Bustard, but King's Farm as well. When they left the village after the First World War, their chapel was given by the late George Waters to the Catholic community at Bulford where it was re-erected as the garrison church.

Not a stone remains of the church at Tidpit. Neither its foundation nor its dedication is known, nor, with certainty, even the site upon which it stood. The earliest documentary evidence of it occurs in 1255, when Ralf de Baskerville, who held part of the knight's fee at Tidpit, devised the manor of Tidpit together with the advowson of the church in frankalmoin to the Abbot and Convent of Glastonbury.[83] It may be conjectured that the church had been founded by one of the Martin family[84]

[81] *Wilts N & Q,* II, p. 289.

[82] Churchwarden's Presentations.

[83] Dugdale, I, p. 33. The grant was made in the same year as the Bull of Pope Alexander IV licensing the appropriation of the churches of Damerham and Martin.

[84] Possibly by Robert Fitzmartin, who in the first half of the twelfth century founded the Abbey of St. Dogmael in Pembrokeshire.

upon whom the hide of land held by Serlo at the time of Domesday at Tidpit had descended. It was designated a church throughout the Middle Ages until the presentation of the last rector in 1525, when it was called a chapel.[85] Patronage throughout its existence was vested in the Abbot and Convent of Glastonbury.

John Holwaye, the last incumbent, signed the *Valor Ecclesiasticus,* and was still alive in 1548, when the chapel was sequestrated, as 'the free chapel of Tudpytt in the parish of Marton'.[86] But it had already been described as 'destructa' at the suppression of the abbey, destroyed, as Sir Richard Colt Hoare thought, though without citing his evidence, by fire.

The church was a rectory, but not a rich one. Its value for papal taxation in 1291 was £4.6.8, and it was assessed at the same figure in 1307, when John Stykelynch was admitted, the first rector whose name is known. At the time of its destruction it was valued at £4.8.0. The tithes, which in 1281 had been worth 8/-, in 1518 increased to 9/-. About 1341 the rector had the use of his house with a close adjoining, the tithe of hay, flax, hemp, honey, cheese, milk and other small tithes, oblations and mortuaries, worth together 40/-.[87] Although disused as a residence for the incumbent some 250 years previously, Tidpit parsonage paid an annual rate of 2/- as late as the first quarter of the 19th century. The poverty of the living induced several of the rectors to advance themselves by exchange to richer benefices, as, for instance, Cammell to Damerham, Gargrave to Edmondsham and Pykerell to Broadchalke. The exchange of benefices was a very common, and often a lucrative practice in the fourteenth century, in which these rectors held their livings. After the confiscation of the abbey's estate, the advowson was granted in 1549 to John Barwick and Robert Freke,[88] and afterwards to Richard Audley. In 1557 it was sold to John Webb, a citizen of Salisbury;[89] the glebe was thirty-four acres.

The traditional site of the church is west of the Allen stream and north of Tidpit pond in a field called Chapel Plot, a moist situation, unlike those usually chosen for church buildings. According to a newspaper account, written in the last century, when Chapel Plot was ploughed, there were exhumed an urn, since destroyed, and a dark brown brick supposed on account of its size to have been used as paving of the floor.[90]

[85] *Wilt. Inst., supra*, Chap. V. The word *Capella* supplants *Ecclesia.*

[86] *W.A.M.*

[87] *Inquisitio Nonarum*, also Hoare, *S. Wilts.*, p. 15.

[88] *V.C.H. Hants.*

[89] *I.P.M.* (ser. 2) CLIX, p. 74.

It is said to be preserved in the floor of a farmhouse dairy. This field, however, being a valuable water-meadow, is not likely to have come under the plough. According, however, to the tithe map of 1840, Chapel Plot is shown on some elevated ground to the right of the Cranborne road, south-west of the house now called the Gamekeeper's Cottage.[91] Adjoining it was another field, called on the same map Chapel Piece.[92] Both have for many years been arable land. This site more appropriately corresponds with the description given in Thynne's Survey of 1549 of 'the free chapel a quarter of a mile from Sudpett (Tidpit) in the parish of Martyn'.[93] It seems more probable that one of the fields was the site of the church, the other the graveyard.

APPENDIX I

PATRON	DATE	VICARS OF DAMERHAM
The Abbot and Convent of	c.1235	Robert of Sottingdean
Glastonbury	c.1252	Henry of Wyngham
	1270	John Burnell
	1282	Richard of Chisingbury
	1315	Stephen de la Haye
	1321	John Cutel
	1342	Walter de Molton
		John Irelond
	1361	Walter de Kynardsleigh
	1391	Hamon atte Soler
	1398	Gilbert Neele
	1399	Nicholas Partout
	1422	Robert Camel
	1446	Walter Copeland
	1453	John Tregonson
	1459	William Colyns
	1468	Morgan Vaghan
	1470	William Bladon
	1488	William Banyster
	1507	William Pickname
	1535	Peter Horsey

90 Neville Henderson's Scrap Book.
91 Tithe Map, 531.
92 *Ibid.*, 532.
93 *W.A.M.* 28, p. 17.

PATRON	DATE	VICARS OF DAMERHAM
William, 1st Earl of Pembroke	1554	Thomas Pope
	1570	George Kenweye
	1600	Thomas Wilson
	1603	John Humphrey
William Cecil, 2nd Earl of Salisbury	1622	Thomas Buckley
	1630	William Buckner
	1659	Thomas Balham
	1673	William Mayo
	1674	Thomas Derby
	1677	Samuel Godfer, B.A. (Curate)
	1678	John Hancock, B.A. (Curate)
John Holles, 1st Duke of Newcastle	1698	Henry Pinke
	1723	John Nourse
	1754	Samuel Ogden
	1766	Charles Mein Hayes
	1822	Thomas Longland
Thomas Pelham, 1st Earl of Chichester (1801)	1849	Richard Allnutt
The Hyndman Trustees	1862	W. Owen
	1916	G. H. Moule
	1922	H. W. Moule

APPENDIX II

CURATES OF MARTIN

DATE		DATE	
1606	William Maurice	1684	Silas Ayles
1615	James Jones	1686	Roger Saunders
1625	John Bishop	1687	Charles White
1639	Luke Parry	1689	Joseph Munday
1643	Edward Deare	1691	Richard Highmore
1665	Edward Watson	1716	Joseph Hosse
1669	T. M. Kingsman	1744	Thomas Staples
1676	Thomas Ellis	1754	Henry Bennett
1678	John Hancock, B.A.	1769	William Horsey
1680	Oliver Horsey	1773	Benjamin Pepper

CURATES OF MARTIN

DATE		DATE	
1782	— Rigby	1820	John Lawes
1792	M. Honwell	1830	Henry Taylor
1805	Anthony Davidson	1845	H. Knowles

VICARS OF MARTIN

1854	G. W. B. Daniell	1910	Price
1871	N. Honiss		Jones
1872	John Harding	1927	Hollius
1881	E. W. Michell	1931	Skillbeck Smith
		1944	E. Corke

APPENDIX III

DATE	RECTORS OF TIDPIT
c.1255	Robert, 'persona de Todeput'
1307	John of Stykelynch
1316	Thomas de Hoghton[1]
1393	John Taylor
	John Wylmington
	John Pykerell – rector of Broadchalke 1394
1401	John Nettleton
1411	William Plonte
1411	Robert Cammell, app. vicar of Damerham 1422
1422	John Sowy
1427	John Elmore
1433	John Hows
	Humphry Clark
1453	William Gargrave, app. rector of Edmondsham, Dorset, 1463
1467	Walter Wilde
1471	Robert Elle
1496	John Dale
1498	Thomas Saye
1510	Stephen Dowes
1511	William Wilton
1525	John Hollowaye, rector at the suppression of the Monasteries in 1535

[1] There is apparently a lacuna in the institutions at this point. It is improbable that Thomas de Hoghton was Rector for 78 years.

APPENDIX IV

DATE	CHURCHWARDENS	
1614	Charles Reade	and Matt. Stoop
1615	George Reade	and Matt. Stoop
1616	— Compton	and — Busher
1638	William Harris	and John Short
1640	Bernard Blandford	and Thomas Holloway
1657	Henry Prince	and John Grove
1662	Richard Compton	and Robert Harris
1668	William Yeadley	and John Thorpe
1674	John Thane	and Richard Compton
	Sidesmen: John Grove	and Henry Parker
1682	Thomas Grove	and Nicholas Street
1683	Thomas Blandford	and Richard Compton
1686	Simon Thane	and Henry Prince
1688	Thomas Blandford	and Henry Loxley
1690	W. M. Newman	and Edmund Gray
1696	John Bagus	and Henry Parker
1744	James Shrimpton	and Joseph Haiter
1805	Richard Williams	and John Williams
1807	Richard Williams	and John Sweetapple
1808	John Williams	and Richard Williams
1809	Richard Williams	and Luke Shrimpton
1811	Richard Williams	and Edmund Bound
1812	Richard Williams	and John Waters
1813	Richard Williams	and George Batt
1816	Richard Williams	and William Saunders
1819	Richard Williams	and Edmund Bound
1820	Richard Williams	and John Hewett
1832	John Hewett	and Edmund Bound
1837	John Hewett	and William Brooks
1838	John Hewett	and Edmund Bound
1841	Martin Sweetapple Friend	and Thomas Waters
1842	Martin S. Friend	and William Cull
1846	Martin S. Friend	and William Street
1850	Martin Friend	and George Waters
1868	Martin Friend	and William Street
1870	Martin Friend	and George Waters

DATE	CHURCHWARDENS	
1873	Martin Friend	and G. S. Tasker
1884	G. S. Tasker	and George Ford
1885	George Waters	and George Ford
1886	George Waters	and William Kendall
1888	George Waters	and Christopher Ryall
1896	W. Bennett	and — Thompson
1925	George Waters	and Lush
1938	George Waters	and J. Poore
1944	W. Dowse	and J. Poore
1952	J. Poore	and T. Hibberd

X

THE POPULATION, POOR LAW AND AGRARIAN RIOTS

THE late Heywood Sumner speculated upon the probability that the density of earthworks, barrows, ditches and ancient village sites suggested evidence of a population in the prehistoric era larger than that of today.[1] The magnitude of the earthworks presuppose an effort of a very large labour force; on the other hand, the total population of England at the time of Domesday is placed at no more than two and a half million souls.[2] It seems scarcely credible that the population of Martin could have exceeded its present-day figure of about 400.

In the accompanying table an attempt is made to estimate the population at Martin at different dates since Domesday.

1086	*Domesday Book*	180
1189	*Liber Henrici de Soliaco*	394
1225	Eileen Power, *Medieval Wool Trade*	475
1235	*Rentalia* of Michael of Amesbury	427
1518	*Terrarium Abbatis Richardi Beere*	370
1676	Bishop Compton's Census of Nonconformists	367

[1] Sumner, *Earthworks of Cranborne Chase*, 6.
[2] A. L. Poole, *Domesday Book to Magna Carta*, p. 36.

1801	First decennial census	394
1821	Decennial Census	528
1851	Decennial Census	599
1858	Report on Labouring Classes in Wilts	602
1861	Decennial Census	586
1881	Decennial Census	507
1901	Decennial Census	396
1921	Decennial Census	420
1941	Decennial Census	391
1951		

The influx of population which followed the Conquest is clearly illustrated in the surveys of the twelfth and thirteenth centuries by the frequency with which occur such names as William Novus, William Francus or Richard Francigena. The estimates at these dates are based upon a formula devised by Maitland,[3] whereby multiplication by five of the persons named is thought to produce the total population. Yet, even though this formula may tend to exaggerate rather than understate the total figure, the population seven hundred years ago was much the same as it is today and possibly even larger.

A decline followed the Black Death, when the mortality is believed to have been not less than one third, reducing the population at Martin to well below three hundred, but it has been estimated that this loss had been made good by the middle of the succeeding century.[4] The figures for the sixteenth and seventeenth centuries reflect the change from arable to sheep farming and show little fluctuation.[5] But a calculation based upon the ship money subsidy of 1642 suggest a figure of about 400.[6]

The first decennial census was taken in 1801, but that in the following decade reveals that there had been much evasion, due perhaps to a fear of being impressed by the recruiting officers, and a suspicion of the real purpose of the inquiry. After the cessation of the Napoleonic war the population rapidly increased, maintaining a steady rise in the era of peace

[3] Maitland, *Domesday Book and Beyond*, p. 437. His formula, however, is strictly applicable only to Domesday statistics.

[4] *Camb. Econ. Hist.*, 'Agrarian Life in the Middle Ages', p. 520.

[5] In 1676, the date of Bishop Compton's Census, the population of the combined villages is shown in the records of the Diocesan Registry as 503, giving a figure for Martin of 266 only, which is manifestly too low. The figures, however, includes adults only; computations for the inclusion of the juvenile population vary from 40 per cent to 60 per cent.

[6] *W.A.M.* 38, p. 589.

until it reached its culmination in 1858, which coincided with a prosperous decade for agriculture. In the first twenty years of the twentieth century it again declined, but since 1920 has been relatively stable.

Except during the period of the Tudors, when generations of Horseys occupied the manor house, there was never a resident squire at Martin. The Earls of Shaftesbury never, and their relatives or dowagers only seldom and intermittently, lived here. The absence of a squire conduced to the inhabitants becoming self-reliant and independent of charity and relief.

In the Middle Ages, while the church at Damerham was a rectory, relief of the sick and indigent was dispensed by the rector, and a quarter of the tithes was, in theory, allocated for this purpose.[7] The extent by which the sick and suffering benefited depended upon the residence and the benevolence of the rector. At Damerham he must have been often absent; and not all rectors were prepared to sacrifice their tithes for the relief of the sick. After the appropriation of the churches to Glastonbury in 1269, the obligation of the rector was transferred to the Abbey, and it is usually conceded that the populations of appropriated parishes lost in charity more than they gained. But no material has survived from which the condition of the poor may be judged until the last decade of the eighteenth century.[8]

The Poor Law was administered under a series of acts, of which that of 1597, empowering justices to appoint overseers and overseers to levy rates, was still the most important. Efficient and sympathetic administration, therefore, depended upon the choice of overseers, which itself was limited by the necessary qualification of literacy. At Martin this thankless task appears from the evidence to have been carried out with commendable discrimination.

The headquarters of Poor Law administration was the picturesque market town of Hindon, which at this date returned two members to Parliament. Each year the two retiring overseers harnessed a cart and drove the thirty odd miles there and back to give an account of their stewardship and to have their accounts audited by a justice. The justice's signature appended to the accounts during these years was that of the distinguished antiquary and county historian, Sir Richard Colt Hoare. After the Act of 1836 Martin was included in the Salisbury and Amesbury union, and in 1881 was transferred to the union of Fordingbridge.

[7] Moorman, *Church Life in England*, p. 138.

[8] Overseers Accounts for the years 1790–1804 and 1813–1819.

The poor house at Martin was probably that dilapidated structure at College, built on the edge of the parish pound. It had been built before 1790, and between then and 1800 several references to 'Collig housen' prove that the overseers were under an obligation to keep them in repair: 76 feet of elm boards in 1798, and rethatching at the cost of £5.15.9 in 1800. The name College for these and adjacent buildings cannot be explained in the usual way by the fact of their having been the property of a college of one or the other of the universities. But it is possible that the term college may have been used in some places to denote a Poor Law institution.

The poor-house accommodated, it would appear, half a dozen sick, aged and infirm chronic patients, whose maintenance cost the parish in 1790 about £3.15.0 a month, or 5d. each per day. By 1800 after the resolutions of Speenhamland had come into force, the cost had risen to some £5 a month. By the Speenhamland system each union was free to formulate its own scale of relief, and that agreed upon by the magistrates at Hindon was more complicated than most others. This relief allowed one and three-fifths gallon loaves per week to a man, and one and one-tenth gallon loaves per week to a woman,[9] a weekly ration of sixteen and eleven pounds each for the respective sexes. Winter fuel was provided, hauled from as far as Knighton Wood, or Cranborne Chase, at the cost of 10/- or 13/- a hundred faggots. The poor, too, were sufficiently supplied with clothing for themselves and their families. Numerous are the disbursements to some sempstress for making a shift, a shirt, 'a jacket and breeches for Bonapart' [*sic*], – there was also a Nelson in the village at this time – and the like.

Smallpox occurs repeatedly between 1790 and 1800. 'Paid B's family in small pox', 'the Doctor's bill in small pox', 'paid to A.I. for looking after F. in small pox', are typical of several entries. Rum and gin were prescribed by the half pint to those in need of it.

A century before this our local antiquary had written 'not above halfe teeming women are marryed'.[10] As might be suspected in a village so isolated as Martin, the accounts reveal a high rate of illegitimacy. An incentive to illegitimate unions was given by the Speenhamland system, which was applied to Martin soon after its adoption at Newbury in 1795. It put a premium on illegitimacy in that the maintenance of the illegitimate child was made an obligation of the parish instead of the putative

[9] J. L. Hammond, *The Village Labourer*, p. 160.
[10] Aubrey, *N.H. Wilts.*, p. 75.

father. The mother, whose children were supported by the parish, therefore, became a most eligible wife. At Martin the mother of a bastard child was paid a sovereign for her 'lying in' just as at the end of her days there was paid a half-crown for her 'laying out'. The infant received alimony of 2/- a month.

In a less generous spirit the parish defrayed the cost of burial, to the amount of six shillings. The items composing this total were: laying out, 2/-; a shroud, 2/-; cost of beer to the bearers, 2/-. A coffin augmented the bill by 1s. 6d., but the addition of a coffin was at this time unusual in pauper burials.

Unemployment was another problem delegated to the overseers. Like many other social evils, unemployment was accentuated by the so-called Speenhamland 'Act'. But in this village it was attributed by the inhabitants themselves to the 'newly-invented machines', which absorbed all the wool, thus depriving them of the raw material for domestic spinning.[11] The able-bodied were put to work 'by the Stym', i.e. on piece work, for 6d. a day, or half the labourer's normal wage. Such work would usually be on roads, drainage and so forth, except at haymaking and harvesting, when they were readily employed by the farmers at the parish rate and accounted for to the overseers.

The various laws of settlement, in order to stop vagrants and beggars moving from village to village, had put the onus of their maintenance upon the parish in which they were born. In 1684 the manorial court had imposed the heavy fine of £5 upon any person who should introduce one 'that is not an inhabitant and have no yearly estate therein'.[12] Now, about 1800, 'gave a man on the road one shilling' is a recurring entry; it was sufficient to move him on to the next parish, or back to the parish of his birth.

Recruiting for the militia was an urgent and vexatious duty, which sorely exercised the overseers. The method at this time was this: after a quota had been allotted to the county, that number was filled by ballot from among those capable of bearing arms. But it was open to anyone so drawn for service to find a substitute, for whom he and the parish each paid half. Thus, in 1790 W.F. accepted his bounty money, and apparently served his term with the colours. But in 1798 the Overseers paid £5 as their share of the payment towards a substitute, and again in 1800 they paid for the consumption of beer at the White Hart 'when the

[11] Hanvil, *A brief Statement of Facts*.
[12] Court Rolls, 1634.

farmers held a meeting concerning a man of Heytesbury that went a substitute for W.F.', to whom was paid in the following year £4.5.6. In 1797 they paid to the parish of Hindon £10.4.9 for raising two men for the militia instead of Martin.

A few miscellaneous disbursements may be mentioned. In 1790 the sum of £1.11.6 was contributed towards the apprenticeship of a deserving son of one of the regular paupers; in 1798 to 'two men for sitting up at the White Hart all night guarding persons for rioting on Sunday evening'; in 1803 8d. each to members of a Jury; in 1814 to a Mrs. Adams 'for a man W.P. found in the snow'; a subscription to Salisbury Infirmary, afterwards an annually recurrent item, begins in 1817; in 1818 the overseers were required to attend the church and examine the accounts for the past seventeen years; and in 1819 they supplied beer to the value of £2 to 'men who helped with the fire at H.'s house'.

The expense of administering the Poor Law increased progressively. While in the period covered by the seven years 1793–99, the average annual cost was £170.14.7 (highest £240, lowest £136), in the seven-year period 1813–19 it averaged £478.17.7 (highest £631, lowest £200). Consequently the rates, which were the only source of income, rose proportionately from an average of £142 in the earlier to an average of £396 for the later period.

In this there is nothing of inhumanity or apparent neglect. At Damerham, on the other hand, the conditions and treatment of the poor about 1795 were so revolting as to impel the curate of the parish to expose the conduct of the overseers in a pamphlet published in 1796.[13] From this evidence, based on unimpeachable contemporary testimony, the following account has been extracted.

After paying a tribute to the benevolent patroness in a neighbouring parish (presumably the wife of General Sir Eyre Coote, whose mansion at West Park had recently been built in the parish of Rockbourne), who did not disdain to visit the poor and the sick, he attributes the distress at Damerham to the degradation of the squirearchy, the monopoly of land from which ensued the monopoly of food, and to the absenteeism of the vicars. There was, indeed, some substance in his contention. The estate recently acquired by Sir Eyre Coote embraced a very large acreage, but the common lands, it must be remembered, were still unenclosed. The non-residence of the vicars in the sixteenth century was, unfortunately, notorious, and there is no doubt that the pastoral work of the parish

[13] Hanvil, *op. cit.*

fell almost entirely upon the shoulders of the curate. But these strictures could be made applicable to many parishes throughout England at this date, when the unfortunate Speenhamland decision had attempted to remedy the worst conditions of destitution in the history of the poor law.

The poor-house at Damerham was described by the local doctor as the worst in his experience of many parishes. January 1795 has been described as the coldest winter for fifty years.[14] In a room with two entrances the doors had been torn from their hinges and removed; the window casement was an aperture without glass, until someone, more humane than his fellows, hung in front an old mat. Beds, blankets and sheets were lacking and only the embers of an old fire supplied an illusion of warmth to this glacial apartment. Upon the floor lay the human skeleton of a woman, her bones projecting through her skin, the lice feasting on her flesh, in a state of such nudity that the parson was dissuaded, for reasons of pudicity, from visiting her. In another corner a woman in the throes of childbirth was unable from the coldness of the temperature to deliver her child.

In the room for destitute men, one suffering from dysentery lay for days in his own excrement, with a ragged rug for a covering and numerous children at his feet, howling execrations upon the overseer who refused to send for a doctor. The outspoken curate describes another woman, whose hair was so matted with lice as to defy the action of a pair of scissors and yielded only to the application of sheep-shears, and then it was found that the vermin had eaten a large hole in her skull. The money allowance for the sustenance of these wretched people was delivered by the overseer to a disreputable woman of the village, who appropriated the greater part to her own use, and deprived the unhappy patients of such relief as their poor pittance might purchase. Children ran naked in the streets with neither shoes nor stockings, begging.

Today it seems almost incredible that the village could have been the scene of such poverty and neglect, were it not for the eye-witness of this protesting parson. He served Martin as well as Damerham, and his omission to expose either the poor-house or the overseers at Martin suggests that conditions here were less oppressive.

The causes of the agrarian riots of 1830 have been analysed by writers of the social history of the time.[15] The recent enactments of the Poor Law, and in particular the Speenhamland system, which favoured the employ-

[14] The frost lasted without intermission from 24th Dec. 1794 to 24th February 1795.

ment of married rather than single labour and out-door relief rather than regular work are thought to account for the fact that most of the rioters where single able-bodied labourers. Unemployment is said to have been the motive for the destruction of machinery; low wages and semi-starvation the reason for the demand for money. The deprivation of rights of commonage, a consequence of the extensive enclosures, which preceded the riots, and the harangues of Cobbett, whose favourite field for oratory were the counties of Wiltshire and Hampshire, may have been contributory causes. The fact remains of all counties in England Wiltshire and Hampshire were the worst affected, and the tragedy lay as much in the fact that by a more conciliatory procedure the labourers could have obtained all they wanted, as in the transportation to Queensland and New South Wales of so many men from the two counties.

The agricultural wage in Wiltshire averaged only 7/- a week, but Cobbett, an enthusiast for statistics, calculated that in 1826 the bare cost of living for a man, his wife and three children amounted to 18/- a week.[16] The farmers were quite prepared to concede an extra shilling, which was all the labourers demanded. Moreover many of the threshing machines destroyed by the mob were deliberately set aside by the farmers for demolition. A gentleman named Williams, Member of Parliament for Marlborough, wrote 'the greatest number of the threshing machines destroyed have been put out for the purpose by the owners', and another from Market Lavington 'nearly all Wiltshire farmers are willing to destroy or set aside their machines.[17]

The particular prominence given in the local press and in modern accounts of the riots to the episodes at Pyt House, the seat of John Bennett, M.P. for Wiltshire, of whom it was said 'the poor are oppressed more than in any other parish in the kingdom', and at West Park, the residence of Eyre Coote, must not obscure the fact that the rioters were incensed in an equal degree against farmers all over the county, great and small.

The wave of incendiarism and destruction extended in Wiltshire from Cricklade in the north to Damerham in the south. Not the least surprising revelation of the riots is the ubiquity of the threshing machine, an invention of some sixty years previously, even in the smaller villages. Among local villages, machines were destroyed at Downton, Coombe Bissett,

[15] J. L. and B. Hammond, *The Village Labourer*, 1760–1832, gives an excellent account of the riots and their causes.

[16] Cobbett, *Rural Rides*, II, p. 191.

[17] Hammonds, *op. cit.*, p. 241.

Odstock, Homington, Broad Chalke, Ebbesbourne, Tollard Royal and Damerham. This last was owned by John Waters, who also had a farm at Tidpit. The warrant of committal reads: 'William Cheater of Damerham . . . with others riotously, tumultuously, and feloniously assembled and with menaces and force demanded of the said George Masters money, with intent to steal the same at Damerham, and at the same place feloniously and maliciously broke and destroyed a threshing machine, the property of John Waters. Warrant dated 10th December, 1830, on the oath of the said George Masters, and committed by Sir C. Hulse, Justice of the Peace.'[18] William Cheater, whose family at Damerham can be traced back 600 years, was condemned to death, but subsequently reprieved.

But it was from Fordingbridge that that apprehension radiated which induced farmers to put out their machines for demolition. Fordingbridge had not been unaccustomed to militant disturbance. In 1795 women, discontented with the high prices then prevailing, staged what was called the Housewives' Revolt[19] and, having appropriated the goods of the retailers, – butter is specially mentioned – sold them in the market place at what they considered a reasonable price – a precedent ignored in modern days under similar circumstances.

In 1830 the ringleader was one Cooper, the son of a labourer at East Grinstead, but at the time popularly supposed to have been the notorious Swing himself, who was credited with the inspiration and organisation of the whole movement. Swing's technique was to despatch a letter in advance under his signature demanding money, with an assurance that compliance with the demand would leave the recipient immune from interference.[20]

Cooper demolished machines at two factories at Fordingbridge and next reappears at West Park. The attack was made on 24th November, by which date most people had concluded that the riots had been suppressed. That evening Coote was twice visited by parties of rioters, and for the third time at 2 a.m. the following morning. This mob, consisting of some forty persons, some armed with iron bars, presented themselves before Coote's front door. Coote had taken up a position with his ten

[18] Calendar of Prisoners at Special Commission of Assize (*Wilts. Tracts.*, vol. 59) in the Library of the Wilts. Arch. Soc. at Devizes.

[19] Hammonds, *op. cit.*, p. 97. Sarah Rogers of Fordingbridge was sentenced to three months for this offence at Winchester Assizes.

[20] An example of Swing's threatening letters addressed to Mr. Castleman of Chettle may be seen in the Pitt-Rivers Museum at Farnham.

servants in the porch, and when they arrived, demanded their business. 'Money', they replied, and Coote refused. Whereupon one of them tried to strike Coote, but was captured. Nine others were knocked down and taken prisoner and the rest fled.[21]

Mr. Dowding, a governor of Fisherton Gaol, published a few more details in 1855. He adds that Coote was relieved by the Salisbury troop of Yeomanry under the command of Lord Arundel, and that Lieut. Peniston was left on guard to enable Coote and his party, exhausted after a contest that had lasted all night, to sleep. Ten of the assailants had been captured.[22]

A special Commission of Assize under Sir John Vaughan and Sir James Parke, Justices of the King's Bench, was sent to Winchester and Salisbury for the trial of prisoners. The Attorney-General in person led for the prosecution. A contemporary newspaper account states that six men were transported for life for the riot against Sir Eyre Coote.[23] At Winchester six men were sentenced to death, but four being reprieved, only Cooper and Eldridge, who had taken part in the riots at Fordingbridge as well as in the affray at West Park, were hanged. At Salisbury both the men sentenced to capital punishment were reprieved. On the other hand 95 at Winchester, and 154 at Salisbury, were sentenced to transportation (33 for life), in addition to those committed to imprisonment. An examination of the lists of the convict ships, sailing to Tasmania and New South Wales has disclosed that 151 convicts came from Wiltshire, 100 from Hampshire, and 206 from all other counties.[24]

As a result of the riots, Sir Eyre Coote raised wages to 9/- a week, increased to 12/- for the harvest, or 8/- for reaping an acre of corn. At Martin wages were 1/- less than at Damerham, and a favourite response to a greeting was said to be 'We hold on, and do not quite die'.[25]

The last of the great surveys before the advent of the Blue Book was made in 1836. This was the Tithe Award, accompanied by a tithe map, a monumental compilation, which has justly earned its description as the 'title deeds of the parish'. In its detail and information given it is comparable to the great terriers of the Middle Ages. In parallel columns are tabulated the owner, occupier, field name, acreage, its nature, whether

[21] Hammonds, *op. cit.*, p. 256,

[22] *Salisbury & Winchester Journal*, 12 September, 1930, contributed by Mary Eyre Matcham.

[23] *Ibid.*, 27 Dec. 1830.

[24] *Hammonds, op. cit.*, p. 284.

[25] *S. and W. Journal*, 2 December, 1844.

arable, meadow, pasture or woodland, and finally the rent charge due to the impropriator and the chaplain. There is also a supplementary award to Henry Brounker, who seems to have been overlooked in the first instance, in respect of his property at North Blagdon Farm (now Kite's Nest), and in Martin woods.

The history of the tithes at Martin may be briefly noticed. Up to 1269 the church at Damerham with the chapelry at Martin had been a rectory, and the rectors received the tithes. The effect of appropriation at that date was to transfer the greater or predial tithes, viz: a tenth of wheat, barley and oats, grown on the soil of the parish, to Glastonbury Abbey. It was, however, one of the stipulations of the appropriation that the lesser tithes, the tenth of the issue of stock, should be retained towards the subvention of the vicar's stipend. This disposal of tithes continued until the suppression of the abbey in 1536, when the greater tithes became vested in the crown, and at the prerogative of the sovereign were granted to lay rectors or impropriators. From now on the tithes of Damerham and Martin, which had, at any rate in part, been devoted to ecclesiastical, and at least to some extent, to the repair and embellishment of those churches, now came to be diverted to lay purposes, the only obligation imposed upon the lay impropriator being the duty to keep in repair the chancel of the parochial church.

After the suppression of the abbey, it seems probable that the tithes were paid to the Horseys at the manor house of West Martin, for, at the death of Sir John Cooper, who had bought the Horsey property, the tithes of Martin are disclosed as part of his estate.[26] They were received throughout the seventeenth, eighteenth and the greater part of the nineteenth century by successive Earls of Shaftesbury.

In 1291 the greater tithes of Damerham with Martin amounted to £4,[27] an exact tenth of the valuation of the two parishes about forty years earlier. In 1518 the tithes of West Martin were 16/-, of East Martin 8/-, and of Tidpit 4/-, and of the four tithings of Damerham 28/-. At the dissolution of the monasteries the tithes of Damerham were returned at £18 and those of Martin at £10.13.4.[28] At Toyd there was paid a modus of 6s. 8d. a year, that is a commutation of tithe, fixed at an early date by agreement between the farmer and the tithe owner,[29] and was not altered by the Act of 1836.

[26] Collins, *Peerage*, III, p. 393.
[27] *Taxatio Ecclesiastica*, p. 181.
[28] *Valor Eccles.*

The Act for the Commutation of Tithes in 1836 affected the incidence, not the payment of tithes. From this date the liability for tithe became a corn rent charge, payable in cash instead of in kind. The rent charge was calculated at the average price of wheat, barley and oats over the preceding seven years, and was so correlated with the purchasing power of money that it fluctuated with the price of corn. At Martin, when the Act became operative, these prices were for wheat 7s. 0¼d., for barley 3s. 11½d., and for oats 2s. 9d. per bushel. On this assessment the Earl of Shaftesbury received an annual cash payment of £550, the Chaplain £145 in lieu of his lesser tithes, and Henry Brounker of Boveridge £10.11.0. The total tithes were valued at £705.11.0.

The tithe barns, the office of tithingmen and many quaint customs, derived from the Middle Ages, disappeared with the passing of the act. The medieval tithe barn of Glastonbury Abbey had stood in what was then called Grange Field, and in more modern times Vicarage Lawn, between Bustard Farm and Angel lane, from which it was approached. The site remained an extra-parochial island until recent years.

When the Earls of Shaftesbury became the impropriators, a tithe barn was built next their stables, across the road from the manor house, upon a site known as Parsonage Ground.

Tithingmen were annually appointed by the court leet, sitting at The Compasses, Damerham, or the White Hart, Martin, for each of the three tithings of Martin, and for the four tithings of Damerham. In theory, no cereal crop could be carried until the tithingman had taken the tithe for the rector, but in practice his presence was often dispensed with. To facilitate the business, every stock or hyle (as it is here called) had to be made of ten sheaves, four on each side and one at each end. The tithingman had the option of taking either every tenth hyle, or one sheaf out of each hyle, with this proviso that every sheaf must be taken from the same position; for instance, if from the first hyle the tithingman selects, say, the second sheaf on the left, he must take the second on the left from every hyle in the field. The purpose was to prevent him from choosing the largest and fattest sheaf from the hyle. After the passing of the act, the duties of the tithingman were purely perfunctory.

---

[29] Brocklehurst, *Tithes*, gives Lord Coke's definition as follows: 'a *modus decimandi*, is when an annual certain sum or other profit, always time out of mind, has been given to the Parson and his successors in full satisfaction and discharge of all tithes in kind in such a place; and such manner of tithing is a good bar of tithes in kind.'

The Tithe Award furnishes the following figures of the parish of Martin, inclusive of Tidpit, but exclusive of Toyd and Allenford.

	Tithe Awards
Arable	3,059¼ acres
Meadow & Pasture	371½ acres
Downland	909¾ acres
Woodlands	553¾ acres
Houses, roads, waste	6½ acres
Total area	4,900¾ acres

XI

SHEEP FARMING

With a preface on the Wiltshire Horn

WILTSHIRE has long been preeminent for its flocks of sheep. Eighteenth-century writers waxed ecstatic about the incredible numbers they saw grazing on Salisbury Plain. Yet, in the earliest times of which we have record, other animals than sheep predominated. The excavations of General Pitt-Rivers at sites surrounded by downland sheepwalks have revealed that skeletons and bones of oxen and often also of horses were in excess of those of sheep.[1] From measurements recorded by him the animal some two thousand years ago stood at the shoulder not more than two inches shorter than a modern Hampshire Down sheep.[2] They cannot, therefore, have been insignificant animals.

Sheep in the Middle Ages were classified in two types, those carrying a long wool represented by the Lincoln and Cotswold breeds and those with a short staple derived from the mountain sheep of Wales and located in England chiefly in Shropshire and Herefordshire. It is from the Welsh mountain sheep that the Wiltshire-bred flocks with a medium staple are thought to have originated. By the Middle Ages, although no description of them has survived, a distinctive Wiltshire breed had been evolved. A

[1] Pitt-Rivers, *Excavations in Cranborne Chase*, IV, p. 16.
[2] *Ibid.*, p. 233.

civil servant, named Davis, making a report on agriculture in Wiltshire to the Government in 1794, describes the Wiltshire sheep as the tallest in the country, and attributes its large size to judicious breeding from a smaller animal.[3] Their distinctive characteristic, apart from their great height, was a horned poll, with horns set close together and falling back to form a semicircle, similar to the Dorset horned sheep of today, with which in the days before flock books they were often classified. They were uniformly white, with naked bellies, carrying a fleece of fine and good quality wool. At the beginning of the eighteenth century the wool provided employment as a domestic industry to all the local villages, and was manufactured into 'fine flannels and long cloths, for the Turkey trade, called Salisbury Whites'.[4] At the end of that century we are told the wool was much in demand for 'super-broadcloth', which sold at 10/- to 12s. 6d. a yard.[5] But an average fleece weighed only about two and a half pounds.

A select Parliamentary Commission had found that in 1710 the average carcase weight of this large beast was no more than 28 lb.[6] The improvement during the century is shown by the fact that it is on record that a Wiltshire Horn lamb was sold on Easter Monday of the year 1800 at Smithfield market turning the scales at 96 lb. The exceptional weight was attributed to the maturing lambs being put out to graze on the water meadows in spring at the time when the grasses were richest and most succulent.

Their capacity for travelling long distances made them especially suited to downland grazing, but they were greedy feeders and when they were later replaced by Southdowns, it was estimated that 300 Southdowns could be put to grazing which was sufficient for only 200 Wiltshire Horn.[7] They were folded every night of the year on arable,[8] a practice which persisted since the thirteenth century, when writers on agriculture advised farmers to lay down straw or marl in the folds to enrich the manure.[9] That versatile author of *Robinson Crusoe*, Daniel Defoe observed in 1724 that this practice had so improved land that was otherwise impover-

[3] Davis, *A General View of Agriculture in Wilts.* (1794), p. 18; *v.* also Marshall, *Rural Economy of the Southern Counties.*

[4] Defoe, *A tour through England and Wales* (1724) I, p. 189.

[5] Marshall, *op. cit.* III, p. 345.

[6] Prothero, *op. cit.*, p. 188.

[7] Davis, *op. cit.*, p. 143.

[8] Arthur Young, *A six weeks tour through the Southern Counties* (1769), p. 190.

[9] Walter of Henley, 19, p. 143.

ished and hitherto regarded as not worth ploughing, that it was rapidly being converted to arable. As a consequence of the curtailment of the pastures even in his day the number of sheep on Salisbury Plain was diminishing.[10] So valuable was this method of manuring the ground that, he tells us, a farmer would rent a thousand sheep at 10/- a night to fold on his land.[11] The Wiltshire sheep were hurdle sheep, and their principal purpose was not wool, but dung. A writer on agriculture in the eighteenth century enumerated the uses of the Wiltshire Horn and places them in the following order: first their dung, second their wool and third their carcase. 'So long as South Wiltshire remains a corn country', he wrote, 'the sheep fold must be the sheet anchor of husbandry.'

Medieval sources show that even then the flocks of Wiltshire sheep were by no means negligible. About the time of Magna Carta the Bishop of Winchester kept a flock of 1,764 at Downton,[12] and in another Wiltshire village the tenants of the Abbot of Glastonbury possessed between four and five thousand.[13] Sheep increased rapidly under the Tudors. No one could travel across Salisbury Plain without being amazed at the spectacle of sheep grazing there. John Aubrey, writing towards the end of the seventeenth century estimated that the number of sheep to each tithing was between one and two thousand,[14] and he was probably not far wrong. In 1724 Defoe wrote "Tis ordinary for these flocks to contain from three to five thousand in a flock' and noted that they were then decreasing.[15] Arthur Young, later to become a secretary to the Board of Agriculture, met in 1769 flocks of 3,000, the largest within his experience. Some fifty years later on his Rural Rides to his favourite Uphusband, as he called Hurstbourne Tarrant, Cobbett encountered a single flock of 4,000.[16] Davis in 1794 estimated a summer stock of half a million sheep in south Wiltshire alone, and remarked that fifty years previously there had been 'many thousands more'. Another writer described them by such epithets as 'myriads'. Defoe believed that a figure of 500,000 sheep sold at Weyhill, 'the greatest sheep fair the nation could shew', to be a slight exaggeration, but agreed that the number was 'prodigious'.[17] A century

[10] Defoe, *op. cit.*, I, p. 285.
[11] *Ibid.*, p. 286.
[12] *Pipe Roll of the Bishop of Winchester* (1208), p. 22.
[13] Eileen Power, *Medieval Wool Trade*, p. 30.
[14] Aubrey, *N.H. Wilts.*, p. 108.
[15] Defoe, *op. cit.*, p. 283.
[16] Cobbett, *Rural Rides*, II, p. 62.
[17] Defoe, *op. cit.*, p. 233.

later Cobbett recalled having seen 200,000 sold at a single sale,[18] and as late as 1860 110,000 were put up for auction at a single Wilton Sheep Fair.[19]

It was to remedy the defects of the Wiltshire breed that Southdowns were introduced into Wiltshire. The multiplying population of England demanded mutton for its food; the rapid conversion of the open arable fields into enclosures enabled the farmer to improve his livestock; and the introduction during this period of clover and turnips went a long way towards solving the problem of winter fodder. The experiments of Robert Bakewell with his Leicester sheep were soon emulated by John Ellman with his Southdowns. It was noted by a writer in 1798 that 'the long established breed of Wiltshire are routed in every quarter and may soon be extinct'.[20] About half a century later this prophetic utterance was fulfilled. In the museum at Devizes may be seen an exhibit of a pair of horns of the old Wiltshire breed. They belonged to a sheep bred by John Nalder of Berwick Bassett in North Wiltshire and were presented by him in 1853.[21]

But though they disappeared from Wiltshire they became popular with Midland and Welsh farmers, and today the Wiltshire Horn, rechristened the Wiltshire Horn or Western, is especially common in Wales and Anglesey,[22] where it is kept for its early-maturing fat lamb.

It is recorded that Southdowns were first introduced by a farmer named Mighell of West Kennett on the Marlborough Downs in 1789,[23] and in the following decades either displaced or were crossed with the Wiltshire Horn flocks. The change was remarkably rapid. By 1813 the Wiltshire Agricultural Show advertised a special class for Southdowns,[24] and in 1828 Cobbett could write 'Southdowns are the great stock of these counties' (Wilts and Hants).[25] In 1844 it was authoritatively reported in the *Journal of the Royal Agricultural Society* that Southdowns were nearly the universal breed in Wiltshire.[26] The Southdown fleece of fine, soft curly wool sold for almost twice as much as that of the old Wiltshire

[18] Cobbett, *op. cit.*, II, p. 193.
[19] *The Field*, Jan. 12th, 1946.
[20] *Marshall, op. cit.*, III, p. 345.
[21] *W.A.M.* 38, p. 107.
[22] *Flock Book of Wiltshire for Western Horn Sheep*, Vol. II.
[23] Davis, *op. cit.*, p. 147.
[24] *W.A.M.* 43, p. 483.
[25] Cobbett, *op. cit.*, II, p. 48.
[26] *Journal of R. Agr. Soc.*, 1844.

animal, and its carcase fetched a penny a pound more in the market. The Southdown thus supplied the chief deficiencies in the old Wiltshire Horn. But its era in Wiltshire was not long. Before many decades had passed farmers had begun to deplore the disappearance of their large native sheep and the substitution of a much smaller animal. They perceived before it was too late that by judicious crossing they might retain the large frame, the early maturity and hardihood of the Wiltshire breed without losing the finer fleece and marketing qualities of the Southdown. The last breeding flock of pure Southdowns in Wiltshire is said to have been kept by William Sainsbury of West Lavington, on whose death it was dispersed.[27]

By crossing the old Wiltshire Horn and the Berkshire Knot with Southdown ewes (in north Wiltshire with Cotswold Ewes) the Hampshire Down sheep was evolved.[28] By 1857 the Hampshire Down had become a distinctive breed, and by 1890 a registered flock book was started.

Not since the pestilential epidemic of scab in the past (and Wiltshire suffered less than many counties) have the flocks of sheep been so decimated as by the last war. The sheep walks of Salisbury Plain have been reclaimed to arable; Wiltshire has long ago lost her native breed. But we should not be ungrateful to that long and lanky animal which brought the county to agricultural prosperity in past centuries.[29]

The first documentary reference to sheep at Damerham occurs in 1189, when, according to the Glastonbury survey of that year, there was a flock of 617 breeding ewes, 'but' the writer continues 'there should be a thousand, and at Martin 500 ewes.'[30] This flock belonged to the abbey and the latter would have been pastured on what was later known as Bustard Down, which was at Martin the only demesne pasture. Already, at the end of the twelfth century the Glastonbury Officials were aware that these Wiltshire pastures were much understocked. But little improvement was made in the following generation. In the next document,[31]

[27] *W.A.M.* 154, p. 338.

[28] *Hampshire Down Flock Book,* Vol. I. *Standard Encyclopaedia of Modern Agriculture,* VI, p. 215. The Dorset Horned Sheep are said to have been the result of the opposite, viz. a cross between the Wiltshire ewe and the Southdown ram.

[29] The fleece of a Wiltshire Horn ewe weighed no more than 2½ lb. at the end of the eighteenth century, that of a Southdown ewe only 3 lb. in the middle of the nineteenth century, but by the end of that century the fleece of a Hampshire Down ewe averaged between 6 and 12 lb.

[30] Inq. 1189, p. 133.

[31] E. Power, *op. cit.,* p. 30 from p. 195 in P.R.O. ref. E17/242/47.

which is dated 1225, it is learnt that whereas 198 villagers possessed flocks totalling 3,760 sheep, the abbey's flock numbered only 570, a surprisingly small flock in the century when demesne farming reached the culmination of its prosperity. While consistent with the enumeration made in the previous century, it shows that none of the recommendations for increasing the flock were carried out and reveals the depth of stagnation to which the abbey had been reduced by the disturbances inflicted by Savaric and the want of a conventually elected abbot. At about this time in the neighbouring parish of Downton, the Bishop of Winchester's flock numbered 1,764,[32] 1,497 fleeces were sold in the year and sheep from Lincolnshire were imported to improve the breed. The paucity of the abbot's flock at Damerham and Martin was not typical of monastic herds elsewhere.

Of the tenants' sheep perhaps 2,600 belonged to Martin, and the balance at Damerham. A few years later we read a good deal about the shepherds and the sheep folds. Among the privileges of the shepherd at Martin was 'an acre of corn and another of oats, one lamb, one fleece, one cheese, the right to graze 50 ewes and one wether in the lord's pasture and one old sheep at drafting time' as his perquisite.[33] The shepherd at Toyd enjoyed the same benefits, with the addition of a seed-box of wheat and another of oats.[34] Wool and cheese, which was made of sheep's milk, were now being exported to Winchester and Southampton.[35] About this time, also, a freeholder at Martin made a grant to the abbey of four acres 'in the field called Tohyde [Toyd], where the lord's wethers are folded in stormy seasons'.[36] By 1252, under the enterprising policy of Abbot Michael, the Abbey owned 6,717 sheep[37] distributed over all its manors.

Recent research has modified the opinion formerly accepted that after the Black Death, owing to the scarcity of agricultural labour and the high wages demanded, an impetus was given to sheep farming. It is now held that sheep farming not only did not expand, but may even have declined.[38] But the survey of 1518 shews that it revived rapidly under the first two Tudor kings. At Damerham the abbey kept 200 ewes and 240 shearlings; at Toyd, where we now read of a grange for the ewes, a

[32] Pipe Roll of B. of Winchester (1208), p. 22.

[33] *Rentalia*, p. 113.

[34] *Ibid.*

[35] *Ibid.*, p. 108.

[36] Hoare, *H.S.D.*, p. 27.

[37] Adam, p. 522, John of G., p. 223.

[38] E. Power, *op. cit.*, p. 38; Payne, in *Bull. of Inst. of Hist. Research*, No. 54, p. 116: 'Agrarian conditions on Wiltshire estates in thirteenth century.

paddock two perches in extent, there were 500; at Allenford, 600, where there was an enclosure called Lordescroft, in which the farmers of Toyd and Allenford might fold their flocks at lambing time; Boulsbury, from having been chiefly a forester's lodge, had developed into an extensive ranch, supporting on Blackheath down no less that 1,000 ewes and shearlings;[39] while at East Martin Bustard Down supplied grazing for 500 sheep 'at a cost to the lord of nothing but tar and paint and sufficient straw in winter and a smock for the shepherd or 3s. 4d. in lieu thereof'.[40] The firmarius, indeed, was reprimanded for not keeping the full flock of 500 as required by the terms of his copyhold.[41] The flocks kept by the abbey within the hundred numbered at the end of the Middle Ages 2,800.

The organisation for the disposal of fleeces had reached in the Middle Ages an extremely high standard. On the adjoining manor of Downton, belonging to the Bishop of Winchester, excellent arrangements were made for the marketing of fleeces, their sale to the merchant staplers and final export to the Continent. According to Aubrey, during the fifteenth and sixteenth centuries Sir William Webb of Odstock held almost a monopoly of this business on Salisbury Plain,[42] fulfilling the same function in Wiltshire as the better known Greville family in Gloucestershire. After the decline of the guilds and the merchant staplers, sheep were driven to and disposed of at the local fairs, of which the most important were Weyhill, Wilton and Britford.

Yet, since the abbey relied largely upon the fallow for supplementing its down pasture,[43] the grazing was not overstocked. At this date (1518) the available downland supported at East Martin 2.3 sheep to the acre, at Boulsbury 2.2, at Allenford 1.8 and at Toyd 3.4, an average of about 2¾ sheep to the acre. After the suppression of the abbey, when Toyd became the property of Lord Pembroke, this rate increased to exactly three sheep to the acre of pasture. The survey in 1569 records: 'At Toyd and Allenford there are 240 acres of pasture, upon which may be grazed 720; the value of the pasture, is 1/- and the value of a sheep 4d.'[44] Clearly

[39] *Beere*, p. 42.

[40] *Ibid.*

[41] *Ibid.*, p. 64.

[42] Aubrey, *N.H. Wilts.*, p. 113.

[43] *Beere*, p. 41. Of Toyd, 'unde coluntur 50 acre et residue pro pastura domini cum La Downe'; *Ibid.*, p. 41, of Boulsbury . . . 'coluntur C acre et residua ad pasturam bidentum'. Cf. also *Pemb. S.*, p. 312, 'auxilio terre arabilis post tonsuram.'

[44] *Pemb. S.*, p. 312. It has been pointed out to me that this formula dated from the twelfth century when 4d. was the market price for a sheep; *v.* A. L. Poole in *E.H.R.*, April 1940.

the equation of three sheep to the acre was an economic formula, generally accepted as correct in the business of sheep farming at this time.

Although there are no statistics of the number of sheep kept by the customary tenants, it may be assumed not to have exceeded the rate of three sheep to the acre of pasture. The pasture available was:

At West Martin	Martin Down	767 acres	
East Martin	Bustard Down	420 acres	
Tidpit	Tidpit Common	165	237 acres
	Whitcombe	72	
		1,424	

But Bustard Down was shared by the flocks of the abbey; and Whitcombe Down by the flocks from Damerham, and in practice there were never more than 500 sheep at East Martin, nor more than 700 at Tidpit. Applying to West Martin the formula quoted above, there was grazing available for a maximum total of 2,300 sheep. Evidence from other sources, however, suggests a rather lower figure. The medieval fields of the old open field cultivation carried sheep rights on the down at the rate of almost exactly 1½ sheep to the acre, and by this reckoning the number would be 1,858. Again, as will be seen later, if the number of sheep requisite for manuring the arable was fifty to each virgate, as is postulated hereafter, then the figure is 1,819 – a sufficiently close approximation. If these figures are at all correct, it appears that the tenantry were more provident of their herbiage than their monastic landlord.

Aubrey, who delighted in sheep, writing in the late seventeenth century, shrewdly estimated to every tithing between 1,000 and 2,000 sheep.[45] His maximum would not be an exaggeration for West Martin with its expansive pasture. By 1846 the stint on Martin Down was 2,516[46] and by 1920 had risen to 2,957.[47] These numbers, it is true, represent sheep rights rather than sheep, but that sheep rights were exercised to the full is evidenced by the number of persons fined for exceeding their stint.

At the close of the Middle Ages, the number of sheep kept in the parish of Martin and the extra-parochial district of Toyd and Allenford may be tabulated as follows:

[45] Aubrey, *N.H. Wilts.*, p. 108.
[46] Tithe Awards.
[47] Coote sale catalogue, 1920.

	West Martin	East Martin	Tidpit	Toyd	Allenford	Total
Glastonbury Abbey	—	500	—	500	600	1,600
Tenantry	2,000	500	700	—	—	3,200
	2,000	1,000	700	500	600	4,500

The stint, or the number of sheep permitted to each tenant to graze on Martin Down, was determined by sheep rights. Sheep rights had their origin in the number of sheep requisite by their manure to maintain arable land in a proper state of cultivation. They are included in the word *pertinencia* (appertenance),[48] which occurs constantly in customaries and conveyances of the Middle Ages. As has already been said, the manure of sheep was an essential to the sheep and arable husbandry, traditional on Wiltshire chalk soils. It was, therefore, a natural consequence that sheep should be attached or apportioned to land in a definite proportion to the size of the arable holding. A document dated 1243, relating to Christian Malford, another Glastonbury manor in the Hundred of North Damerham in Wiltshire, clearly sets out this allocation. It is entitled *De admensuratione pasturae*, and was extracted by Aubrey from what he called 'the Legier Book of Glastonbury'.[49] The case in issue was where three persons had overstocked the common pasture,[50] and a sworn jury pronounced that for every virgate of arable there belonged, for its proper cultivation and sustenance, four oxen (for the plough team), two cows, one draught horse, three pigs and twelve sheep. In another case, where the parson was charged with overstocking the pasture the number of animals is laid down on a higher scale in respect of a hide of land (160 acres) for the abbot and the incumbent.

It will be noticed that the jury does not say that a virgate will support that number of animals, but that those animals are required to keep the virgate in good heart and in good cultivation:[51] the oxen for the plough team, the horse for harrowing and carting and sheep for treading the soil, when folded and hurdled.

A uniform rule for obvious reasons could not be made applicable to all manors, and we should be cautious of transposing it from the North to the South Hundred of Damerham without modifications. For instance,

48 Vinogradoff, *Villeinage*, p. 263.

49 Aubrey, *Top. Coll.*, p. 423 gives the full text; *v.* Vinogradoff, *op. cit.*, p. 262 for a commentary.

50 'superoneravit communam pastruae'.

51 'ad tantum excolendam et sustinendam'.

the virgate varied in size from manor to manor, even under the same lordship, and there is evidence to show that at Christian Malford it was unusually small.[52] But the inference to be drawn here is that this or a similar custom, in written or unwritten form, must have been operative on all manors for the regulation of stock and for the prevention of overstocking the pasture. The expressions 'according to the rate for six virgates' (1518),[53] and 'according to the ancient rate' (1609)[54] are evidences of a similar formula in use at Martin.

The conclusion has been arrived at elsewhere that at Martin the unit of arable was a virgate containing thirty-three to thirty-four statutory acres.[55] The sheep rights attached to the original open field cultivation are almost exactly one and a half to the acre. The deduction, therefore, is that the number of sheep requisite to keep land in a proper state of cultivation was fifty sheep to the virgate.[56] Here, then, is the origin of sheep rights on Martin Down. The allowance of sheep which a tenant might keep was conditioned not by the pasture available, but by the extent of his arable land.

In the sixteenth and seventeenth centuries there was, as has been said, a great expansion of sheep-farming. Field names with the sheep prefix chiefly belong to this date. Although sheepdown and sheepland belong to the Middle Ages, sheepfurlong, sheephill, sheepcroft and sheepsleight[57] first occur about this time, indicative of enclosure of adjoining downland. The earliest to be reclaimed, as might be expected, were those fields adjacent to the old open fields, and were named after the individuals who reclaimed them, e.g. Hawkins' Down, and many others.[58] Next came the old cow down and last the Blackheath grounds near Kite's Nest Farm.

The enclosure of the commons had an important bearing upon sheep rights. First the common land was curtailed by the extent of the enclosure. West Martin was not affected because the new enclosures were excised from the Cow Down or from waste.[59] But at East Martin the commonage on Bustard Down was extinguished and with it the immemorial right

[52] A. L. Poole, *Domesday Book to Magna Carta*, p. 48.

[53] *Beere*, p. 56.

[54] Court Rolls, *sub anno*.

[55] *Infra*, Ch. XII.

[56] Davies, *The Early Stuarts*, p. 276 quotes Leonard in *Trans. R. Hist. Soc.* (new series), xix., pp. 104–106 for 50 sheep to the virgate at Daventry.

[57] *I.P.M.* 18 Chas. I, (1642), p. 326. The earliest date for this name given in *P.N.W.*, p. 454, is 1702.

[58] *Supra*, Ch. VIII.

[59] Rotherdown, now the Lodge Down fields, Nos. 308–321 in Tithe Map.

of the villagers to pasture 500 sheep there. At Tidpit, too, the common was reduced by about a quarter of its area.

Moreover, the augmentation of arable affected sheep rights in another way. The new fields were not only endowed with sheep rights, but in a higher proportion than formerly. Freshly opened land, of course, needed the dung of sheep, but this in itself seems hardly sufficient to explain the increased number of sheep attached to the arable acre. It is probable that a generous endowment of sheep rights was held out as an inducement to those who undertook the clearance of waste or assart.

The progressive increase in the number of sheep rights attached to the arable acre may be summarised as follows:

Enclosure	Arable Acreage	Sheep rights	per arable acre
Medieval Open Fields	1,800	2,700	1.5
17th cent. reclamation	123	197	1.6
Lodge Downs	134	262	2.0
Burnbake (Tidpit)	45	85	1.9
Blackheath	84	176	2.1

The number of rights at the present date is 2,957, made up from:

Coote estate sold in 1920	2,382
Coote estate sold in 1941	135
The Manor House (Street's)	380
Glebe (Vicar of Damerham)	60
	2,957

So long as sheep-farming offered lucrative prospects, there must always have been present a strong temptation to exceed the permissible stint. *Numeratores ovium* – later called sheep-tellers – are mentioned in the Court Rolls of 1609, whose duty it was to count the flocks four times a year. A fine, which rose from 6d. per sheep in this year to 1/- at the end of the century and 5/- by 1900, was imposed on those who depastured sheep in excess of their allocation. Two such officials were appointed from West Martin and two from Tidpit, to enforce the orders of the court leet. So jealous of their succulent turf were the graziers that animals straying on to the down from other parishes were promptly impounded by the Hayward. Some amusing instances may be found in the Court Rolls.

A wether (*vervio*) from Coombe Bisset, a bull calf (*bovulus*) from Alderholt (1609); a bullock from Boveridge and a ewe from Rockbourne (1611); many remained in the pound, unclaimed, e.g. a gray mare (*equila coloris graya*), a heifer (*vacula*) in 1609, a black horse and a ewe with lamb in 1610, a bullock, two heifers and a bay pony, 'having a halfpenny branded below his near ear' in 1612. In 1685 Lord Pembroke's keeper was presented for 'suffering deer to come into our liberty to eat upon our land and grasses . . . to our great damage and detriment'.[60]

Watering of sheep must have presented a problem. There had existed a well on the down before 1778, when it was dangerous and in need of repair, but there may also have been dew-ponds at the northern and southern extremities. The practice of dipping sheep in Bustard Pond was prohibited in 1754.

A regulation made in 1684 forbade rams to run with the flocks on Martin Down, until Woodbury Hill fair,[61] and every grazier depasturing twenty ewes was obliged to run one ram with them. Sheep folds were removed 'from wheat and fresh-eared land' on St. Luke's Day (old style),[62] which was also the prescribed date for the 'flocks going together'.

[60] Court Rolls, *sub annis*.

[61] I am indebted to Major Woolley for the identification of this fair with Woodbury Hill, near Bere Regis. It was held annually on 21st September, until 1921, when it was discontinued.

[62] October 6th in the Old Style or Julian calendar, October 18th in the Gregorian calendar.

XII
THE FIELD SYSTEM

THE pattern of the Open Field system in the Middle Ages has been described by the thirteenth-century authority, Walter of Henley in a familiar passage. 'If,' he wrote, 'your lands are divided in three, one part for winter seed, the other part for spring seed, and the third part fallow, then is a ploughland nine score acres. And if your lands be divided in two, as in many places, the one half sown with winter and spring seed, the other half fallow, then shall your ploughland be eight score acres.'[1] That this was the usual and recognised agricultural plan is proved by another thirteenth-century writer on husbandry. 'Each plough ought by right to plough nine score acres, that is to say, sixty for spring seed, and sixty for winter seed and sixty for fallow'.[2]

Our knowledge of open field agriculture at Martin is derived from the *Terrier* of Abbot Beere, dated 1518 – at the close, therefore, of the Middle Ages. The survival of the medieval ploughland of 180 acres, indicating a three-field system, appears from several pieces of evidence. The total land under cultivation at West Martin was 986 acres or 5½ ploughlands (180 × 5½). The east field at East Martin was 360 acres (180 × 2). The division of the land to the west of the village illustrates this yet more

[1] Walter of Henley, p. 7.
[2] *Ibid*. p. 85, by the author of *Seneschancie*.

remarkably. Here the land is intersected by four droves, roughly parallel with each other, leading from the main street to the downs. In order from north to south they are Middleend Lane, Townsend Lane, Sillens Lane and Smallend Lane.[3] These droves divide the land into four divisions:

1. Between Middlend lane and Townsend lane	192 acres
2. Between Townsend lane and Sillens lane	193 acres
3. Betwen Sillens lane and Smallend lane	170 acres
4. Between Smallend lane and the Tidpit boundary	89 acres

The first three average 181 acres, the last is half the size of the others and therefore called, as far back as 1235, a Smalelon, smalelande, i.e. a small ploughland.[4] In addition to their primary purpose as sheep droves, they also served the ancillary purpose of accommodation lanes to the arable furlongs. It is suggested that the droves were deliberately sited and cut to demarcate the areas into ploughlands.

Within the ploughlands were the furlongs (furrowlongs) elsewhere often called selions or shots.[5] In theory, the furlong measured forty poles by forty poles and contained ten acres.[6] Ten, however, was no more common than any other denomination of acres with one exception. The Dole fields in East Martin, the strips in which were allocated annually by lot, were ten acres exactly. Fields called 'Ten Acres' were not unusual by the time of the Tithe Awards, but seldom contained ten acres. In Martin the furlongs varied from half an acre to seventy acres, the former usually being land newly reclaimed from assart, and situated on the perimeter of the open field. Dr. Orwin found at Laxton furlongs from two to twenty-five acres.[7] But his explanation that the size of the furlong was conditioned by the configuration of the terrain does not altogether account for the variations at Martin, where there is nothing to prevent several furlongs of fifty acres and more. The majority varied from sixteen to thirty acres and only five exceeded the latter figure. The survival of the old field-names Cackenhulle and Grattenstichen,[8] now Cacknells and

[3] In their original forms Middleland Drove, Townend Lane, Southland (Sutland) Lane and Smaleland Drove. The termination land has become corrupted to end.

[4] *Rentalia*, p. 109.

[5] The expression often used at Tidpit of furlongs 'shooting' to the down or 'shooting' to Toyd is presumably the verb formed from *Shot* the noun.

[6] Prothero, *English Farming*, p. 24.

[7] Orwin, *The Open Fields*, p. 36.

[8] Nos. 203, 204 and 205 on map.

Grattenstiches, both situated on the margin of the Downs, prove that modern cultivation has not advanced beyond the medieval boundary of the open fields.

Within the furlong were the strips of the tenants, which at West Martin averaged four-fifths of an acre.[9] The number of strips allotted to a tenant in each furlong was based on his status. Thus the tenant of a virgate might receive two strips, to one for the tenant of a half-virgate and one half to the tenant of a ferling. But a number of factors militated against this being an invariable rule.

Wiltshire, it has been asserted, is predominantly a county of the two-field system.[10] The commissioners of Beere's *Terrier*, moreover, all local men and themselves cultivators, invariably refer to an east field and a west field only; the tenants are recorded always as having strips 'in both fields'.[11] But the ploughland, as has been seen, postulates a three-field system. How, then, are these conflicting propositions to be reconciled?

The distribution of acres as between the two fields is tabulated as follows.

	East Field		West Field		Totals	
Tithing	Acres	Strips	Acres	Strips	Acres	Strips
Damerham	531½		567		1,098½	
W. Martin	236¼	293	750¼	917	986½	1,210
E. Martin	359¼	288	120½	112	478¾	400
Tidpit	118¼	90	227¼	145	343¼	235

The reason for the considerable disproportion is not deliberate design, but topographical necessity. To the east and west of the two tithings of Martin there was room for unlimited expansion towards the Downs, more and more of which, as the centuries passed, was brought into cultivation. But the east field of West Martin and the west field of East Martin were conterminous, so that the enlargement of either field was impossible. Thus the two fields which marched together were about one-third only of their respective counterparts. Clearly, if this were a two-field system, where one half of the arable lay fallow each year, the villagers every alternate year when the larger field was rested, would have been seriously undernourished.

[9] *Supra*, Ch. XI. At East Martin 9/10 of an acre, but at Tidpit 1 1/4 acres.

[10] Gray, *Field Systems*, 70.

[11] The fields in the original are invariably 'campus orientalis' and 'campus occidentalis'. The tenants always hold strips 'in duobus campis'.

Now, a two-field system of rotation presupposes an equal acreage in either field, whereas here except at Damerham there is a wide disparity. The explanation lies in the fact that at each place the commissioners for their own convenience enumerated the furlongs on either side of an artificial datum line, in this case the village road, irrespective of whether those furlongs were in an east, west, north or south field. The words east field and west field did not mean that a two-field system was employed: they meant that the furlongs were located geographically to the east or west of the village road.[12]

With this prefatory observation we may proceed to examine first each village and next the demesne.

Damerham supplies the only example of an approximately normal two-field system, because the terrain on either side of the road afforded space for an equal acreage in both fields. The 531½ acres in the east field was supplemented by closes to equate with the 567 acres in the west field.[13] About 1761 each field was divided in half to form a four-field arrangement.

At *West Martin*, the east field contained 236 acres only, and the west field no less than 750, a ratio of about one acre in the former to over three in the latter. The distribution of the tenants' strips, moreover, presents a bewildering diversity:

Thus 2 tenants have 1 strip in the east field to 1 in the west
3 tenants have 1 strip in the east field to 2 in the west
10 tenants have 1 strip in the east field to 3 in the west
8 tenants have 1 strip in the east field to 4 in the west
1 tenant has 1 strip in the east field to 5 in the west

A four-field system might be indicated by this distribution were it not for chronological difficulties. It is said to have been developed not earlier than the Elizabethan and Jacobean periods, and then because agricultural improvements demanded it. But there is no known and undoubted four-field arrangement as early as Abbot Beere's survey.[14] A fourth field originated from a division of two fields of equal area, as, in fact at Damerham about 1761, or by the addition of land brought freshly under cultivation, as was done at Tidpit about the same time. But by no conceivable

[12] Beere's Survey was made in response to an enquiry from Cardinal Wolsey who was alarmed at the public unrest occasioned by Enclosures; *v.* Statute, 10 Henry VIII.

[13] *Beere,* p. 40.

[14] Gray, *op. cit.*, p. 406.

manipulation of acreages could it have occurred in 1518. A three-field system is subject to adjustment feasible, but the one thing that is absolutely negatived is a two-field plan.

A third of the total acreage of both fields (986 acres) is 329 acres, which must be the approximate area of each of the three fields. If to the east field (236 acres) be added the small ploughland of 88 acres, we arrive at a field of 324 acres. The other two fields lying together in the west field were, perhaps, separated by one of the droves. Some such compromise seems to be the only solution of the distribution of acres at West Martin.

The problem was similar at *East Martin*, though of the 480 acres the Abbey held no less than 230 in demesne, which will be considered later.

Finally the twelfth-century knight's fee at *Tidpit* provides conclusive proof of a three field system here. Although the commissioners here as elsewhere denote the fields as east and west, their survival until relatively recent times reveal that there were, in fact, three. Whereas in the east field there were 118 acres,[15] in the west there were 227¼, raising at once the presumption that there was not a two-field system as the Terrier states, but three fields. This is proved beyond doubt in the Tithe Awards and by the tithe map. The east field was known as Toyd field: the larger west field comprised two separated by the Tidpit-Cranborne road and known as Chalk Hill and Allenford Field.

The demesne was of three kinds. First there were the outlying farms, all leased to farmers, with the exception of Toyd which the abbey still appears to have kept in hand. Since there was no village population, the question of growing crops for sustinence did not arise. Moreover, since they were all predominantly sheep farms, a disproportionate and often excessive area of fallow was let to supplement the sheep grazing on the the downs.

Stapleton, let to Johanna Moreys of Damerham, was already largely enclosed, for it contained 133 acres in ten closes; Boulsbury was leased to John Rode and half of its 188 acres was given over to sheep: Allenford was also a sheep farm, let to William Tokarde, who also farmed the demesne at Damerham and held the tenancy of the *hospitium* at Martin. At Toyd two-thirds of the arable was set aside for sheep to supplement the grazing.

Secondly, demesne land consisted of strips in the open fields interspersed with those of the tenants. There was no demesne land at West Martin,

[15] Exclusive of a furlong called Sonderton (a detached or sundered farm containing 13 acres of demesne land let on lease).

but at East Martin the dominical strips amounted to nearly half the total land under cultivation and at Tidpit rather over a quarter. There are no signs of any preferential treatment accorded to the abbey in the selection of strips. But where an adjoining strip came to be surrendered, through death or other cause, the abbey appears to have annexed it so as to form a compact block of land.

Lastly, certain strips in the open fields were known by the term 'overland'. Overland is found at Damerham, Tidpit and East Martin. It is defined as 'demesne land, that is to say, Overlonde, over and above the aforesaid farm of lands'.[16] By implication, therefore, it was not leased or farmed out with the rest of the demesne, nor was it farmed by the abbey, but by the rent-paying tenants on behalf of the abbey, which received the produce.

At Damerham there were thirty-six acres, which included three acres of nut-grove, called 'thrushes',[17] at Tidpit twenty-four acres of which two were pasture, and at East Martin five and a half acres. At Tidpit eighteen out of the twenty-four acres were in furlongs called Curtelawe and Nether Curtelaw (later Courtland fields), which must have discharged some special liability in connection with the court of the abbey at Damerham. The pasture was called Lordiscrofte and was reserved for the folding of the abbey's flocks.[18] It may perhaps be inferred that the remainder of the overland, in the same way, carried with it certain obligations, which made it advisable for the abbey to retain it in its own hands, even when the rest of the demesne was at farm.

There was nothing servile attaching to the cultivation of overland. While John Strete and Richard Chatoure, it is true, were classified as *nativi domini*, the chronological descendant of the villein, nine others similarly designated did not have overland. On the other hand, the largest landholders and those of greatest consequence were charged with it: Agnes Wykes who farmed the demesne at Tidpit, Bernard Ashley, John Atteford and Johanna Moreys at Damerham. Between the cultivation of the demesne where it lay in strips and the cultivation of overland there was this difference: that while the former was cultivated by communal effort, the latter seems to have been cultivated by the individual effort of the tenant.

Some conclusions may be drawn from this analysis of the field system

[16] *Beere*, p. 43.
[17] *Ibid.*, 'Alnetum vocatum Turdelles alias Pleycrofte.'
[18] *Beere*, p. 42.

obtaining in the hundred. First, a caution should be enjoined against accepting without further examination that the terms east field and west field necessarily imply two open fields only. The example of Tidpit decisively proves the contrary. The proposition can only be accepted if it is accompanied by an equality of acres and strips in either field. The terms in the survey we have been considering are purely conventional. The open fields at Tidpit had names: Toyd field, Chalk Hill and Allenford field. But even these were seldom used. In colloquial discourse the villager would speak of the wheat field, the barley field or the summer (i.e. the fallow) field, and later the clover field. These were never the same from one year to another, but alternated with the rotation of crops.

Nor was this only the language of the villager; they are also the expressions of the court leet. Examples may be found every year in the court rolls: the fence in Tidpit wheat field is in disrepair (1610); the hedge between the barley and the summer fields is in disrepair (1611); the people to go abounding of Tidpit summer field on the first Thursday in May (1755); horses and beasts to feed in Tidpit barley field a week before the sheep (1813). The terms east field and west field find no place at all.

The impact of sheep farming affected rather the demesne farms than the open field cultivator. But, since the number or rights for grazing sheep on the downs was dependent upon the extent of arable, farmers were anxious to enlarge their arable holdings. Since the thirteenth century not only had the number of tenants decreased, but their status had materially altered. In 1235 the may have been about eighty-four at Martin; in 1518 there were only thirty-six. At the former date they were customary tenants, owing labour services. At the latter, they had become copyhold or rent-paying tenants. Moreover, they were also gentlemen of substance, like John Garrett of Alderholt Park, or Lavenham and Sevior whose affluence brought their wills within the probate of the prerogative courts. Such persons were not, like their predecessors dependent upon their strips for subsistence: rather, they farmed for profit. Their holdings were usually much in excess of the medieval virgate, and were managed in conjunction with the lucrative business of sheep-farming. The new method led to a deviation from normal practice, to an unequal distribution of strips and to an irregularity in the field system.

APPENDIX I
THREE GLASTONBURY SURVEYS

The old controversy between the long hide of Maitland and the short hide of Kemble has ended in the recognition by historians of a hide widely diverse, not only from county to county, but also from manor to manor. While even for a particular county opinions have been divergent, the most recent computation of the Wiltshire hide is forty acres.[1] The Glastonbury Use, as the method of superficial land mensuration employed upon the Glastonbury manors came to be called, has hitherto not claimed much attention. It is given as follows:

10 acres	–	1 Ferling or Ferdel
4 Ferlings	–	1 Virgate
4 Virgates	–	1 Hide
4 Hides	–	1 Foedum

Ferdellum	Virgate	Hide	Foedum
10 acres	40 acres	160 acres	640 acres

Hearne, who prints it in the *auctorium* to *John* of *Glastonbury's Chronicle*,[2] says that this table is appended to the codex in possession of Lord Charles Bruce in a later hand, presumably by the monk who wrote the *auctorium*.[3] The formula recurs in the glossary annexed to *Peter Langtoft's Chronicle*, with a not very informative disquisition upon it.[4] In the preface to the *Rentalia of Michael of Amesbury* the late canon Jackson, sometime librarian to the Marquis of Bath, is quoted as having stated that the table was extracted from page 406 of the great cartulary,

[1] Tait, in *E.H.R.*, XVII, p. 280; Stenton, *Anglo-Saxon England*, p. 276. These opinions are based rather on Domesday statistics than on post-Conquest surveys. Prof. Gray, *Field Systems*, p. 25, offers evidence of another Glastonbury manor in Wiltshire, Kington St. Michael, having a hide of 80 acres.

[2] John of G., II, last page.

[3] 'manu equidem antiqua, diversa tamen ab illa qua scriptus ipse fuerit textus Johannis.'

[4] Hearne, *Peter Langtoft's Chronicle*, II, p. 600.

parts of which were published by Dugdale and Hearne.[5] Writing about 1674 Aubrey found the same formula 'written in a special note on the margin of the Legier Book' of the Hundred of North Damerham.[6] Sir Richard Colt Hoare accepted it without question and commented upon the parity of acreage under cultivation in 1518, the date of Beere's *Terrier*, with that at the time of the Enclosure Act of Damerham exactly three hundred years later.[7]

The Glastonbury Use is, therefore, too authoritatively documented to be summarily discarded on the grounds that the land areas of the medieval surveys, when measured by its terms, become too large to be contained within the ambit of the average manor. It is, indeed, tempting to relate it with the frequently quoted passage of Walter of Henley distinguishing the three from the two field systems: 'and if your lands are divided in two, as in many places, the one half sown with winter seed and spring seed, the other half fallow, then shall a ploughland be eight score acres.'[8] It had, at least, this advantage, not shared by some other computations for Wiltshire, that the hide is exactly divisible by sixteen, the quarter virgate. The fourth part of a virgate, the ferling or ferdelle, was on the Glastonbury manors the most ubiquitous of all holdings.

The ferlingus or ferdella (the terms are synonymous) was a fourth part of a virgate, and that it contained ten acres may be inferred from the fact that whereas tenements of three, four, five (very common), six, eight, twelve and sixteen acres frequently occur, a tenement of ten acres is scarcely ever mentioned. The omission of holdings of ten acres is intelligible only by the substitution of the word ferling or ferdelle. It follows, therefore, that the virgate contained forty acres, as stated in the Glastonbury Use. Though large, a virgate of forty acres was not unusual. In the south of England, for instance, it is found on the manors of Eynsham.[9]

In the preamble to the *Terrier* of Abbot Richard Beere in 1518 is a note to the effect that while woods are measured by the large perch, containing eighteen feet, as is the custom of the country and of arable, the meadow and pasture are measured by a perch of fifteen feet only.[10]

[5] *Rentalia*, Introduction, XXV. The Great Chartulary has now been published by the Somerset Record Society.

[6] Aubrey, *Top. Coll.* 127.

[7] Hoare, *Hundred of South Damerham*, p. II.

[8] Walter of Henley, p. 7; *vide supra*, (Ch. XII).

[9] Vinogradoff, *Villeinage*, p. 238.

[10] Hoare, *op. cit.* p. 41.

Consequently, the Glastonbury acre by which woods and arable were measured was about one-fifth larger and the acre by which meadows and pasture were measured about one-fifth smaller than the statutory acre in use today. The following table illustrates this:

	Statutory	Long Perch (Woods & Arable)	Short Perch (Meadows & Pasture)
Lineal perch	16½	18	15
Acre in sq. yds.	4,840	5,760	4,000
Excess in sq. yds.	—	920	—
Deficiency in sq. yds.	—	—	840

Therefore to convert the Glastonbury arable acre into modern acres, it must be reduced by approximately one-fifth:

	Glastonbury	Statutory
Knight's Fee	640	523
Hide	160	130–1
Virgate	40	32–3
Ferling	10	8

Other evidence supports this conclusion. By the time of Beere's *Terrier* in 1518 virgates were fast becoming obsolete and were being replaced by acres. But there was still tenants denominated *nativi domini*, the descendants of the medieval villein. Their average acreage is thirty-nine Glastonbury acres, or, applying the necessary adjustment, thirty-one and a half statutory acres.

Again the virgate in terms of the statutory acre probably survives in the glebe, attached at the time of the commutation of tithes to the disused rectory of Tidpit and to the chapelry at Martin. The former was thirty-four and three-quarters, the latter thirty-five and a quarter acres, within one rood, that is, in each case of thirty-five acres.[11] Another equation is supplied by the manor house estate at Martin. In 1518 Sir John Horsey held six virgates;[12] a century later it was bought by Sir John Cooper with 204 acres, making the virgate to contain thirty-four acres. The court rolls

[11] Tithe Awards.

[12] Beere, p. 42.

of the seventeenth and eighteenth centuries provide instances of the use of the words virgate or yardland, and in every case their content varies from twenty-nine to thirty-eight acres.

Walter of Henley wrote that a man could easily plough an acre a day and be home at three o'clock in the afternoon.[13] He has not found many people to agree with him. On the other hand, a day's ploughing has been equated not with the acre but with the strip. The strip has been computed to average two-thirds to three-quarters of a modern acre;[14] elsewhere seven-eighths of an acre has been suggested.[15] At West Martin at the end of the Middle Ages the strip was about four-fifths of an acre and at the hamlet of Tidpit the medieval dominical strips, interspersed in the common field with those of the tenants, averaged between half and three-quarters of a Glastonbury acre. More recently a theory has been advanced by which the strip is equated with the 'lands', the ridge and furrow formation still visible on many of our fields.[16] According to this view, the strip measures twenty-two feet by 220 yards, or one-third of an acre only. To this attractive theory the chief objection is that the strip becomes too small. But any of these calculations are more within the capacity of the ox-drawn plough than the full acre.[17] Forty strips, such as are found at West Martin, dispersed among the furlongs of the open fields, will amount to thirty-two acres, a close enough approximation to what at Martin we have concluded to be the size of the virgate.

The calculation of the exact content of the virgate is, howevere, little more than an academic exercise. The virgate was an area of arable, varying from manor to manor, to which certain rents, services and dues were attached and, primarily, it connoted liability to such services rather than denoted a definite acreage. To a person living in the thirteenth century the mention of a virgate would as much suggest the status and obligations of the tenant as the extent of his tenement.

In the table set out below are shown first the classes of tenement and against each the number of tenants at the date of the two earliest surveys under discussion.

13 Walter of Henley, p. 9.

14 Orwin, *Open Fields*, p. 36.

15 *Camb. Econ. Hist.*, I, p. 129.

16 *Antiquity*, 95 (Sept. 1950), p. 115.

17 Massingham, *Country Relics*, p. 99, cites an instance within memory of the long wooden wheelless plough, drawn by oxen, ploughing in Gloucestershire ¾ of an acre a day.

Villein Tenants	*Inquisition* 1189	*Rentalia* 1235
½ hides	10	5
1½ virgates	8	—
Virgates	52	62
½ virgates	48	58
Ferlings	11	24
Gotsettles	8	—
5 acres and under	27	26

In the interval between the two surveys certain changes had been introduced conducing to a greater efficiency of estate management and simpler accountancy. First, whereas in the *Inquisition* of 1189 the tenants of Damerham and Martin were inextricably intermixed, in the later survey there is an attempt, not uniformly successful, to distinguish the tenants of one village from those of the other, and further to enumerate them in compact lists according to the size of their tenements.

Another significant reform was the reduction in the number of different tenements from seven to five, by the elimination of the holdings of one-and-a-half virgates and that of the Cotsettles. What happened to the tenants of one-and-a-half virgates? The only case of which the descent can be traced with certainty is that of John Clericus, and that only because, being an exceptional one, it justified a special note in the *Foedary* of Abbot Monyton.[18] In the twelfth century he received a grant from Henry of Blois of one virgate at Damerham and another at Stapleton. For his own convenience he exchanged the latter for half a virgate near his home, and is thus assessed in the 1189 *Inquisition* for one-and-a-half virgates. But he also about this time enclosed a piece of heathland for which he paid a rent of 1 lb. of cummin. At the time of the second survey the piece of heathland was reckoned as half a virgate and the tenement is valued at two virgates. At this date it had passed to Peter the son of Geoffrey, who is shown as a freeholder. A century later his successor, John de la Sale, did homage for two virgates to the abbot, Adam of Sodbury (1325–33).

The case of John Clericus does not help in the solution of the disappearance of the one-and-a-half virgates, but it does illustrate how the succession of holdings changed hands, how the holding itself was subject to additions. It seems probable that most of the one-and-a-half had been degraded to the category of virgates in 1235, which had increased by ten.

[18] *Foedary*, p. 26.

This is the obvious inference to be drawn from Nicholas Mai of Martin, who in 1189 held one-and-a-half virgates and in 1235 only one virgate. On the other hand, a scrutiny of the second survey suggests that the tenants of one-and-a-half virgates may have been entered in two categories, as the tenant of one virgate and again as the tenant of a half virgate.[19] A reclassification on this basis would account for the half virgates increasing by ten between the two dates. It has been contended that the subdivision of units, unaccompanied by a reduction of services attached to them, was a favourite device of Glastonbury to obtain more labour from its tenants.[20]

The other villein tenure that was suppressed in 1235 was that of the cotsettlers. In 1189 there had been eight, by 1235 there were none, but the ferling tenements had increased by thirteen. But whereas the usual rent for the ferling was 1s. 3d., nine holders of a ferling paid an enhanced rent of 2s. A 2s. rent was paid by cotsettlers at Deverill (a detached part of the South Damerham Hundred), one of the last of the Glastonbury manors in Wiltshire on which cotsettlers survived, and the conclusion is almost certain that at Martin the cotsettlers of 1189 became assessed as tenants of a ferling at a slightly higher rent to cover the value of the cottage.

The services due from the cotsettler had always been the same as those rendered by the tenants of ferlings. In the 1189 *Inquisition* at Damerham we read: 'Joceline holds a cotsettle and works as other Cotarii, and again Aluredus the son of Hoppesort holds a ferling and works as other Cotarii.'[21] The conclusion to be deduced from this syllogism is that the services of the cotsettler and the ferling tenant were the same. They were, also, *operarii*, because the essential part of their service was the obligation to do week-work.

It is seldom that the same name occurs in both surveys; where it does, the tenement held is usually the same: Robert of Stapleham, Reginald Hatchwell, William Hoppesort, Robert Mai and William Carpenter each held a virgate at both dates. On the other hand, Seman junior held a half virgate in 1189, while his relict held four acres only in 1235, and the widow Christina's half virgate diminished to a ferlng. But the enlargement of a family's holding is well illustrated by the case of Alfred

[19] William Gilbert held one virgate only in 1189, but in 1235 is entered as the holder of one virgate and again of a half virgate.

[20] Postan, in *Trans. R. Hist. Soc.* (4th series) XX, p. 187.

[21] Inq. 1189, pp. 130 ff.

True, who held one virgate in 1189. In 1235 we find William, Ralph, Nicholas and Ralph Junior True, each holding one virgate and Hugo True holding a half virgate, a total of four-and-a-half virgates in the family.

By the suppression of intermediate tenures, and by the determination of rent proportionate to each tenement, the abbey was able by 1235 to comprehend within an intelligible scheme the great majority of its tenants at Damerham and Martin, as the following figures illustrate:

Virgate			Half virgate			Quarter virgate		
No. of tenants	Rent	Donum	No. of tenants	Rent	Donum	No. of tenants	Rent	Donum
62	5/-	10d.	56	2s. 6d.	5d.	17	1s. 3d.	2½d.

There were, of course, several holdings smaller than the quarter virgate; there were also exceptional rents like the ex-cotsettles, to which reference has been made; there were also a few half hides. But seventy-eight per cent of those holding in villeinage are covered by these terms.

Many other Glastonbury manors aimed at the same uniform system, but no other achieved such good results. It may be that Damerham, the chief, the largest and most profitable of Glastonbury manors thus set a model for imitation by lesser estates.

Any analysis of the two surveys of 1189 and 1235 must start with the view propounded by Professor Postan in his *Chronology of Labour Services*.[22] Briefly his conclusion is that whereas in the twelfth century rent was preferred to labour services, in the thirteenth century services were preferred to rent. It must not, however, be inferred, on this manor at any rate, that by the later date labour services were substituted for rent; rather they were exacted in addition to rent. In 1189 there was no uniform system; nineteen tenants paid rent and discharged no services; seven more paid rent and performed only the essential bed-ripe or boon services. On the other hand, twelve tenants gave labour service but paid no rent at all. Those whose labour service was remitted were chiefly the smaller tenants of ten acres or less. By 1235 every tenant, without exception, paid rent and performed labour services in addition; the former practice of exacting service as the sole discharge of rent was discontinued.

Customary tenants at Damerham and Martin discharged their obliga-

[22] Postan, *loc. cit.* His conclusions are accepted with reservations by the *Camb. Econ. Hist.* 'Agrarian Life in the Middle Ages', p. 509.

tions to Glastonbury Abbey in two ways: they made certain money payments and they rendered certain labour services. These dues, though their incidence varied according to the size of the tenement, were universal.

Monetary payments, exacted universally from the whole community, were three in number:

(i) Rents of villein tenements increased from £28.1.4 in 1189 to £32.17.5 in 1235. At both dates the basic rent was 5s. od. for the virgate, 2s. 6d. for the half virgate, and 1s. 3d. for the ferling. The increase was due in part to the admission for the first time of the cottsettlers as rent-paying tenants (hitherto their tenure had been by service only), to a slightly higher rent paid by the small holders of under ten acres, and to a small increase in the population.

(ii) Rents were augmented by a contribution called the *donum ad lardarium*. Theoretically it was paid gratuitiously, and as such was, in a sense, supplementary to boon work.[23] In 1189 it was levied on the whole community (*tota villata*), and at Damerham and Martin was compounded for the lump sum of £5.[24] In the following century assessment was made on the individual. By this method it was calculated at one-sixth of the rent, and collected personally from each tenant. Thus the virgator paid 5s. od. rent and 10d. *donum*, the half virgator 2s. 6d. rent and 5d. *donum*, and the tenant of a ferling 1s. 3d. rent and 2½d. *donum*. Collected in this way the revenue from the *donum* amounted to £4.18.8, which shows that the earlier composition had been a very fair estimate.

It has been suggested that the *donum* may have been a commutation of all customary food rents.[25] Food rents had disappeared before the earlier of the two surveys, and only survived incidentally in the form of contributions of hens to the church[26] (churchscot), the gift by the reeve and berebrit of eggs at Easter[27] and in such tenancies chiefly of freedom where the rent was paid in honey or pepper.[28]

The juxtaposition of the words *reditum* and *donum*, in the invariable formula 'he shall pay rent 5s. od. and to the *lardarium* 10d.' suggests

[23] Vinogradoff, *Villeinage*, p. 293.
[24] Inq. 1189, p. 133.
[25] Neilson, *Customary Rents*, p. 32.
[26] *Rentalia*, p. 110. For Berebirt, *v. infra*, p. 17, *note*.
[27] *Ibid.*, p. 113.
[28] *Ibid.*, p. 112.

two payments closely associated as we might say 'rent and rates' or 'rates and taxes'. It seems possible that the*donum ad lardarium* was an exaction, intended to equalise rents at a fixed round figure. There is some indication on other manors, besides this, that the sum of the combined payments was intended to be about 6s. od. for the virgates and proportionally for the smaller tenements. Thus where the rent is high, as here, the donum is low – the lowest, in fact, of all Glastonbury manors. And where the rent is low, the *donum* tends to be high.

(iii) A third cash payment was involved in the enforced attendance at *scotales*. In 1189 it was expressly required of virgate tenants, of some others,[29] and, inferentially, of the remainder. Where a tenant has commuted all services for rent, he still drinks *scotale*.[30] In 1235 it was an obligation incumbent upon everyone except the reeve, the berebrit and the hayward.[31] The passage is given below in full, because our knowledge of the practice of drinking *scotales* on the Glastonbury manors is derived from this description, and a slightly different one at Deverill.

'Also he shall drink three *scotales*, that is to say, one before the feast of St. Michael for two days with his wife, for which he shall pay threepence. And if he has a male or female servant and Undersettles, each shall pay one half-penny and drink for one day. Also he shall drink two Scotales after the feast of St. Michael, and for the one he shall give for himself and his wife 2½d., and for the other 2d., and shall drink for two days. And if a male or female servant or Undersettles come, each shall pay one halfpenny a day. And if a stranger come, he shall give a halfpenny.'[32]

There were, however, differences in practice at the two dates: in 1189 there were two *scotales* only, one before and one after Michaelmas, each lasting for two days, Sunday and Monday. In 1235 there were three, one before and two after Michaelmas, each lasting two days. Thus two more days of compulsory drinking had been added. The charge for drinks remained the same at both dates for the first two ales, viz. for a married man and his wife 3d. for the first ale and 2½d. for the second. But

[29] Inq. 1189, p. 129: 'Radulfus ibit scotalium et sic utilius domini.'

[30] *Ibid.*, p. 131: 'Edmund redit ii solidos pro omnibus serviciis, sed dat donum et bibit siceram'.

[31] *Rentalia*, p. 113. The Parkarius 'potabit mediatatem scotaliae' is a unique entry.

[32] *Ibid*, p. 108.

additional revenue was derived from the third ale in 1235, when the charge for a married man was 2d. Whereas in the first survey the total disbursement on *scotales* was for a married man 5½d., at the second survey it was 7½d. No extra charge was made for a wife accompanying her husband, but no mention is made of a lower rate for young unmarried men, who at Deverill were admitted at half price on the first day and free of charge on the second.[33]

While the other universal payments, the rent and the Donum were graduated according to the status of the tenant and the size of the tenement, the payment towards *scotales* was uniform for all tenants irrespective of the size of their tenement. The only distinction made is between a villein tenant and a servant, and those associated with him, the undersettle[34] and the stranger. The 7½d. charged in 1235 was the equivalent of an eighth of the rent of a virgate, quarter the rent of the half virgate and half the rent of a ferling. It was an excessively severe imposition upon the small holder, and reversed the abbey's normal procedure of graduating the burden according to the size of the tenement.

The liquor consumed at *scotales* is termed either *cervisia* or *cicera*.[35] The former is translated by the English word 'ale' and the latter by the word 'cider'. The expression '*bibere plene*' or '*bibere ad libitum*' means attendance on every day at every ale. The occasion, coinciding with the end of the harvest, before and after Michaelmas, has all the characteristics of a harvest festival and, perhaps, the inauguration of the autumn ploughing. Beer drinks of this kind have their parallels in many primitive races. Besides celebrating with festivity the conclusion of the harvest, Michaelmas was chosen because then the apple crop had been picked for the cider and the barley had been garnered for the brewing. This date, however, was not immutable; in the neighbouring Hundred of Chalke *scotales* were held after autumn and before Christmas.[36]

Whenever a tenant brewed ale, he had to surrender to the abbey two gallons,[37] which must have made a substantial contribution to the stock behind the bar at the ales.

There were, of course, numerous other payments due from the tenants

[33] *Ibid*, p. 143.

[34] Neilson, *op. cit.*, p. 173. interprets undersettle as a hired labourer.

[35] Cicera is the word used in Lev. X. 9. and translated from the Vulgate as 'strong drink'. Also in Luke I. 15 (H. W. Moule).

[36] *Rot. Hund.* II, p. 249.

[37] *Rentalia*, p. 108, and *cf. ibid.* p. 37, where at Sturminster 9 gallons were surrendered.

in cash such as *faldicium*, the payment for the privilege of grazing cattle or sheep on the demesne, pannage, the fee for depasturing pigs on the waste, at the rate of a penny a pig or ½d. for a porker under six months. The above analysis has been confined to those cash payments, the incidence of which fell upon all tenants without exception. To summarise them, rents increased from about £28 to £33; the *donum*, from being a compounded contribution, levied upon the whole village and assessed at £5, came to be collected from each individual at the rate of one sixth of the rent, and produced ¼d. less; and scotales, by an addition to their number, produced a revenue of perhaps £5 or more compared with about £3.15.0 or less fifty years earlier. The value of the manor at this date, it may be added, was £40.[38]

In 1235 the cash payments for typical tenements were as follows:

Typical of	Rent	Donum	Scotale	Total	Levy per acre
Virgate	5s. od.	10d.	7½d.	6s. 5½d.	1 15/16d.
Half-virgate	2s. 6d.	5d.	7½d.	3s. 6½d.	2⅛d.
Quarter-virgate	1s. 3d.	2½d.	7½d.	2s. 1d.	2½d.

The labour services due from the various tenants at the two material dates are here given in full, not solely for purposes of comparison, but because they are typical examples of villein services in the twelfth and thirteenth centuries and repay close examination.

Inquisition 1189, p. 127.

Radalfus, son of Maheld holds one virgate at Martin. He ought to reap, load and carry the corn crop. In autumn he ought to reap half an acre every day until the whole crop is cut, and carry it and collect straw for thatching the houses and to help in the thatching and to drink one of the lord's scot-ales for threepence, and another for twopence halfpenny.

Ibid. p. 129.

Every ploughteam ought to plough the fallow, and one acre for oats and one acre for the winter sowing; one acre gratuitously [*de dono*] and two acres precariously [*ad preces*], and the men shall have their rations. Every horse shall harrow one acre for the winter sowing and another for the summer crop.

38 *Ibid.* p. 169 *Ibid.*, p. 108.

Ibid. p. 133.

Every ploughteam ought to fallow one acre and plough another acre for the summer crop, and, besides, to plough for the winter sowing gratuitously and two acres at the request of the lord, and the men shall have their rations, and every horse ought to harrow one acre for the winter sowing and one acre for the summer crop.

Rentalia 1235, p. 108

Robert Palmer holds one virgate and pays an annual rent of 5s. od. in three instalments, viz. at the feast of St. Michael 1s. 8d., at Xmas 1s. 8d., and at Easter 1s. 8d., and a contribution of 10d. to the *lardarium* on the feast of St. Martin.

If he owns a complete ploughteam, he shall plough by himself between Michaelmas and Christmas three acres and shall harrow one acre with his own horse with his own corrody or twopence. If he has his own horse or mare he shall harrow one acre in Lent. Every plough shall fallow one acre in estate. And the said Robert shall hoe one acre.

He must dip and clip the Lord's sheep three times a year.

He must mow the meadow, pick up and carry the hay.

He must reap every day except Sundays and Feast days from the feast of St. Peter ad Vincula to Michaelmas. On the day he carries, he need not cut.

When he threshes wheat or barley, he shall thresh two bushells; if oats, four bushells.

If he collects wood for fencing in Haywood, he shall collect one cartload, or he shall cart one cartload and have two handfuls of faggots. If he cuts wood for the lord's work he shall split one cartload and cart it to the court, and he shall have his own pule[?]. If he cuts wood or collects fencing after Michaelmas he shall have the help of men with horses.

If he collects 'kauman' [? thatching straw], he shall gather fifty sheaves, and each sheaf shall be as much as can be carried under one arm.

Moreover, if he carries corn at Deveril or Niunetone [Sturminster Newton] between the feasts of St. Peter and St. Michael, he shall carry only half the amount and then have two days rest.

When he works in the lord's garden, he shall be there till the third hour. When he works on the park enclosure, he shall enclose to the length of ten paces.

And he shall carry once before Xmas from Hampton to Glastonbury, and once in Lent. Also, he must carry once after Pentecost salt or corn to Glastonbury. Further, he must carry wool or cheese to Winton or Hamton or within a radius of twenty leagues, and in default of carrying he shall pay one halfpenny.

If he owns a pig over the age of one year, he shall pay one penny towards pannage, and if of six months only, a halfpenny.

He shall not sell without a licence from the lord any ox, horse, cow, hen, or pig. Nor can he give his daughter in marriage without his lord's permission.

From any brewing which he brews for sale he shall give to the lord two gallons of beer.

And the said Robert shall move four hurdles from the fold of the lord once a year.

And, if he dies his lord shall have a horse or an ox or a cow or the better sown acre of his arable.

And if he comes on account of the lord's or the seneschal's corrody, he shall have his own corrody.

Lastly, he shall not keep any ox in the lord's pasture, except such as he shall be entitled to by ploughing work.

[Then follow the names of sixty-four others]

Ibid. p. 109.

Ranulfus War' holds half a virgate and pays an annual rent of 2s. 6d., that is 10d. at Michaelmas, 10d. at Xmas and 10d. at Easter, and he contributes 5d. to the *lardarium*. And he shall do half the customary services of husbandary, which Robert Palmer is bound to do, but yet he shall drink three *scotales* like the said Robert.

[Then follow the names of fifty-seven others]

Ibid. p. 110.

Adam Episcopus holds one ferling for an annual rent of 1s. 3d., and a payment to the *lardarium* of 2½d. Between the feast of St. Peter ad Vincula and Michaelmas he must reap for three days in every week four acres. And he must hoe three half acres, and plough, fallow and harrow, stack and carry the lord's crop in autumn, dip and shear the lord's sheep three times, and drink *scotales* as does the aforesaid Robert. And he shall not give his daughter in marriage, except with the licence of his lord, nor sell cattle or a horse or a fowl without licence. And he must carry wool and cheese to Winton or Hamton or in a radius of twenty leagues, as much as applies to his holding.

[Then follow the names of fifteen others]

The form in which they are set out is in itself significant. While the inquisition of 1189 is directed to the ploughteam, the *Rentalia* is addressed to the owner of the plough. In the first there is imposed a collective responsibility for the prescribed task; in the second the onus is placed upon the individual to perform it. In the first, the words used are 'Every ploughteam shall plough'; in the second 'Richard Palmer, if he has a plough'. The implication that a gradual transition from communal to individual cultivation of the demesne was perhaps taking place is scarcely justified at this date, but the emphasis is now being placed on the individual rather than on the community. A plough team consisted of eight oxen, for the abbey possessed 92 oxen or 11½ plough teams.[39]

The only agricultural operations common to both surveys is the essential duty to plough and harrow and to reap and carry the crop. In 1189 every plough team was obliged to plough five acres, three for the winter crop, one for the spring crop and one of the fallow, of which three were ploughed *de dono* and two *ad preces*. In 1235 the virgator had precisely the same work to do. Similarly, at both dates there was an obligation to harrow two acres, one for the winter and one for the spring corn, but in 1235 the possessor of a horse had to harrow an extra acre in Lent. A new operation mentioned for the first time is weeding with a hoe (*serclare*) of one-and-a-half acres, also in Lent. In effect, therefore, the virgator of the thirteenth century stirred the soil of two-and-a-half more acres in Lent than did his predecessor. The additional cultivation of the ground in Lent may only be a sign of improved husbandry; but it may signify that more barley and oats were now being grown,[40] and it may indicate that a transition was taking place from a two-field to a three-field system of rotation; in other words, that two-thirds of the field were cultivated instead of one half only. It is clear evidence that more work was exacted from the tenants under Michael of Amesbury than had been the custom under Henry de Sully.

Formerly harvest work, not only cutting the corn, but also carting and ricking the crop, and even the haulage of straw to houses needing thatching, fell upon the virgate tenants. In the thirteenth century part of

[39] John of G. p. 223. 8 oxen formed the plough-team in Domesday Book.

[40] But *v.* Knowles, *Religious Orders,* p. 37, where it is said that in general wheat was being grown at the expense of barley.

this work was assigned to the smaller tenants, and they were required to work harder. Whereas half an acre a day had been the prescribed task before, now it was four acres in three days every week.[41] The operation, however, usually included the binding of the sheaves with a whisp of straw by another workman. The thirteenth-century Anonymous Author of Husbandry informs us that the economic unit was a band of five men,[42] who in combination could reap and blind two acres a day. The conjunction of the verbs to mow, pick up and carry[43] may perhaps imply cooperation of this kind, and does not impose an excessive task.

The long catalogue of services particularised in the *Rentalia* comprehends almost every contingency of agricultural routine or manorial custom which the prescience of its compiler could foresee. Operations of husbandry from the ploughing of the soil to the threshing of the grain; the care of sheep; the winter tasks of fencing and carting; the delivery of letters and the marketing of produce; the potation of scotales; fines, heriots and merchets. Because many of these things are omitted from the 1189 *Inquisition*, is it to be supposed that they were not then rendered; that they were the innovations of some despotic official at Glastonbury, resolved to extract from the customary tenants their maximum effort? Some, indeed, like the export of cheese to Winchester and Southampton, in pursuance of the policy of exploiting the demesne, may have been new. But most of them must necessarily have been done before, or manorial economy must have collapsed. The reasonable conclusion is that this statement of services imposes few new obligations, but rather recapitulates in writing what it had always been the custom to exact. But whereas these tasks, hitherto rendered from ancient and traditional custom, lacked definition, now they were given the minutest precision. It is stipulated with exactitude the number of feet of fencing to be done, the number and size of sheaves of thatching straw to be collected, the number of messages to be delivered or the number of bushells to be threshed. The substitution of piece-work for unspecified week-work is the outstanding characteristic of the list of services in the *Rentalia*.

Piecework is usually reputed to be the hardest form of manual labour. It is pertinent, therefore, to inquire how onerous were the tasks set in 1235. It has been argued elsewhere that if Walter of Henley's acre be the equivalent of a day's work, or a strip, which at Martin was always a

[41] Inq. 1189, p. 127. *Rentalia*, p. 110.
[42] Walter of Henley, p. 69.
[43] Inq. 1189, p. 127; *Rentalia*, p. 108.

fraction of an acre, then the service of ploughing, for which a wide margin of time was allowed, was not an excessive burden. As with the cultivation of the soil, so with the harvesting of the product, more and harder work was expected of the tenants in the thirteenth century, but still within the limit of their capability. From 174 tenants of Damerham and Martin at this time, the attendance of a few at the sheep dip or the wool clip of about 600 sheep, which is all the abbey is likely to have possessed, was not an exacting duty. Few country gentlemen today would be content with their gardener stopping work at nine in the morning,[44] and few modern farmers with their threshers ceasing work at the same hour.[45] Despite, therefore, the comprehensive list of obligations, and the precise calculations of piecework, the services rendered were, except perhaps at the critical seasons, neither exceptional nor arduous. Irritating they must have been, even exasperating when the tenant was anxious to progress with his own business. To the objection that such a daily routine left the tenant little time in which to harvest his own crops, the sentence 'on the day he carries he shall not reap'[46] probably supplies an answer. For, he would start reaping when the dew was on the ground, from 3.0 a.m. to 9.0 a.m., and have the rest of the day at his disposal; likewise, he would not start carrying the corn until it was dried out by the sun, in the afternoon, thus having the morning to work in his own field. If to this is added that the tenants on Glastonbury manors were not required to work on Sundays or feast days or in unseasonable weather;[47] that they had the assistance of tenants from Idmiston, who were under an obligation to carry an eighth of the crop at Damerham or Deverill,[48] the people at Damerham and Martin were not unduly oppressed by their labour service.

At the end of the 1235 survey is given a list of the skilled staff, which on behalf of the abbey was entrusted with special duties on the estate.[49] In number they were twelve, graded in relation to the land, in respect of which they were excused rent and services. They fall into three classes; in a class by himself is the reeve, a fact which, apart from all other evidence, stamps him as the superior manorial official. The forester, too, was in an exceptional position, living remote from the manor's centre.

[44] *Rentalia*, p. 108, 'ad tertiam horam'.
[45] *Ibid*, p. 114.
[46] *Rentalia*, p. 108.
[47] Vinogradoff, *Villeinage*, p. 296.
[48] *Rentalia*, p. 165.
[49] *Rentalia*, p. 113.

The perquisites attached to their office correspond with their gradation, the higher posts receiving more, the inferior less.

I		Reeve	exempted from rent and services for 1 virgate
II	(i)	Berebrit	exempted from rent and services for ½ virgate
	(ii)	Hayward	exempted from rent and services for ½ virgate
	(iii)	Park keeper	exempted from rent and services for ½ virgate
	(iv)	Shepherd	exempted from rent and services for ½ virgate
	(v)	Blacksmith	exempted from rent and services for ½ virgate
	(vi)	Forester	exempted from rent and services for 1 virgate
III	(i)	Ploughmen	exempted from rent and services for ¼ virgate
	(ii)	Dairymen	exempted from rent and services for ¼ virgate
	(iii)	Swineherds	exempted from rent and services for ¼ virgate
	(iv)	Gardeners	exempted from rent and services for ¼ virgate
	(v)	Threshers	exempted from rent and services for ¼ virgate

An example from each of the last two classes may be given:

The berebrit, the person in charge of the grange,[50] shall be exempt from payment of rent for half a virgate of arable, viz. 2s. 6d., and he shall give to the *lardarium*. And, like the reeve, he shall be relieved of all works, and customs, and shall have an acre of corn from the lord's demesne, one young pig, one lamb, one fleece, one cheese, a quarter and a half of oats at mid-Lent and one sheaf of corn of the prescribed size every day they carry. And for his own lamb he must find a man to work at the sheep-fold from the beginning of the lambing season to the time of weaning. And he shall have an allowance of meat like the reeve, and like him, also, give 200 eggs.

The swineherd shall be exempt from rent and services for one ferling of arable, except 2½d. *donum ad lardarium*. And he shall have one young pig and half an acre of corn, and everything that belongs to one pig except the bacon. And he shall plough, harrow and drink scot-ale.

[50] Latham, *Revised Medieval Word List*. Neilson, *Customary Rents*, offers no translation. In the notes annexed to Adam of Damerham a grange is defined as 'domus seu aedificia ubi reponatur grana.' This seems to be the meaning in Beere's Terrier, where it is applied to the Tithe Barn. Knowles, *Religious Orders*, 75, believes a grange to be an outlying demesne farm, and in this sense it is applied to Toyd, a remote demesne farm.

After the comprehensive list of services which the customary tenants were obliged to discharge, a list of perquisites which these persons were entitled to receive comes as a refreshing contrast. Though expressly exempted from services appropriate to their tenement, they still had some services to render, based on a principle which baffles logical explanation. They all paid the *donum* in money at the usual rate, except the reeve and the hayward, who in lieu thereof contributed the now obsolescent food rent, in this case 200 eggs at Easter,[51] and then only if they lived at Martin. They were all required to drink *scotales*, except the reeve, the berebrit, the hayward and the gardener. The Park-keeper was excused half, presumably one day's potation.[52]

Again, all were liable to service of ploughing except, apparently, the berebrit and the threshers (the omission to state this may be inadvertent), and all in the second grade also of harrowing. Such other services as are mentioned are peculiar to the vocation of the individual, and they are not many. The blacksmith, for instance, must shoe the lord's riding horse once a year, and the horse of his servant; he must shoe one cart-horse throughout the year with his own iron, and make five ploughs with iron provided by the lord.

What we have called perquisites were of two kinds. First there was what might be called a subsistence allowance, applicable only to those in the higher grade, whose work precluded them from providing for their own needs. It might consist of the yield of an acre of corn from the demesne, a young pig, a lamb, a fleece and cheese. But it was not quite invariable. The reeve for instance and the berebrit got in addition an allowance of meat and the former a cartload of corn at harvest time. The hayward, on the other hand, had to do without the cheese, the shepherd without the pig and the park-keeper without either, but they were usually compensated in other ways peculiar to their calling. The lower grade, exempt from the rent of 1s. 3d. only, received none of these things, or else only a small part. The swineherd and ploughman received some produce from the demesne. The dairyman and swineherd each got a young pig and the ploughman a lamb. Only the swineherd and ploughmen received two items, the dairyman one and the gardener and threshers none.

The other kind of perquisite is incidental to the exercise of a particular vocation. Only rarely is one of these perquisites shared by another. The

[51] *Rentalia*, p. 113.
[52] *Ibid*.

hayward, for example, was allowed a seed box of corn, and of barley; the park-keeper had the right to take all old wood, not suitable for fencing or hurdles; the shepherd was given an old sheep at drafting time; the blacksmith was allowed a tree trunk from the abbey's woods; the foresters had hayebote and husbote and top and lop of the trees felled; the swineherd all that belonged to a pig except the bacon; the gardener's share was all the apples on one tree and two flagons of cider at brewing time; and to the thresher fell a quarter of a bushell a week during the time of threshing.

Such perquisites, each appropriate to his particular calling, may, of course, have been merely an additional remuneration for the work done. But the impression is also left that the system was devised to prevent pilfering. The gardener, it might be argued, might be less likely to steal his master's apples if he had plenty of his own, less likely to steal his master's cider if he had enough of his own to get drunk upon. So too the shepherd would be less tempted to report the mysterious death of a sheep, if he were provided with a carcase that would provide him with salted mutton throughout the winter. To the park-keeper and forester the opportunity to steal was always present, but could be lessened by permission to take freely a certain quantity.

After a century of extremely prosperous dominical farming, during which labour services were preferred to rent, a reversion to commutation of services for rent was made in the fourteenth century.[53] In a work, in which a special study of the Glastonbury manors has been made, this change is assigned to after 1287, precipitated, perhaps, by an epidemic of sheep scab about 1276, accelerated by a famine in 1314 and by a cattle plague in 1327.[54] It continued until the Black Death, when the economic situation was again rudely changed.

The evidence from the Damerham manor, however, indicates little change between the abbacy of John of Taunton (1274–90) and that of Adam of Sodbury (1322–35), by whom expensive buildings were erected, markets established, and land, usually pasture, reclaimed for the demesne. On this manor the change does not seem to have occurred until about the year 1335.[55]

Among the many causes tending towards commutation of services was

[53] Postan, *loc. cit.*, p. 186.

[54] Knowles, *Religious Orders*, p. 48.

[55] Since this was written, the editor of the Glastonbury Great Chartulary, I, xiii, arrives at the same conclusion.

the expansion of sheep farming both by lords and tenants. At Damerham, whereas in the first half of the thirteenth century it was chiefly arable land that was reclaimed, in the second half it was mostly pasture. The population was increasing, but sheep farming employed less labour, and labour services could, consequently, be dispensed with. Cash payment, moreover, was becoming more and more an element in economics; sheep were disposed of for cash through the agency of instaurators,[56] cheese and fleeces were exported from Damerham to markets at Winchester and Southampton. The introduction of a money economy showed that a greater profit could be obtained from renting the demesne than by farming it.[57]

The Black Death and the consequential Statutes of Labourers again altered the situation. Agricultural labour became scarce and wages doubled.[58] Even sheep farming may have declined.[59] Tenants are now found leasing the demesne, and the lord did everything possible to retain such labour services as still survived. This was the situation when Abbot Richard Beere in 1518 caused the *Terrier* which bears his name to be compiled.[60]

This *Terrier* discloses that the demesne at Damerham and Martin and on most, if not all, the dominical farms were leased to farmers (*firmarii*) for a money rent. Of labour services none were left. But there were still eight tenants, all except one at Damerham, who were described as *nativi domini*, signifying their tenure in villeinage, so that should dominical farming revive, labour services might still be exacted from them. Rents were assessed at about 6d. an acre, though this rate was far from universal, but may be compared with 1½d. per acre in 1235. The *donum ad lardarium*, which had been as obligatory as the rent, has now entirely disappeared. Fines on admission, which were such a feature of the copyhold tenure in succeeding centuries, were rendered usually in fractions of a mark, 6s. 8d., 3s. 4d. and 1s. 8d. especially being common. But to many holdings there was no fine on admission at all, and at West Martin, in particular, it survived in the medieval form of one or two capons. Fines

[56] R. C. Payne, 'Agrarian Conditions on Wiltshire Estates', in *Bull. of Hist. Research*, XVIII, 54, 116.

[57] *Camb. Econ. Hist.* 'Agrarian Life in the Middle Ages', p. 503.

[58] *Ibid*, p. 573.

[59] Payne, *op. cit.*

[60] *Terrarium Abbatis Ricardi Beere*, printed in Hoare, *Hundred of South Damerham*, p. 41.

were lowest at East Martin, where the abbey held a larger interest and exercised a greater control.

There were only three exceptions to the payment of a heriot on death, a custom which on this manor lasted until the twentieth century. Where more than one heriot was paid (there are instances of five, three, and two) more than one holding was involved, acquired by inheritance or reversion of the copyhold. 'The best good the tenant die possessed of is due to the lord for a heriot, if his tenement be heriotable' is the presentment of the jury at the court leet from the beginning of the seventeenth century onwards.

The demesne at Damerham was leased to William Tokerde, who also kept the *hospitium* at Martin and farmed the demesne farm at Allenford. At East Martin the large demesne, which lay in strips in the open fields, was let to John Storke, and that at Tidpit to Walter Lavenham. John Rode rented Boulsbury and Toyd alone seems to have remained in the hands of the Abbey. The Reeve was John Hollowaye, who farmed 148 acres of his own at Damerham. The medarius of Glastonbury held the abbey's estate at East Martin in freehold, as well as half a hide at Damerham. The pitancarius[61] of Glastonbury received the revenues from the medieval field called Peytwynsfielde, in Toyd Field.

Since the last survey in the thirteenth century, the number of farmers was reduced by half; the land under cultivation had diminished; virgates are displaced by acres; hired labour has superseded communal efforts, and Glastonbury Abbey was interested only in the rents, fines and heriots it received from the leases. We may conclude this chapter with a statistical picture of Martin, as it was in the year 1518.

SUMMARY

	No. of farmers	Acres	Rents	Fines	Heriots
West Martin	24	999½	£22.12.2	£8.10.6[62]	26
East Martin	7[63]	479¾	£8.13.0	£6.18.8	13
Tidpit	7[64]	357¼	£6.8.10	18.4	8
	38	1,836½	£37.14.0	£16.7.6	47

[61] These were obedientiary offices in the monastic establishment. The Medarius was, possibly, connected with the collection of rents in honey. Latham, *op. cit.* translates: 'obedientiary in charge of mead'.

[62] Plus 5 capons.

[63] Inclusive of demesne farms.

[64] Inclusive of demesne farms.

WEST MARTIN

		Acres	Rent	Fine	Heriot
1.	William Harries	49¾	24s. od.	3s. 4d.	2
2.	William Sevyar	23	12s. od.	3s. 4d.	1
3.	John Storke	68	32s. od.	—	3
4.	Robert Storke	28	10s. 8d.	—	1
5.	John Garrett (Sen.)	212	71s. 4d.	100s. od.	2
6.	Richard Thorne	9¾	6s. od.	1/-	1
7.	Robert Lavenhame	57¾	12s. od.	6s. 8d.	1
8.	John Garrett (Jun.)	64	30s. od.	—	—
9.	Thomas Sevyar	46	24s. 8d.	6s. 8d.	2
10.	Richard Harries	23½	1s. od.	—	1
11.	Robert Fychett	10¼	6s. od.	2 capons	—
12.	Thomas Compton	25	1s. od.	1 capon	1
13.	John Curteys	87	40s. 4d.	26s. 8d.	1
14.	Robert Godwyne	23¾	12s. 4d.	3s. 3d.	1
15.	William Pore	32	16s. od.	1s. 8d.	1
16.	John Swetapulle	45¾	24s. 2d.	—	1
17.	John Blysse	21	12s. od.	10s. od.	1
18.	Edith Harries	11	6s. od.	2 capons	1
19.	John Sevyar	12	6s. od.	7d.	1
20.	Valentine Carpenter	33	16s. od.	2s. od.	1
21.	Edmund Nycholas	52¼	24s. od.	—	1
22	William Marlowe	34¼	1?s. od.	2s. od.	1
23	Thomas Prynce	22	12s. od.	3s. 4d.	1
24.	William Tokerde	8½	34s. 8d.	—	—
		999½	£22.12.2	£8.10.6 plus 5 capons	26

EAST MARTIN

		Acres	Rent	Fine	Heriot
1.	John Storke (demesne)	229¾	56s. 8d.	133s. 4d.	5
2.	John Storke (own)	46½	24s. od.	—	2
3.	Richard Kyng	26	12s. od.	1s. 8d.	1
4.	John Thorne	23	12s. od.	—	1
5.	William Blake	81	36s. 6d.	1s. 8d.	2
5.	Robert Laurence	43½	19s. 2d.	1s. od.	1
7.	John Yonge	30	12s. 8d.	1s. od.	1
		479¾	£8.13.0	£6.18.8	13

TIDPIT

	Acres	Rent	Fine	Heriot
1. Agnes Wykes	94	35s. 6d.	—	2
2. Walter Lavenham (own)	41	20s. 8d.	3s. 4d.	1
3. Walter Lavenham (demesne)	62	16s. 0d.	—	1
4. Radulfus Gifford	59	22s. 9d.	4s. 0d.	1
5. John Strete	48	13s. 8d.	5s. 0d.	1
6. John Lavenham	23½	8s. 0d.	2s. 0d.	1
7. John Harryes	29¾	12s. 3d.	4s. 0d.	1
	357¼	£6.8.10	18s. 4d.	8

APPENDIX II

DAMERHAM CHURCH

The oldest part of the church is its tower, which is ascribed by the *Victoria County History*, in an account much in need of correction and amplification, to about 1130. In my opinion, which receives corroboration from the recent survey made by Professor Stuart Piggott, it belongs to the early period of Norman architecture and may be assigned to a date not later than 1100, and may even have been in existence in Saxon times. Its position at the east end of the south aisle is, if not unique, at least most unusual. The proposition that it is a transeptal tower has been rebutted by many authorities: there remain no vestiges of a corresponding transept; there is no trace of a crossing; the archway subsequently pierced to connect the south aisle with the tower chamber is, on the assumption of a transept, purposeless.

The tower leaves the impression of having been built for defensive purposes, commanding, as it does, the hill slope and the ford over the stream beyond, independent of the church and possibly an outpost of the buildings at the court house, which must have been standing long before the Conquest, as the centre from which the sixteen hides, farmed by Glastonbury Abbey at the time of Domesday, were administered. Some medieval field-names suggest that there may have been defensive fortifications, e.g. Portway, Gardelande, Wardeland.

The stages of the tower suggest that at one time it may have been inhabited, a circumstance which might explain the curious apertures on its west face, characteristic rather of pre-Conquest architecture, permitting of access by means of external stairways or ladders. Both have the appearance of doorways rather than windows: one has a typical norman round arch, the other is pointed. The diagonal wall tooling on the interior faces is a sign of thirteenth century restoration, and may well be contemporary with the pointed doorway.

The nave was built in the late eleventh or early twelve century. Apart from its architectural features, the reasons for assigning an early date may be recapitulated; first, it must have been standing for some time to have been in need of renonvation (renovare is the word used) by Henry of

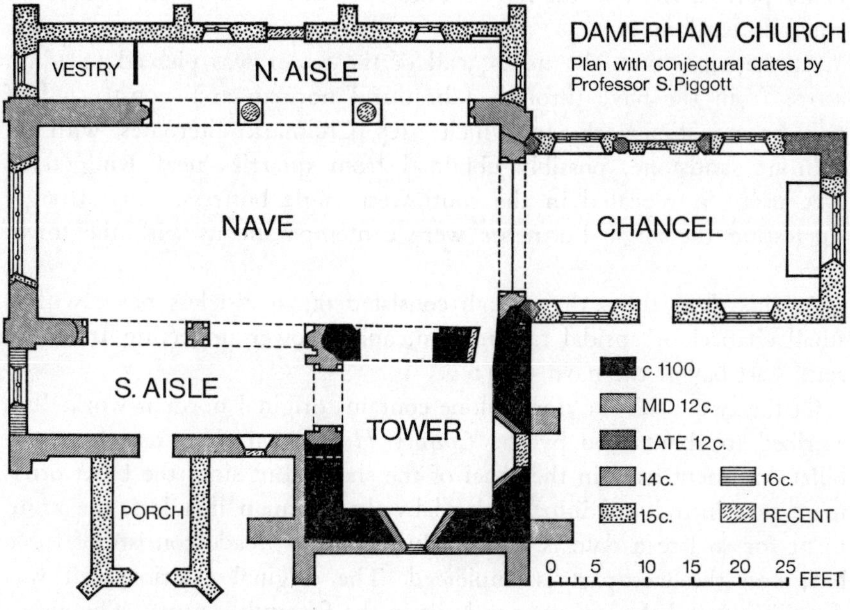

Blois in c.1130. Secondly, its foundation cannot have been later than its daughter chapelry of Martin, which has been ascribed to between the years 1080 and 1120. Finally, at the time of the visit of Henry of Blois it was of sufficient size and importance to merit unusually fine church ornaments.[2]

The nave was built adjacent to and conterminous with the tower, utilising its north face as part of the south wall. The original limits of the nave, as has been pointed out to me by Mr. Moule, are marked by early Norman angle buttresses at the south west, north west and north east corners, the tower serving the purpose instead at the south-east corner. In this view, these angle buttresses delimit the church as it was planned about the year 1100 or earlier.[3] They enclose a space of approximately 50 × 25 feet, conforming, therefore, closely to the building formula

[2] *Supra,* Ch. V.

[3] Professor Piggott inclines to the view that these buttresses belong to the middle of the twelfth century, and is supported by The Victoria County History. In his view, as I understand it, the only part of the original church which has survived is the tower, built over a transept, and every stone of that church which Henry of Blois restored has disappeared.

of the period, viz. that the nave should contain two superficial squares of equal dimension.

At the same time the north wall of the tower was pierced to admit access from the nave through a beautiful norman arch constructed of polychrome stonework, in which grey Chilmark alternates with an ochrous sandstone, possibly obtained from quarries near Ringwood.[4] The motif is repeated in the south-west angle buttress, thus strongly suggesting the angle buttresses were contemporaneous with the tower arch.

At this date, then, the church consisted of an aisleless nave, with a small chancel or apsidal termination, and a tower projecting from the south-east bay of the nave – c.1100.

Of the two aisles the north alone contains original norman work. It is ascribed to about 1260 by the *County History* on the strength of the billet ornament used in the abaci of the shafts. But since the billet ornament was introduced into England by the Norman invaders, the argument for so late a date is not conclusive.[5] The arcade consists of three bays and the west-part is unpierced. The original exterior wall was demolished and the present one built in the fifteenth century. The aisle's east window also belongs to this century and proves that the north chancel chapel had been removed before its insertion.

After the completion of the north aisle during the period when norman round arches were still the vogue, the south aisle was constructed. About 1245 there was at Damerham a rector with an enthusiasm for building who invoked assistance from his sovereign.[6] Much reconstruction was done at the chapelry of Martin, and it is improbable that Damerham was neglected. There is a consonance between the arcade of the south aisle, the archway opening from the aisle to the tower and the chancel arch, which suggest a series of building operations carried out contemporaneously or nearly so. But the presence of the tower interrupted the normal arrangement of the roof. It did more than that. The aisle enclosed the exterior entrance to the tower, and from this time onwards the tower was accessible only from inside the church. And at this very time we find

[4] There are two similar arches of polychrome stone at Cranborne Manor. This type of ornamentation is said by Clapham to be rare. (*Romanesque Architecture after the Conquest*, p. 117). It is at least remarkable that three examples of this rare ornamentation should be found within five miles of each other, and suggests that they were not only contemporaneous, but designed by the same builder.

[5] Clapham, *op. cit.*, p. 125.

[6] *Supra*, Ch. V.

the rector obtaining loads of timber from the king's forest at Clarendon to build himself a house. It is possible that up till now he had lived in the tower? We do not hear of a manse until 1270.[7]

Most perplexing in this baffling church is the chancel. It was flanked by two chapels, of which the *County History* noticed only the northern and assigned a date of about 1230. The south chapel was obscured by ivy and plaster. Professor Piggott attributes them to the end of the twelfth century, a date with which Mr. Greene agrees on the evidence of a 'bowtel' at the north-east angle. Each chapel consisted of two bays and contained elaborate ornamentation. On the south side there are apparently two series. The first, judging from those parts that have survived, round and disproportionately lofty. They seemed to have formed part of a more pretentious conception. They were superseded by a more beautiful, if more modest, arcade corresponding with that on the north side.

The absence of entrances into these chapels from the north aisle or from the tower indicates that these chambers were chapels rather than aisles. Whatever their purpose, they were singularly short-lived. The east window of the north aisle ascribed to the fifteenth century could not have been inserted if the north chapel were still standing: the fourteenth century buttress against the tower, as Mr. Moule has pointed out, could not have been erected if the south chapel were still in situ; moreover if the *County History* is correct in attributing the labels of the south-west and north-east windows to the thirteenth century, these elaborate chapels can only have survived a bare hundred years.

In 1270 the church was appropriated to Glastonbury Abbey, which thereafter received the greater tithes and became responsible for the maintenance of the chancel. As has been said elsewhere, monastic houses in general took a good deal more than they gave, and the care given to the chancel was often much less than what the parish lavished upon the nave. The demolition of these chapels may have been deliberately carried out to avoid the cost of maintaining them.

The original north door was replaced by another in the fifteenth century, which in its turn was blocked in the nineteenth century. Above it is a circular patch in the masonry, into which the tympanum representing the Majesty *in vesica* would seem exactly to fit. It seems to have been transferred from here to its present position above the south porch, possibly when the door was blocked. Such tympana can all be dated to

[7] *Ibid.* The manse was secured to the Vicar when Damerham was ordained a perpetual vicariate.

the second half of the twelfth century, and, indeed, if the one at this church originally surmounted the north door, it assigns a date to this wall.[8]

The other tympanum, the history of which is given in Mr. Moule's notes, represents St. George on horseback, annihilating Saracens on the field of Antioch, and closely resembles a similar one at Fordington.[9] It can be definitely assigned to the second half of the twelfth century, and must have surmounted the south door, admitting to what was then the nave. Its present position is above the porch.

[8] Clapham, *op. cit.*, p. 137.
[9] *Ibid*, p. 138.

BIBLIOGRAPHY

Among contemporary authorities, William of Malmesbury[1] (c.1096–c.1143) was chiefly interested in proving the antiquity of the Abbey's foundation and in describing its treasures, but he makes a few references to Damerham.

Adam of Domeram, a native of Damerham,[2] who died about 1291, professes to continue 'the history of the Abbey' from the point where William of Malmesbury ended, therefore about 1126. He confines himself to a strictly veracious account of the acts of the Abbots, and has not allowed a single sentence of autobiographical reminiscence to intrude. His first conventual office was that of Cellerer, and later as Sacristan he was present at the exhumation of the legendary bones of King Arthur. His work incorporates extracts from the *Scriptura Henrici Blessiensis*, the record left by Henry of Blois (1126–1171).

In the following century John of Glastonbury[3] abbreviated in a less polished style the history of Adam of Damerham and continued it to about the year 1400. The *Auctorium*, which covers events in the fifteenth century, is thought to be the work of a monk named Wason.

Four surveys emanated from Glastonbury during the Middle Ages. The first, usually known as the *Inquisition* of 1189, was produced in that year by the Abbot, Henry de Sully.[4] It contains a list of the tenants of Damerham and Martin, together with the extent of their tenements and the rents and labour services due from them.

This was followed half a century later by a survey by Abbot Michael of Amesbury (1235–52)[5] which, while furnishing the same information, also supplies a very detailed description of the customary services rendered by the tenants, and an informative account of the skilled hands on the manorial staff.

[1] *De antiquitate Glastoniensis ecclesiae*, embodied in the history of Adam of Damerham.

[2] *Historia de Rebus Glastonie*, printed by Hearne, 2 vols., (Oxford, 1727), from a MS. in the library of Trin. Coll. Camb.

[3] John of Glastonbury, *Chronica Sive Historia de Rebus Glastionensibus*, Hearne, 2 vols. (Oxford, 1726), from a MS. in possession of Lord Charles Bruce.

[4] *Liber Henrici de Soliaco*, Roxburgh Club, 1882.

[5] *Rentalia et customaria Michaelis de Ambresbury* (Somerset Record Society, V (1891).

'The Extente of Roger Forde' (1252–61) is for the Somersetshire manors appended to the *Rentalia*, but pecuniary support from Wilthsire did not justify the expense of printing it for that county.

The *Foedary of Walter Monyton* (1341–74),[6] prefixed to his still unpublished Secretum, is dated 1342. As its name implies, it is concerned with the knights' fees held of the abbey. It supplied for the abbey much the same information as the *Book of Fees* did for the crown. It traces the descent of the fees from the time of Domesday, and later monks have added to the original script marginal notes giving the names of their successors up to the middle of the fifteenth century. It history is not uninteresting. Lost from the collection of the Earl of Arundel, it was discovered among books lying in the vestry of St. Clement Danes Church, and was bought by Sheldon, together with other manuscripts, for £30 on behalf of the Vice-Chancellor of Oxford University.

There has recently come to light among the MSS. of Trinity College Cambridge the *Inquisitio Hilberti Cantoris* which gives a summary of the Glastonbury Estates at the time of the death of Henry of Blois, Bishop of Winchester, in 1172.

Towards the end of the monastic regime, in 1518, appeared the last, and most detailed survey, compiled by Abbot Richard Beere.[7] This *Terrier* records after the name of every tenant his message, his enclosures, his meadow and pasture, followed by an enumeration of the arable strips, their area and location in the open fields. Every field is named, and its format resembles that of the *Tithe Awards*.

Finally, the great accumulation of MSS. at Longleat, which the late Canon Jackson, librarian to a former Marquis of Bath, once described as sufficient to fill a waggon, is in process of publication.[8] The first volume appeared in 1947, and two further volumes are now published.

After the suppression of the abbeys there is a paucity of original material. The *Pembroke Survey*[9] of 1569 furnishes an account of the former demesne lands of Wilton Abbey. The *Tithe Awards*[10] of 1846 is a document of fundamental importance to the student of parochial history. *Inclosure Awards*[11] exist for Damerham only, and, passed into law in 1818, where put into operation in 1830.

[6] *Monyton's Foedary* (*Som. Rec. Soc.* 1910, Vol. 26).

[7] *Terrarium Abbatis Ricardi Beere*, printed in Hoare, *Hundred of South Damerham*, p. 41 et seq.

[8] *The Great Chartulary of Glastonbury*, Ed. Dom Aelred Watkin, Vol. I. (*Som. Rec. Soc.* LIX, 1947).

[9] *Survey of the lands of the first Earl of Pembroke* (Roxburgh Club, 1909).

These sources are supplemented by a valuable series of Court Rolls,[12] which survive for the periods 1609 to 1613, 1684 to 1685 and 1706 to 1921, which, besides illustrating the procedure of lifehold tenure, afford interesting information about the management of the open fields. Two volumes of overseers' accounts have survived, for the years 1790 to 1804, and 1813 to 1820, which reflect the changes in a critical period of Poor Law administration.[13]

Aubrey (1626–97), though his accuracy was often at fault, records in his individual style anecdotes especially in the neighbourhood of Martin, which, but for him, would have been lost to posterity.

Sir Richard Colt Hoare's (1758–1838) *Hundreds of Wiltshire*,[14] though of unequal merit rank with the best of county histories. He has made use of Monyton's *Foedary*, and had access to the Glastonbury MSS. at Longleat. It concludes with a transcription of Beere's *Terrier*, and is indispensable to a parish history of the two villages.

Much miscellaneous matter may be found in the library of the Wiltshire Archaeological Society at Devizes, an unexhausted quarry of information relating to the county.

THE COURT ROLLS

By the courtesy of Mr. Philip Jackson, solicitor at Fordingbridge, I have been privileged to examine the court rolls of Damerham, Martin and Tidpit in the old Hundred of South Damerham which before being transferred to Hampshire in 1895 formed one of the administrative divisions of Wiltshire and is, therefore, historically connected with that county.

The rolls are in four chronological series : (i) from 1609 to 1612 on parchment rolls of eight skins, (ii) from 1684 to 1685 on parchment rolls of three skins, (iii) from 1706 to 1744 on parchment rolls of thirteen skins, and (iv) from 1746 to 1921 in six volumes bound in calf, the first and second volumes being bound together.

These manors had belonged to the Abbey of Glastonbury until its suppression in 1539. It is not necessary to enter into the descent of the

---

[10] Those for Martin are in the custody of the Vicar.

[11] 58 Geo. III. Cap. IV. A copy with map is in the Public Record Office; another without a map in the County Archives at Winchester.

[12] In the custody of a member of the Coote family.

[13] In the Library of the Wilts Arch. Soc. at Devizes.

[14] Colt Hoare, *The Hundred of South Damerham*.

capital ownership during the years in which it remained with the crown. It will suffice to recall that in 1574 Edmund Gheast, Bishop of Salisbury, exchanged his ancient manor of Sonning with Eye in Berkshire for the manors of Damerham and Martin in Wiltshire. At a survey made during the Commonwealth the Bishop owned in the two parishes (for Tidpit had become united with Martin) 3,855 acres, which by 1818 had become augmented to 5,750 acres. In pursuance of the policy of the Long Parliament of sequestrating ecclesiastical property the manors passed by a deed of conveyance dated 1648 to Sir William Litton for £2,335.14.0½, but were restored to the bishops on the accession of Charles II. They remained with the successive Bishops of Salisbury until in 1762 General Sir Eyre Coote purchased the Damerham property and his successors the Martin copyholds in 1863, having held the leases since 1810.

In the years covered by the first series of rolls in the reign of James I the lord of the manor was Sir Anthony Ashley. There are extant no rolls for the period of the Civil War, but it is known from that *Fragment of Autobiography* which has survived that Ashley Cooper held and frequently presided at his court at Damerham. Following, however, a law suit with his trustees he lost the manors to Denzil Holles. In the second series of the rolls the court in 1684 was held by Lord Holles, Baron Ifield in the county of Kent, and thereafter by the Dukes of Newcastle to whom Bishop Seth Ward granted a lease for three lives, subsequently extended by Bishop Burnet to five with a substantial fine on the admission of the last two, for a rent of £74.1.0 and a corn rent paid in kind of 20 bushels. The lordship of the manor passed, as has been said, in 1762 to General Sir Eyre Coote on his return from his victorious campaigns in India and remained with his descendants until 1921.

Attending the courts were the freeholders and a jury of twelve men appointed for Damerham and an equal number from Martin and Tidpit. Their first duty was to appoint a constable for the hundred who held office for two years and a tithing man for each of the four tithing at Damerham two for the tithings of Martin and one for the hamlet of Tidpit. The jury next made their presentments and the first four which are the same for both manors begin in 1684 and are annually repeated with only slight verbal/alterations until the dissolution of the court in 1921. Since they embody the custom of the manor they are worth setting out in full.

(i) Their custom is to have fireboot, plowboot, hedgeboot and cartboot without leave of the lord and timber for repairs with the leave of the lord.

(ii) Their custom is to have three lives and a widow's estate to every life that dieth seized or possessed.

(iii) The best good of any in possession dieth possessed is due to the lord as a heriot if the estate is heriotable.

(iv) If any tenant dieth upon the feast of St. Michael or upon the feast of the Annunciation of the Blessed Virgin Mary or on any day after the Executor shall have and enjoy the estate for the half year ensuing.

A comment on the development of these customs may be added. In the later years of the nineteenth century the last clause of the first presentment was omitted. It was argued that the obligation to do repairs rested upon the tenant and the omission to repair constituted a waste and therefore involved forfeiture.

Lifehold tenure was especially common in the West of England intended to provide against the contingency of the tenement falling in through the premature decease of the tenant. In theory a lease for three lives was equivalent of fourteen years purchase of the rental value. On the death of a life the tenant might introduce another, which the landlord could not normally refuse, but such admissions were usually accompanied by a fine which theoretically the value of eight years' purchase was often much in excess of this. There appears to be little correlation between the fine and the acreage but an average of admissions during the eighteenth century gives a figure of about £5.10.0 an acre. The fine might be paid by the sitting tenant for the admission of his son at his death.

From the fact that in the first series of rolls in the reign of James I tenants hold *pro vita sua ar pro vidualitate*, for their own life or for widowhood, and in the second series in the reign Charles II 'for three lives and the life of the longest liver of them successively one after another', it may be inferred that lifehold tenure was introduced at some period between those two dates. The nomination of 'lives' passed through an evolution illustrative of the copyholder's determination to prolong his tenancy at all costs. At first it was usual to enter besides the wife a close relation, a son or a brother. Later grandsons and minors frequently occur. In the eighteenth century the choice of persons quite unconnected with the family seems to have been an innovation; thus George Reade, the largest copyholder in Martin nominated two sons of his gardener, aged five and seven. Finally when most of the copyholds fell into the hands of a single person in 1855 they were taken on the lives of H.R.H. Princess

Helena Augusta, aged nine and H.R.H. Princess Louise, aged thirteen, the daughters of Queen Victoria.

The heriot was a relic of Anglo-Saxon times. A complete list of the heriots due under the Glastonbury regime was made by Abbot Beere in 1518; a hundred years later it might be a horse of the value of £3.6.8 or two cows valued at only 16s. 8d. It continued to be exacted in kind until about the middle of the nineteenth century when it was commuted for the sum of £5.5.0, but it was demanded as late as 1915.

The rolls throw much light on the working of the Open Fields. Damerham was enclosed by an Act of Parliament in 1818, but it was not put into effect until 1830, after which date every transfer of land was accompanied by the words 'and all allotments of land allotted and awarded in respect of said premises by the award of the Commissioners under the Damerham Enclosure Act'.

INDEX

LIST OF SUBSCRIBERS

Mrs. E. R. Adams
Mr. & Mrs. R. K. Adams
P. A. Allison
E. J. Bailey
B. R. Baker
Captain R. C. C. Baker
Dr. M. Barnes
William Bate
The Reverend G. H. Baverstock
James M. Beatty
Mrs. B. Sylvia Beckett
Miss Nora S. Beckwith
G. B. Berry
Bishop Wordsworth's School
T. H. Blank
N. A. Bourne
Mrs. J. J. Bouskell
D. S. Bowles
Mrs. Fiona Breeze
Mr. & Mrs. J. C. Brocklebank
Mrs. M. A. Brown
Mr. & Mrs. P. W. S. Brown
Mrs. G. E. Bryant
Mrs. Yvonne Buckland
N. Bush
R. H. Callaway
Hugh Cecil
Miss Elizabeth B. Clarke
G. Colbourne
Lord Congleton
A. T. P. Cooper, B.A., A.C.P., F.R.S.A.
Rear Admiral Sir John R. Coote, Bart., C.B., C.B.E., D.S.C.
Mrs. M. V. Crispin
Mrs. Margaret D. Currie
David J. Dampney
David Davies
Mrs. Dorothy Densham
Mrs. Catherine Dupré
P. F. J. Edlin
Mrs. Dorothy M. Egremont
M. J. Egremont
R. G. Egremont
John Felton
R. Fitzherbert-Brockholes
John Flemington
H. S. Frampton
Mrs. Susan Gibson
Mrs. C. M. Godber
J. Goodwin
Mrs. N. M. Gouldsbury
Mrs. Margaret Guido
F. C. Hall
Miss L. E. Hall
Mrs. B. Hall-Smith
P. Hippisley-Cox
P. R. Hooper
Captain A. P. M. Horsey
Miss A. Hutchison
Captain M. H. Hutton, O.B.E., R.N.
H. H. Jackson
J. F. James
Mrs. B. Jarvis
Mrs. Doreen M. Jones
Mrs. R. T. Jones
Colonel R. J. A. Kaulback, D.S.O., M.A.
Mrs. M. A. Kenyon
Richard Lamb
Leicester University Library
R. P. Letcher
A. Light
Mrs. E. M. Lloyd
Mrs. Susan D. Love
L. C. Lush

Miss P. M. L. Lush
Mrs. Eileen Macey
Mrs. E. M. Main
C. H. Margetts
Mrs. S. Marlow
Air Chief Marshal Sir W. H. Merton, G.B.E., K.C.B.
Mr. & Mrs. J. F. Millar
Derek C. Mills
J. W. Morgan
W. A. Morris
G. W. Murray
R. P. de B. Nicholson, C.ENG., M.I.MECH.E.
E. H. North
J. A. O'Sullivan
R. Owen
Mrs. G. Penny
T. Penny
Professor Stuart Piggott, C.B.E., D.LITT, F.B.A.
M. A. Pitt-Rivers
Miss Susan J. Preston
Mrs. G. Phelps
Queen Elizabeth's School
The Earl of Radnor
S. J. Rayner
Z. M. Rayner
J. A. Reeves
C. Rhodes
Colonel H. D. Rogers, O.B.E.
Mr. & Mrs. K. Rooney
Salisbury & South Wiltshire Museum
Mrs. E. I. Say
G. V. Seymour
M. A. Shallcross
Mrs. P. A. Shepherd
Miss K. T. Shearing
A. Shering
Mr. & Mrs. John Shering
South Damerham C. of E. Aided Primary School
Mrs. Patricia M. S. Spooner
T. H. G. Stamper
J. M. Stratton
Anthony Sykes
John Sykes
Mrs. M. H. Trickett
A. J. Taylor
C. R. Tubbs
A. C. Waskett
A. J. W. F. Wallace
R. O. Waterfield
B. Waterman
E. C. Whidden
M. J. White
R. E. White
D. S. Whitelegge
M. H. Whitelegge
B. I. Wilcox
E. C. Williams
Mrs. M. P. Woodvine
Peter M. Woolley
I. S. Wylie
Miss Diana H. Young
Mrs. M. Young
M. R. M. Young

Mrs. Alison Lane Poole is very grateful to the subscribers whose names are printed above, whose support has made the publication of her late husband's history of Damerham and Martin possible.

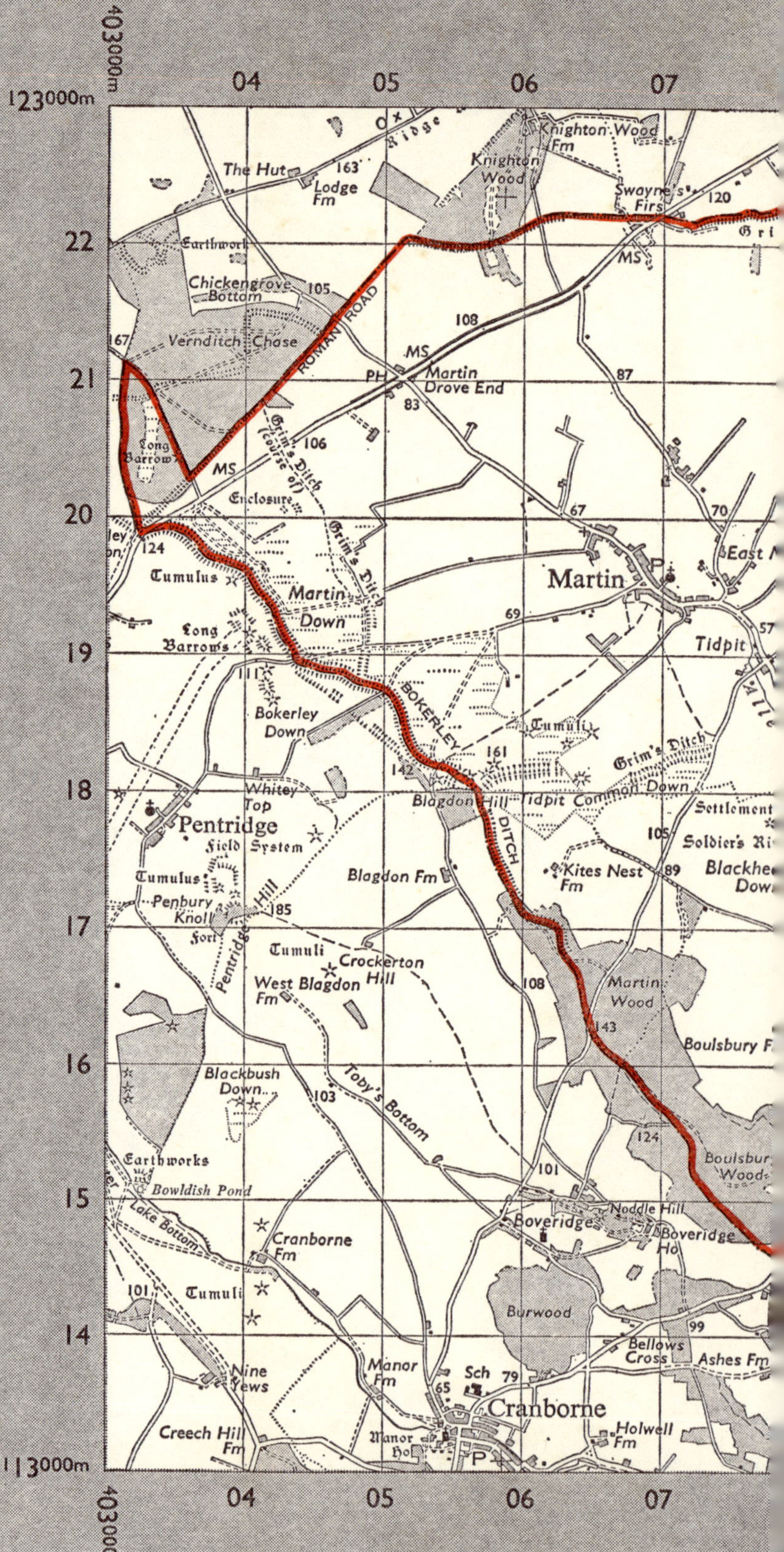
403000m
123000m
113000m
04
05
06
07
22
21
20
19
18
17
16
15
14
Ox Ridge
The Hut
163
Lodge Fm
Knighton Wood Fm
Knighton Wood
Swayne's Firs
120
Gri
MS
Earthwork
Chickengrove Bottom
105
ROMAN ROAD
108
167
Verndit ch Chase
MS
PH
Martin Drove End
83
87
Long Barrow
Grim's Ditch (course of)
106
MS
Enclosure
67
70
124
East
Tumulus
Martin Down
Grim's Ditch
Martin
69
Long Barrows
Tidpit
57
111
Bokerley Down
BOKERLEY
Tumuli
161
Grim's Ditch
142
Whitey Top
Blagdon Hill
Tidpit Common Down
Settlement
Pentridge
DITCH
105
Soldier's Ri
Field System
Kites Nest Fm
89
Blackhe Dow
Tumulus
Blagdon Fm
Penbury Knoll
185
Pentridge Hill
Fort
Tumuli
Crockerton Hill
West Blagdon Fm
108
Martin Wood
143
Boulsbury F
Blackbush Down
103
Toby's Bottom
124
Earthworks
Boulsbury Wood
Bowldish Pond
101
Noddle Hill
Lake Bottom
Boveridge
Boveridge Ho
Cranborne Fm
101
Tumuli
Burwood
99
Bellows Cross
Ashes Fm
Nine Yews
Manor Fm
Sch
79
65
Cranborne
Creech Hill Fm
Manor Ho
P
Holwell Fm

1¼" to 1 mi